372.5 PAL

TH
ED

This book is due for return on or before the last date shown below.

Don Gresswell Ltd., London, N21   Cat. No. 1208   DG 02242/71

D1464637

feminist educational thinking

Series Editors:
Kathleen Weiler, Tufts University, USA
Gaby Weiner, Umeå University, Sweden
Lyn Yates, University of Technology, Sydney, Australia

This authoritative series explores how theory/practice and the development of advanced ideas within feminism and education can be fused. The series aims to address the specific theoretical issues that confront feminist educators and to encourage both practitioner and academic debate.

Published titles:

Britt-Marie Berge with Hildur Ve: *Action Research for Gender Equity*
Jill Blackmore: *Troubling Women: Feminism, Leadership and Educational Change*
Jacky Brine: *underEducating Women: Globalizing Inequality*
Pen Dalton: *The Gendering of Art Education: Modernism, Identity and Critical Feminism*
Kaye Haw: *Educating Muslim Girls: Shifting Discourses*
Bob Lingard and Peter Douglas: *Men Engaging Feminisms: Pro-Feminism, Backlashes and Schooling*
Petra Munro: *Subject to Fiction: Women Teachers' Life History Narratives and the Cultural Politics of Resistance*
Georgina Tsolidis: *Schooling, Diaspora and Gender: Being Feminist and Being Different*
Kathleen Weiler and Sue Middleton (eds): *Telling Women's Lives: Narrative Inquiries in the History of Women's Education*

THE GENDERING OF ART EDUCATION

Modernism, identity and critical feminism

PEN DALTON

OPEN UNIVERSITY PRESS
Buckingham · Philadelphia

Open University Press
Celtic Court
22 Ballmoor
Buckingham
MK18 1XW

email: enquiries@openup.co.uk
world wide web: www.openup.co.uk

and
325 Chestnut Street
Philadelphia, PA 19106, USA

First Published 2001

A catalogue record of this book is available from the British Library

ISBN   0 335 19648 9 (pb)   0 335 19649 7 (hb)

Library of Congress Cataloging-in-Publication Data
Dalton, Pen, 1944.
The gendering of art education/Pen Dalton
    p. cm.
  Includes bibliographical references and index.
  ISBN 0-335-19649-7 – ISBN 0-335-19648-9 (pbk.)
    1. Art–Study and teaching–History–19th century. 2. Art–Study and teaching–History–20th century. 3. Feminism and art. 4. Women in art. I. Title.

N90 D35 2001
707'.1–dc21   00-065270

Typeset by Type Study, Scarborough
Printed in Great Britain by St Edmundsbury Press Ltd, Bury St Edmunds, Suffolk

Contents

Series editors' preface

At the end of the twentieth century it is not a new idea to have a series on feminist educational thinking – feminist perspectives on educational theory, research, policy and practice have made a notable impact on these fields in the final decades of the century. But theory and practice have evolved, and educational and political contexts have changed. In contemporary educational policy debates, economic efficiency rather than social inequality is a key concern; what happens to boys is drawing more interest than what happens to girls; issues about cultural difference interrupt questions about gender; and new forms of theory challenge older frameworks of analysis. This series represents feminist educational thinking as it takes up these developments now.

Feminist educational thinking views the intersection of education and gender through a variety of lenses: it examines schools and universities as sites for the enacting of gender; it explores the ways in which conceptions of gender shape the provision of state-supported education; it highlights the resistances subordinated groups have developed around ideas of knowledge, power and learning; and it seeks to understand the relationship of education to gendered conceptions of citizenship, the family and the economy. Thus feminist educational thinking is fundamentally political; it fuses theory and practice in seeking to understand contemporary education with the aim of building a more just world for women and men. In so doing, it acknowledges the reality of multiple 'feminisms' and the intertwining of ethnicity, race and gender.

Feminist educational thinking is influenced both by developments in feminist theory more broadly and by the changing global educational landscape. In terms of theory, both post-structuralist and post-colonial theories have profoundly influenced what is conceived of as 'feminist'. As is true elsewhere, current feminist educational thinking takes as central the intersecting forces that shape the educational experiences of women and men. This emphasis on the construction and performances of gender through both discourses and material practices leads to an attitude of openness and questioning of accepted assumptions – including the underlying assumptions of the various strands of feminism.

In terms of the sites in which we work, feminist educational thinking increasingly addresses the impact of 'globalization' – the impact of neo-laissez-faire theories on education. As each of us knows all too well, the schools and universities in which we work have been profoundly affected by the growing dominance of ideas of social efficiency, market choice, and competition. In a rapidly changing world in which an ideology of profit has come to define all relationships, the question of gender is often lost, but in fact it is central to the way power is enacted in education as in society as a whole.

The books in this series thus seek to explore the ways in which theory and practice are interrelated. They introduce a third wave of feminist thinking in education, one that takes account of both global changes to the economy and politics, and changes in theorizing about that world. It is important to emphasize that feminist educational thinking not only shapes how we think about education but what we do *in* education – as teachers, academics, and citizens. Thus books within the series not only address the impact of global, national and local changes of education but what specific space is available for feminists within education to mount a challenge to educational practices which encourage gendered and other forms of discriminatory practice.

Kathleen Weiler
Gaby Weiner
Lyn Yates

Acknowledgements

I would like to thank the following who have in different ways helped me in the production of this book:

John Kaler, Diana Gittins, the late Arthur Hughes, John Daniel, John Swift, Anthea Dalton, Susan Stanway, Elaine Benbow, the art staff at KEVICS in Totnes, and the students at the University of Central England's School of Art Education.

Introduction

The chapters in this book cover a wide range of issues that go beyond the usual themes of the histories of art education, yet at the same time they focus on a specific and localized concern: the art education of the 'average girl' in the specific context of modernization and modernity.

Although modernity is said to be 'over' and we are now in the cultural context of the postmodern, the residues of many unexamined traditions and habits of modernist practices are still evident in art education. This, I suggest, is not altogether pernicious. Although there are aspects that have been oppressive and discriminatory and which need to be rethought, challenged or discarded, for the generation of women who were subjected to a modernist art education, there has been much that was beneficial and transformative: more women than ever are active in the arts today and for the first time there are a significant number of women gaining international repute as artists. Girls do well in art, however, but adult working class women of all races and cultures in England are concentrated in low paid, low status feminized jobs: in textile related industries, light crafts, services, entertainment, cleaning, leisure, fashion and caring industries, as well as in domestic and consumer work in the home. These areas of employment find their educational precedents in the school subjects of Art, Design, Crafts, Home Economics (HE), Fashion and Textiles. Art education not only has been concerned with educating artists, but also, I contend, plays a part in shaping the identities of working class women as subordinate.

There are some aspects of modernism in art education that need to be rethought in the light of contemporary ideas. Postmodern debates in art practice, culture and aesthetics, postcolonial and feminist critiques of identity and subjectivity, and psychoanalytic interpretations of vision and creativity have all in recent years begun to undermine many of the assumptions about art and the child that are held in art educational discourse.

What this book sets out to do is to revisit modernist art education, to untangle its discursive themes and preoccupations. By taking on board these postmodern insights, I aim to demonstrate that modernist art education is gendered through and through, and that it has played a part in constructing specifically modernist, feminine identities.

I aim to review critically contemporary trends and their gendered themes and at the same time argue for a continuation of some older modernist pedagogic practices and suggest a reactivation of some of modernity's lesser known discourses. Modernism in art education, I maintain, is an unfinished project and it, together with a critical postmodern approach, could be the means of imagining and constructing an art education that would be less complicit in producing feminine identities as subordinate.

Writing strategies

I am structuring the book as a chronological account of the changes that have taken place in art education over the hundred years or so between the late nineteenth and the late twentieth centuries: a period synchronous with a culture of late modernity in the West. I intend to trace Enlightened modernity's gendered thematic threads of discourse, demonstrating how these discourses persist today. They have changed their gender codes, they appear in different guises but are redeployed and reactivated in new forms in different historical contexts and continue to play a part in supporting and maintaining gender difference.

Constructing the past as a chronological narrative is problematic. It imposes a linear structure on what are complexly interrelating and overlapping events that are not progressive or logically forward moving. A narrative inevitably selects and privileges certain information while it excludes and overlooks others. It avoids contradiction and ambiguity. But, as I think most teachers are aware, the narrative form – with a beginning, a middle and an end – continues to be the most coherent way of introducing and organizing a large body of heterogeneous and complex material. This book has been written for those not familiar with new psychological and poststructuralist theory. It is meant to offer an easily read introduction to busy art teachers, educators and art education students and I have aimed to keep its arguments clear and accessible. What I assume is that readers will bring their own experience and knowledge to bear on this text. To aid this process of 'disturbing' the narrative and to enable the reader to question some of its assertions, I have provided a first chapter which outlines the background of ideas within which this particular account has been structured. Throughout the book I make extensive references to other texts where the reader can find fuller explanations of the issues as well as their counterarguments. These strategies I hope will fill out what is inevitably, in so short a book, a schematic account.

The Gendering of Art Education does not claim to survey the whole field of art education, but focuses on those themes that have received less attention in existing histories and which help to explain gender difference. It is a partial account, told from an interested feminist commitment.

The chapters

The chronology of the book focuses on three significant 'moments' in modernist art education's past. I have chosen first to look at the late nineteenth century, which was the moment when art education began to be taught to working class girls in any significant numbers; then I survey mid-twentieth century art education, a period of 'high modernity' and of expansion and investment in art education; and lastly I look at international movements in art education since the 1980s, where it appears that art education has been embracing some aspects of 'the feminine'. At each of the three moments I briefly survey the contingent social, economic and cultural events within which art education found its contemporary legitimizing meanings and values.

Historians of art education have shown how art education has been variously shaped by different ideas and interests: by Romantic and Classical traditions, by external economic and political forces as well as by the influence of specific personalities and their priorities.[1] While taking these influences into consideration, my account also takes in 'non-legitimate' and non-conscious discourses, such as habit, convention, fantasy and popular assumptions about art and artists expressed in magazines, films, novels and television. I look at the way family relationships have been patterned onto pedagogic relations and have shaped the behaviours and relationships between students and teachers. In doing so I argue that art education has been formed not only by the explicit, well-documented 'big ideas' of modernity or by rational forward moving developments, but as often by hidden, private or overlooked contingencies. It is mainly in these non-explicit, non-conscious pedagogic practices, I suggest, that gender difference is significantly produced.

Dealing with such a vast field of diverse influences inevitably raises the problem of incorporating and explaining the theoretical assumptions that inform this book. A common method in ethnography is to explain the theory first and then use a detailed case study to illustrate it 'in action'. I will to some extent be following this practice by briefly introducing the theoretical background in Chapter 1 and the background in psychology in Chapter 3. But on the whole, the theory is scattered through the text, 'enacted' in the writing strategies.[2] Different theoretical notions are briefly introduced, but will be recalled, repeated, expanded and explained as the events of art education are described. Concepts such as 'discourse', 'deconstruction' and 'ideology' are briefly introduced, but their meanings emerge in use, and in reference to other texts without the need for a separate theoretical explanation. Through this way of telling art education's history, I assume 'theory' to be understood as a process and in practice.

The subject of *The Gendering of Art Education*

I have focused on a very specific concern in this book: the modernist art education of the working class girl, mainly in England. This represents my own interest: part of the story I describe has been my own experience of art education. It has been through my modernist art education that my attitudes to art, my skills, tastes and ideas have been formed. However, this focus has wider implications and is not meant to be exclusive. Growing up in post-war London, the daughter of an Irish immigrant, my art education was shared by the many Jewish, West Indian, Irish, Cypriot and other immigrant families who inhabited South London at that time. The gendered and working class discourses of art education that shaped my identity to some extent, shaped theirs too, although no doubt the meanings they took from the same art lessons were understood and negotiated in different ways which only their own accounts can show. Many of the textbooks, theories and pedagogic practices that informed our art education were shared too by girls in North America, Australasia and Canada.[3] But an English historical perspective is necessary in reviewing and understanding the past in that all English speaking art educational systems share a common history. British art education was exported to its colonies in the late nineteenth century through systems such as the South Kensington model. English culture and its fragmented, classed, gendered and colonial outlook became part of the structuring forms of art education for the United States, Canada and Australasia, as well as parts of Asia and Africa. Any postcolonial, economic or feminist critique of art education has to take into account the European Enlightenment values and the nineteenth-century context of modernization within which art education was formed. At the same time, influences from psychology in North America became absorbed into English art education; towards the mid- and late twentieth century, it has become increasingly shaped within economic contexts of global capitalism and international systems of media and communication. When dealing with these subjects I have not been nationally exclusive in my choice of examples and use of data. I have, in any case, had to extrapolate from empirical and quantitative studies, mainly from North American sources because there has been so little feminist and art educational research in Britain.

The theories which underpin my arguments – from film studies, literary theory, art history, art practice and criticism, psychology and psychoanalysis – have no national boundaries. New ideas that critique the gendered humanist subject,[4] modernist creativity, and the perceptual tradition, have been spearheaded by international contributions from postcolonial, poststructuralist and feminist scholars. Indeed, it has been possible to imagine and write about English art education *as* local and specific only by adopting a vantage point informed by other perspectives.

Chapter 2, then, will be a survey of the European Enlightenment discourses and an introduction to the Romantic/Classical, public/private and gendered divisions of labour that underpinned the emergence of English state-maintained art education in the second half of the nineteenth century.

Chapter 3 reviews the main themes of North American psychology that were structured into English art education at the moment of high modernity in the mid-twentieth century. I briefly introduce the dominant narratives of child development, creativity and perception that have been (and still are) saturated through art pedagogy, and then outline the main points of post-Lacanian, post-Foucauldian challenges to these older paradigms of the self.

Chapter 4 continues this focus on the period between the end of the Second World War and the early 1970s and introduces the cultural and economic contexts in which the aggressive introduction of psychological discourse and expansion in art education occurred, particularly in the new school subject of Design.

The relationship of 'Art' to 'Design' in education is complex and often contradictory. Sometimes Art is considered separately from Design, and sometimes they are combined.[5] The relation between them and their naming is constantly shifting; the historical place of Crafts has been indeterminate. In this book, I include Design, Crafts and Technology as part of my description of the Art curriculum. Any description of the Art curriculum in schools has to take into account design education; since the two have been taught together, their practices overlap. They have explicitly been regarded as 'transferable' skills and they have borrowed their ideological meanings one from another. I have taken, as a paradigm topic, the practice of 'Textiles' education. Textiles is a subject that has been taught at different times across the Art and Craft, Design, Technology and Home Economics syllabus under the heading of 'Art'. It has taken up a considerable amount of time, and its pedagogic practices have been central to the construction of working class feminine identities.

Chapter 5 shifts the focus from England to a more global picture of the influences of corporate culture and a service oriented and consumer economy on art education. I review the expansion of multinational textile and craft production and examine in particular the gendered connotations of these influences in the teaching and management of art education. I contend that art education is assuming an increasingly feminized identification corresponding to increasingly feminized Western forms of culture and employment, that are not always advantageous to working class women and men.

In Chapter 6 I suggest some strategies and tactics for intervening in the economic circle of desire in feminized models of consumer led art education.

To do this I return to some of the theoretical issues raised earlier, and reintroduce some critical modern and critical postmodern tactics and strategies as alternative practices. These tactics and strategies, I suggest, could help to bring about changes in art education, changes which are less likely to produce feminine identities as subordinate.

The invisibility of art education in critical discourse

Art in schools has in many ways appeared to have been successful for girls. It is one area of the school curriculum that is apparently untroubled by gender inequality and lack of opportunity. Girls seem to succeed in Art: they choose it as an option more often than boys, girls outshine boys in art examinations and there is no shortage of girls going on to higher education in the arts. Art lessons, particularly Fine Art – painting, drawing and light crafts – are seen to be the place where girls can express themselves, develop their own interests unrestricted by the gender divisions and formal demands that characterize other academic subjects.[6] Art is taught in relaxed, colourful, playful, creative environments sympathetic to traditional feminine interests and is often regarded, not least by social scientists and feminist educators, as a harmless leisure pursuit, an antidote to real work, and a creative outlet; a place where, with sensitive teaching, the authentic and transparent expression of girls' thoughts, feelings and experiences can be unproblematically encouraged.

While there are a large number of books, articles and feminist projects tackling gender inequality in other school subjects – Maths, Sports, Science, History – there are very few which have identified gender inequality in Art.[7] There has been no drive for compensatory education, indeed, girls have often been discouraged from the traditional feminine arts subjects, towards the sciences, mathematics and technology, subjects which would seem to offer them marketable skills and better paid career prospects. Popular feminist educational propaganda illustrates girls claiming their rightful place in a man's world, handling heavy materials, working with sophisticated laboratory equipment or in machine workshops alongside boys, but there are few pictures of ideal female role models engaged in painting, drawing or sewing.

These subjects have taken up a considerable amount of time in the education of working class girls, and they must be having some effects; they deserve some scrutiny. But there has been little attempt to understand art education's place in relation to the wider social contexts of the family, productive work and consumption or to see how girls' art education relates to women's contemporary art practice.

Art education has been the place where children learn about 'things': about objects and how to create and construct them. They learn how to judge, to discriminate, to evaluate objects for their aesthetic and functional meanings. In short, in art education children acquire meanings about production and consumption.

The invisible girl

One of the difficulties of establishing what art education has been doing to girls has been the lack of any explicit mention of them in art educational histories and textbooks. In art pedagogy 'the child' is always represented as male or as gender neutral. Looking at widely used textbooks, policy documents, government recommendations and popular treatises on art education up to the 1970s, the 'average' girl is absent.[8] She has not always been deliberately excluded: no doubt the authors, who have been almost always men, believed that what applied to 'him' also applied to 'her' and that 'the child' who has been the subject of art education represents both male and female. But as Nicole Claude-Mathieu observed in her research, it is not always easy to include girls logically in the gender neutral discourses of social science:

> Most theoretical or general descriptive writings . . . make no reference to sex categories. What is described in such studies is a human process in its generality, without regard to the sex of the individuals. This is perfectly justified from the methodological point of view, and indeed no-one would imagine that sex membership had anything whatever to do with the problem under review. Yet it often happens that in these works there suddenly appears a 'comment' (five lines after four pages of neutral description, a paragraph in small type, or a chapter added at the end of a book) that reorientates the whole problem in terms of sexual categorisation; 'we know less about how women are affected in this matter' . . . or; . . . 'it would be useful to examine in what ways women are affected . . .'. The reader, naturally enough, becomes perplexed as to the generality of what he has been reading up to that point.[9]

Modernist art education's textbooks and its histories have been written in this way. Each case is in itself trivial, but together they add up to a system of exclusion and omission. There are many examples: the influential Newsom Report, for example, written in 1959, marginalized girls in a mix of 'neutral' and exclusive language. In its main text, it referred throughout to the education of 'children', but when new Design education came under review, it suddenly switched without any explanation to writing about 'the boy'. No corresponding text was available for girls, and what exists is not easily translatable into girls' experience:

> The boy with whom we are concerned is one who has pride in his skill of hand and a desire to use that skill to discover how things work, to

make them work and to make them work better. The tradition to which he aspires to belong is the modern one of the mechanical man whose fingers are the questioning instruments of thought and exploration . . . His is not a narrow vocational interest, but a broad scientific curiosity.[10]

Georgia Collins and Renée Sandell have amassed evidences of the many omissions and examples of this kind of sexism in art educational texts.[11]

Another practice that hides the concerns of girls has been to assume that 'Art' means painting and drawing. Most psychological tests, critical judgements and philosophical ponderings on 'art' construct their arguments with reference to examples and evidences drawn from painting or drawing. Art pedagogy's terminology is vague; 'Art' has meant different things at different times. But education in the art lesson has usually involved a much wider range of practices than painting and drawing. It has included embroidery, weaving, soft toy making, pottery, fabric design, printing and dyeing, fashion, interior design, product design, batik, model making, and so on. Many pedagogic practices and evaluation procedures are, I suggest, fundamentally undermined and their gendered structures revealed when 'girls' subjects' such as textiles, fashion and consumer studies are properly included in discussions of the Art curriculum.

Through gendered textual and pedagogic practices, as well as through silences and omissions, girls' educational concerns, their skills, their modes of knowing and their responses are often hidden. In dismantling art education I attempt to uncover the hidden issues of gender and bring them into feminist discourse, relating them to the contemporary intellectual and artistic field, to social and economic contexts, and demonstrate that Art in schools has had an important part to play in constructing identities as feminine. My focus will be to argue that modernist art education has been and continues to be a complex of gendered discursive practices: saturated through with masculine and feminine divisions and hierarchies which in turn produce gendered identities as hierarchical and working class girls as subordinate, ready to assume subordinate positions in the wider social and economic culture.

1 Theoretical perspectives

Gendering

Art education, as I have suggested, is 'gendered'. This may seem an odd thing to assert since the policy documents, the textbooks and the curriculum these days are not divided into boys' and girls' subject areas, nor do subjects like painting or drawing appear to have anything to do with sexual difference. What follows is a description of gendering in art education, not as an explicit process but as one way that its fundamental ideas are imaginatively organized into binary divisions of masculine and feminine hierarchies of power.

Gendering is not just applied to sexed individuals.[1] Looking around at everyday objects – cars, stereos, clothes, tools and technologies – it can be seen that practically everything is assigned in the imagination with masculine and feminine differences which have obviously nothing to do with biology. Abstract ideas and social institutions are gendered: air and light have been represented in culture and myth as masculine, whilst earth and gross matter have been assigned to the feminine realm. The law is imagined as masculine whilst gossip is feminine in character; intellect is usually agreed to be masculine while intuition is feminine. This binary difference is not equal; gendering also denotes hierarchy, with the masculine term having greater power. Science for instance has no biological sex, yet it is usually imagined as masculine and culturally more significant than the feminine arts; masculine work is seen as more important than feminine leisure; masculine production is a more serious activity than feminine consumption and so on. These are not legally binding, rational, fixed or institutionally necessary categories that can be empirically tested.

Gendering denotes a relationship rather than stable categories fixed to the male or female sex: what is masculine at one time can be feminine at another. Art, for instance, is gendered as masculine when it is related to feminine craft, but is feminine when it is related to masculine science. 'Masculinity', therefore, is a complex of shifting ideological associations which are strongly linked to, but not an essential part of the male sex. Masculinity – in practices of reasoning, logical thought, as well as violence and aggression – can be deployed by women. Feminine behaviours in the form of caring, passivity, emotion and so on can be performed by men.

For the most part, associating objects, ideas and institutions with masculine and feminine is a non-conscious process and operates at a discursive level. But this does not mean that the effects of gendering are insignificant. Gendered associations are widely and firmly established and their shared meanings are understood as accepted conventions without need for explicit justification. Gendering is not just a practice of the unthinking and the uneducated:

> In art-historical parlance . . . it has long been common approbatory lan-
> guage, even the highest level of praise, to describe works of art in terms
> of the exercise of power: as strong, forceful, authoritative, compelling,
> challenging, or commanding; and the masculinist note becomes even
> more explicit with the use of terms like masterful, heroic, penetrating,
> and rigorous. That what is rigorous and strong is valued while what is
> soft or flexible is comic or pathetic emerges again and again in the min-
> imalist's discourse, as it does the everyday language of scholars.[2]

The imaginary assigning of gender to objects, abstract ideas and institutions is a widespread and accepted practice for organizing abstract ideas hierarchically in scholarship, criticism and theory.

The critical psychologist Valerie Walkerdine has demonstrated in her book *The Mastery of Reason* that gendering operates complexly as a way of cognitively organizing information, establishing hierarchies, underpinning and legitimizing relations of social power.[3] Cultural theorists have shown how gendering has real effects in structuring social relationships. It is an imaginary process but has real effects in that it imposes order and structure on an otherwise complex and chaotic world.

In her book *Engendering Modernity*, Barbara Marshall has argued that an understanding of gendering is crucial in understanding the culture of Enlightened modernity. She has suggested that gendering has been at the heart of modernity's institutions, its labour relations, its cultural forms and power structures.[4]

Following from these theoretical positions, I aim to show how the discourses of modernist art education are saturated through with gendered meanings which produce differences between boys and girls.

Patriarchy

The assigning of gender draws its imaginary and emotional force from patriarchal family relationships, based on the division of labour between fathers and mothers.[5]

The discourse of patriarchy appears in these postfeminist times as a some-what irrelevant concept, concerned with inaccessible unconscious childhood events, civilizations long past, or rejected as part of a passé 1970s feminism. It seems to have no part to play in a post-industrial future of fluid gender, work and social relations. But, as Juliet Mitchell observed, although the patriarchal family is 'archaic' in relation to modern capitalist society, its laws nonetheless persist and are maintained 'through thick and thin', sug-gesting that patriarchy still has a contemporary function.[6] Contemporary psychoanalytic theory has returned to a notion of patriarchy in explanations of the construction of gender difference, and contemporary educational theorists include patriarchy as a legitimizing force in normalizing oppressive gender relations in the curriculum.[7] In Chapter 5, I shall suggest that patri-archy can be found in the invisible power of multinational corporations and global finance. Older men continue to hold real legal and economic power, but this patriarchal power is distanced from ordinary people and its work-ings have become less accessible to criticism and change.

There has been much significant debate in psychoanalysis stemming from Lacan's reworking of Freudian theories of the unconscious; about patri-archy, the 'Name-of-the-father' and its crucial role in the structuring of the imaginary symbolic in early childhood.[8] This stress on the unconscious, crucial though it is, and as Hal Foster has argued, has tended to overshadow the effects of patriarchal discourse in the everyday practices of adults.[9] Laura Kipnis comes to a similar conclusion when she argues that in order to make change and take action, we need to focus on conscious experience.[10] Whilst the operations of patriarchy are not conscious, they are not always *un*conscious: that is, they are not inaccessible or available only through deep analysis. Most patriarchal practices (as Kipnis suggests) are, to use Freud's term, 'pre-conscious': habitual, conventional and available to consciousness with a little thought, or with the help of research, investigation, critique and deconstruction and therefore accessible to change. So the emphasis in this book will not be so much on the inaccessible, historical roots of patriarchy, but with descriptions of patriarchy as contemporary discourse operating in everyday practices.

What is patriarchy?

In her influential book, *Psychoanalysis and Feminism*, Mitchell described patriarchy as the symbolic domination of older men over younger men, women and children:

It is the specific feature of patriarchy – the law of the hypothesised pre-historic murdered father – that defines the relative places of men and women in human history. This 'father' and his representatives – all fathers – are the crucial expression of patriarchal society. It is fathers not men who have the determinate power . . . Patriarchy describes the universal culture – however, each specific economic mode of production must express this in different ideological forms'.[11]

So patriarchy means not only a binary pattern of dominance of men over women, but also a pattern of social relations that are complexly organized by age as well as gender. Patriarchy is involved in the organization of gender and generations. It depends on gender difference, but, as Diana Gittins has stressed, it just as importantly depends on differences and antagonisms between older and younger generations, and is active in constructing power relations between adults and children and contributing to the definition of 'the child'.[12]

'The family' has been regarded as a site of oppression for women and children, but what is critiqued in this book is not 'the family' *per se* – families do not have to be organized patriarchally – but its Oedipally organized structures of power, inheritance, authority and legitimacy.

The Oedipal plot

It has often been overlooked that the explanation of the relations of the normally neurotic family was with reference to selected elements of a *story*. The story of Oedipus as retold by Freud has become elevated to quasi-scientific status and maintained as an established model of normal family relationships. It is within this story of a biological family as an imagined ideal that many psychoanalytic and therapeutic practices and popular psychologies have established norms for conducting human relationships and behaviour; relationships which render 'illegitimate' those existing outside the Oedipal triad of a Father, a Mother and a Son.

In the Oedipal story, selectively retold by Freud, it will be remembered that the king, Laius, has a curse put on him that he will one day be murdered by his son. To avoid fulfilling the curse, Oedipus, the son, is exposed to die as an infant, but is rescued and brought up in another country. Oedipus, knowing of the curse, travels to avoid his father's home, but he unknowingly meets King Laius and kills him in a struggle. He then inherits his father's kingdom and unknowingly marries his father's wife – his own mother.

The story of the patriarchal family works as ideology. Ideology, as theorized by Louis Althusser, is the unconscious creation of fantasies and myths which imaginatively account for the relationship of people to the actual conditions of their existence, a notion based on Lacan's metaphoric notion of 'the mirror' stage in early childhood where the child misrecognizes its own reflection, and takes for 'real' an idealized image.[13] Guy Debord takes this notion further in his concept of 'the spectacle' in which relationships among people and classes are disguised in commodified images and visual representations and appear in popular cultural forms which are believed to be 'real'.[14] Patriarchy does not necessarily mean the way that actual families live out their relationships – fathers may be absent or no longer dominant, they may indeed be caring, gentle and feminine – but it is against the patriarchal family as an ideology, as imagined ideal, and the father as authority that law, social policy, medicine and other institutional practices like education have been structured.[15]

Patriarchy works not only in institutional forms and legal prohibitions but also within each individual at a non-conscious level. It is represented in private 'traditions' and personal relationships, performed in unthought-out, everyday behaviours, customs and habits. It does not always have explicitly articulated authority, but the force of custom and received habit. There are no laws for instance which demand marriage or childcare as a female occupation, and no consciously articulated rules saying that a woman should change her name on marriage, or do the shopping. Women are not, by and large, physically forced to do housework, or work in 'caring' occupations, yet daily life can be made intolerable for those – lesbians, gay men, feminists, single and working mothers, women firefighters for instance – who flout its conventions. Patriarchal customs persist as powerful collective social norms and as 'common sense'. Oedipal relationships of a father, a mother and an eldest son form the dynamic and emotional narratives of popular culture: in soap operas, novels, magazines and newspaper journalism, in rituals of courtship and marriage and in the everyday structures and relationships of schooling.

The Oedipalization of the public sphere

In cultural terms, the Oedipal plot is centred around the linear relationship of fathers and their inheriting sons. This myth is represented in the fact that inheritance in all modernized cultures, legally passed from the father to the eldest son – the legitimate heir – who was then displaced in his turn by his son in a linear, hierarchical succession. As Mitchell argued, 'it is this inheriting son whose subjecthood has been the concern of patriarchal culture'.[16] Freud's story excluded any mention of daughters: the figure of the little girl and female relationships remain unsymbolized in patriarchal cultures. Laura Mulvey has observed, 'Looking at the Oedipal myth in detail it is remarkable to what extent it is about the father–son relationship and how marginal the feminine is.' Rosi Braidotti has further suggested that the exclusion of girls from the Oedipal plot has resulted in women's exclusion from history and from civil society:[17] Little girls are indeed absent from modernity's cultural narratives: they have had no part to play in the plots of detective novels, adventure stories, the dominant histories of music and art. They are structurally unnecessary in many war, sports, cowboy and 'rite-of-passage' narratives. As feminist scholars have analysed and interpreted modernist cultural forms, they have found that relationships between women – mothers and daughters, between sisters, between female friends – have been culturally, socially and institutionally, unsymbolized and unrecognized.[18]

On the other hand there are many examples of the privileging of the boy in what has been called the 'Oedipalization of the public sphere'.[19] Sally Alexander, in an historic context, has demonstrated how hierarchical gender and generational relationships were exploited in industrial labour relations in the nineteenth century: the authority of the father in the home was transferred to the authority of older men over women and younger men in the workplace.[20] Michael Roper, in his contemporary analysis of business culture, has described how in mentoring, a strong, affectionate and often unconscious paternal familial relationship is established between older and younger men who are groomed to take their place in a linear process of emotionally suffused inheritance from symbolic father to son that effectively excludes women. Today's business activity, he argues, is steeped in masculine Oedipal pleasures:

> The pleasure of technical innovation or of seeing a new product through to market, the explosive mixture of rivalry and generosity that surrounds management succession, the hard bargaining of industrial relations – at every level, managerial functions involve the dramatization of emotions among men.[21]

The leading contemporary management theorist, Geerte Hofstede, has shown how patriarchal family relationships are reproduced and support hierarchical relationships in the workplace, and continue to be used in postmodern work relations to maintain masculine power.[22] Margaret Tierney has shown how brotherly ties such as those in unions act to bar women from information networks and how a cult of fraternal male cliques and 'laddishness' casually exclude women from power.[23] Feminist theorists have demonstrated the inherently patriarchal structures and practices of modern science and technology.[24] In a subtle and sympathetic analysis of work in the printing industry, Cynthia Cockburn vividly demonstrated how older working class men's skills and traditions were passed on to younger men through elaborate and secret initiations and how masculine identities and emotions of paternal power were bound up in the technologies and manual work they performed with gendered tools and materials, gendered language and work processes.[25]

Patriarchy is not the determining cause of social relationships and caution has to be maintained in transcribing psychic to social realities, but powerful, early acquired psychic experiences in the family underlie patriarchy's strength and persistence. Patriarchy is psychically inscribed in the young, reinforced in the different social roles that mothers and fathers have and in

the different work that men and women do. These family patterns ,   '
everyday – literally 'familiar' – metaphors, normalizing socially convenɪɛ.
patterns of behaviour that save time and thought. And they make the omission and neglect of girls and their concerns seem part of a natural order.

Critical feminism

In this book I am broadly working within an approach known as *critical
feminism*.[26] Critical feminism is appropriate in this context because it is the
field of feminist inquiry that has produced the most sustained critique of
patriarchy, and where the relations between gender identity, the family, culture (including art) in relation to the wider social economic and political
context has been most rigorously examined.[27]

Feminism is a constantly shifting and diverse project. Indeed, as bell hooks
has argued, feminism represents 'theory in the making', always on the move,
open to re-examination and new possibilities.[28] Nonetheless it is useful for
the moment to classify, as a background to critical feminism, two major discourses known as *liberal feminism* and *cultural* or *radical feminism*.[29] Critical feminism shares the emancipatory and progressive aims of liberal
feminisms, but questions the unitary notion of identity that underpins equal
rights arguments as well as the public/private dichotomy on which liberalism has been founded. Critical feminism shares the interest in the aesthetic
and cultural values of cultural feminism, but it resists cultural feminism's
tendencies towards an acceptance of binary patterns of difference. Critical
feminism shares aims and commitments of both approaches: like liberal and
cultural feminisms it has developed within a complex of discourses such as
postcolonial feminist identity politics, lesbian debates on gender difference
and post-Lacanian psychoanalytic theory. Its specific concerns, however,
have primarily been shaped by a third strand of *socialist feminism*. Like
socialist feminism, critical feminism's antecedents are broadly Marxist and
materialist. The economic and class relations of real, embodied women are
always privileged. Critical feminism's main approaches appear in debates in
feminist sociology of education, but with the incorporation of psychoanalytic and cultural theory, greater priority is now given to subjectivity and
the way that popular culture, images, the unconscious imaginary and the
symbolic construct feminine identities.[30]

These categorizations are not always helpful – feminist approaches overlap and recombine in different ways – but they do give a picture of the different historical backgrounds of the different feminist approaches to problems.
Feminism is not, as some critics in art education assume, a monolithic set of
values held in common by all women who claim to be feminists. It can be
said to have a broad aim, which is to improve the lot of real women, but how
this aim is to be achieved, even within one field such as education, differs.

Each feminist approach strategically draws on different historical traditions of practice, struggle and political and cultural engagement.

'Theory'

Critical feminism has been largely an academic activity and has asserted the necessity for theory in bringing about social change for women.[31] Cultural feminists and art educators alike have often been suspicious of theory and overarching belief systems; they have tended to criticize academic theorizing as an overly intellectual, elitist or 'masculine' practice.[32] 'Theory' has been regarded as inappropriate when feelings, the arts, affections, emotions, the unconscious, the body and women's experiences are topics under discussion and there is often a preference for experiential and anecdotal accounts in establishing authentically verifiable truths.[33] Whilst not denigrating the momentum towards personal involvement, and the value of experience as evidence, I maintain that in the case of art education, explicitly articulated and shared beliefs in theories are urgently needed at this particular moment and that critical feminism can offer models of practice and precedents.

Feminism and art education: a similar paradox

Feminists have had to account for and privilege private life – the emotional, the intuitive, the irrational, the body, the unconscious, as well as the trivial, the decorative, the superficial: all those areas of life designated 'feminine'. Yet at the same time, they have striven to bring these hidden and neglected 'irrational' feminine modes into rational and theoretical discourse. 'Theorizing the feminine' is a paradox but is a necessary and always unfinished attempt to bring the private domain of women into the dominant Enlightenment masculine forms of rationality, citizenship and equality before the law, to bring about material progress in the lives of real women.

A similar paradox is at the heart of art education. Art practice is not necessarily tied to moral, logical, ethical, conventional or legal considerations. Postmodern art has been described as rootless and ahistorical, uncommitted; concerned with 'parody, historical quotation, depthlessness, loss of affect, decentering of the subject, eclecticism, and so on'.[34] Postmodern culture and art question and undermine the rational and the progressive, and reject logic and the possibility of civilized and self-aware identity.

Art education has to teach about art, but it cannot work in the same way and with the same beliefs. Education is a social practice which requires selective and hierarchical value systems, accountable priorities, shared meanings and aims. Working with children and students, ethical and critical considerations are involved. In planning curricula, designing courses, evaluating

chronological processes, theory, logic and belief in progress are in
order to take any action: 'definitions are necessary in order to keep us
to allow us to take a stand, however provisional.'[35]

Like feminism, art education needs shared theories, but as Gayatri
Chakravorty Spivak has argued, theories that do not need to be permanent
or regarded as ultimate truths. They can be established 'for the time being'
as the best possible way of doing things, using the best ideas available at any
given time.[36] Feminist theories and strategic practice can offer preceding
models for theorizing art education.

The wider implications of a feminist approach

It has been demonstrated that introducing feminism and including the interests of women and girls into any disciplinary field have the effect of disturbing and changing for ever the basis of the truths upon which that field of
knowledge has been based.[37] The introduction of 'woman' has fundamentally altered the disciplines of art history, literary theory, psychology, philosophy and aesthetics. The cultural theorist, Stuart Hall, wrote vividly of the
moment when it changed the field of cultural studies:

> For cultural studies (in addition to many other theoretical projects), the
> intervention of feminism was specific and decisive. It was ruptural. It
> reorganised the field in quite different ways . . . It's hard to describe the
> import of the opening of that new continent in cultural studies . . . it's
> not known generally how and where feminism first broke in. I use the
> metaphor deliberately: As a thief in the night, it broke in; interrupted,
> made an unseemly noise, seized the time, crapped on the table of cul-
> tural studies.[38]

The inclusion of 'the feminine' and feminist artistic practice and, most
importantly, the inclusion of real girls into modernist discursive practices
of art education reveal the contradictions inherent in those practices, rup-
tures and 'messes up' existing structures, categories and paradigms. But this
is not just a destructive process. Critical feminist theory takes this process
further by holding out and providing examples, strategies and tactics for
constructing progressive and transformative changes for the future.

Critical theory

Critical feminism is itself related to and finds its antecedents in a wider field
of academic study and artistic practice known as *critical theory*.[39] Critical
theory has, since the beginning of the twentieth century, provided theoretical insights and new knowledges about identity, the family, work, art and

popular culture in the modern and post-industrial world. Its debates and theoretical insights implicitly challenge many assumptions that are held in modernist art education.

What follows is a brief review of the background of critical theory for those who are unfamiliar with its ideas. Implicit in this privileging of critical theory is the suggestion that there are many aspects that have profound implications for theorizing transformative change for gender relations and art education and which could be revisited.

Critical theory can be traced back to the Frankfurt School, an institution set up in 1923, forged within what were then new knowledges – particularly those growing up around the ideas of Sigmund Freud and Karl Marx in relation to the effects of modernization in the West. Freud had provided profoundly different ways of thinking about the mind as contradictory, irrational and desiring but ultimately unknowable and inaccessible. This view of a self that can never be fully rational challenged the image of man that had been the basis of the Enlightenment ideal. Marx had exposed and destabilized the established social stratas that supported economic and political social power and upheavals of industrial modernization. He began to theorize the way that personal identities are produced in and bound up in production in work and with new technologies.

For Frankfurt School theorists, culture in all its forms – in the family, in religion, in art, popular film, novels, theatre and so on – was the way that meanings about the economic world described by Marx became internalized as part of the world of unconscious subjectivity and desire that Freud had described. For the first time, intellectuals began to look closely at the effects and meanings of popular cultural forms: at the family, interpersonal relationships, sexuality, consumption, and at new and modern forms of film, jazz, photographs and cabaret.[40]

Critical theory is particularly significant in the context of this book because it began a questioning of the patriarchal family. As Jewish men living and working in Weimar Germany, Frankfurt School members had cogent interest in understanding mass appeal of authority and explaining how it is that people come to collude with and subordinate themselves to authoritarian political regimes such as fascism. The role of the father and paternal authority in the family was examined in particular, for its effects in establishing authoritarian patterns of political life and maintaining the pleasures of identification with dependence and subordination and how personally held beliefs in racism and prejudice are psychosocially formed. Eric Fromm argued in 1932: 'The family is the medium through which the society or the social class stamps its specific structure on the child, and hence on the adult. The family is the psychological agency of society'.[41]

Although the members of the Frankfurt School were concerned with patriarchy, the family, the nature of prejudice, authority and subjectivity – (and perhaps due to its 'monastical atmospherics'),[42] real embodied women had no visible place in its institutions and were accorded a minor and sub-ordinate social role, as outside the major changes of modernization. Aspects of 'the feminine' as well as real women were equated with modernity's weak-nesses and ills, with reactionary political activity, with the conservative, the traditional and with oppressive family life.[43] The increasing public activity of women in consumption and leisure, as Theodor Adorno and Horkheimer observed, was seen as coincident with debased popular culture, with kitsch, sentimentality and cheap mass produced pleasures. As Andreas Huyssens in his analysis of modernist culture perceived:

> It is indeed striking to observe how the political, psychological, and aes-thetic discourse around the turn of the century consistently and obses-sively genders mass culture and the masses as feminine, while high culture, whether traditional or modern, clearly remains the privileged realm of male activities.[44]

But outside the institution of the Frankfurt School, real women were active in social issues in Weimar Germany; women psychologists, sexologists and political activists were concerned with issues of femininity and the patriar-chal family in relation to modernity. Feminists in the 1970s were often unaware that women in the first decades of the twentieth century had already begun thinking and writing critically about women's sexuality, mar-riage, the patriarchal family, matriarchal alternatives, lesbianism and homo-sexuality, prostitution and abortion.[45] Like the classic Frankfurt School theorists, they, in different ways, examined connections between the inti-macy and privacy of the personal: identity, the family, sexuality and the wider social issues of work, culture, politics and modernity. Their work, although not part of Frankfurt School's classic concerns, has formed part of the broad field of critical theory.

Critical feminists have continued working within the same debates since that time and have continued to seek materialist (rather than biologically determined or spiritual) explanations for issues of concern to women in a patriarchal culture, such as family violence, childcare, reproduction rights, prostitution, private and domestic work, sexuality, and oppressive sexual divisions of labour and the effects of popular culture and art in supporting these economic systems. Before the 1970s Women's Studies was not an option in the university syllabus. Feminist issues were not legitimate subject matter for work in the university, art college or in political activism. Women often had to work in the teeth of left-wing opposition, outside the academy, outside the gallery system in unofficial women's study, art and research groups.

Whilst feminists have worked within the broad materialist framework of critical theory, they have not been uncritical of Marxian and Freudian ideas. Jessica Benjamin, for instance, has questioned the androcentric concepts of autonomy and individuality in Adorno and Horkheimer's work.[46] Seyla

Benhabib has argued that the writings of the later critical theorist, Habermas, are inhabited by an image of the ideal human as the disembodied, rational male ego.[47] They and others have highlighted the omission of women from the discourses of classic critical theory. Nonetheless feminist theorists have found in the self-critical, modernist materialist project of critical theory, possibilities for thinking differently about the construction of gender identity, the nature of the patriarchal family and its relation to modern capitalism, production, consumption and art.

Lacan, Foucault and critical feminism

One of the strengths of critical feminism is that it does not, by and large, attempt to begin again with monolithic, new feminist theories that disregard or disparage older ideas.[48] Feminists have always been sceptical of theory written by men but nonetheless they have been able to redeploy it in different contexts, often subversive of its original intent.

There are male theorists whose contributions have in recent years been significant for feminists in shaping their critical agenda. Their work has provided methodological tools for theorizing anti-biologistic, anti-naturalistic accounts of how gender is formed and have influenced a whole range of inquiry about identity and subjectivity and, importantly for feminism, have provided models for thinking of gender as socially constructed and therefore open to change. Two of these theoretical approaches, from Jacques Lacan and Michel Foucault, I shall briefly introduce here.

Jacques Lacan

Before Juliet Mitchell's book *Psychoanalysis and Feminism* appeared in 1973 where she introduced for the first time in English the writings of Lacan, English speaking feminists had tended to dismiss Freud as misogynistic and supportive of normative Oedipal relations. But Mitchell, in her support of neo-Freudian approaches, showed how Lacan in reinterpreting Freud's work had something to offer feminism. He drew attention to the subversive elements always existing in Freudian analysis which popular Anglo-American ego psychology had suppressed.

There are two areas of Lacanian discourse which I introduce here as significant in the context of this book. The first is that Lacan elaborated Freud's description of the unconscious. He made it impossible to think of the individual as ever achieving a rational, controlled and fully conscious identity. Although the unconscious can never be known, never controlled or fully understood, its desires are always insistent, appearing as symptoms ready to undermine, disturb and destabilize rationality, to fragment the fictitious and precariously established image of unity of the self. Second, Lacan proposed that identity and gender difference are effects of language and symbol formation in early childhood constructed in patriarchal relations. He provided a theory of the subject that enabled feminists to theorize gender as an imaginary and a social construct, continually built up in interactions with language, images, objects and other people in the everyday negotiations of patriarchal family life and culture.[49] Lacan's ideas have also changed the face of psychology, producing notions of subjectivity and gender that are socially formed and therefore can be imagined as different.

Michel Foucault

Foucault was hostile to the idea of monolithic determinants of power inherent in Marxist and Freudian theories, but he was, like them in effect, critical of the humanist, civilized subject of the Enlightenment. He questioned the primacy of reason, so highly esteemed in Western science and philosophy.[50] Reason, he demonstrated, had been established precariously as an ideal only with a consequent suppression of unreason, the body, the passions and emotions. Using a method he termed 'genealogy', he traced the complex historical processes of power and knowledge and the ruthless establishment of legitimate 'truths' that maintained the power of the rational as the dominant ideal.[51] He put forward a view of this power exercised not as a monolithic determining force, from 'top-down' or centralized in institutions and the state, but as acted out by everyone, and operating in the networks of discursive practices in everyday life.[52] In this he suggests that marginal political struggles, campaigns, refusals and subjugated discourses of feminists and marginal groups can have destabilizing effects on dominant institutions.

Discourse

The term 'discourse' is associated with speech, but in Foucault's usage it also implies practices: the things people do and make. Objects and structures, theories and institutions, tools and technologies, dress and behaviours are all 'discursive' in that they communicate meanings. Educational 'discourse' does not just consist of explicit writing in textbooks, policy documents, curriculum plans and formally acknowledged government recommendations, or what is said by the teacher. It also consists of meanings communicated through negotiating the structures and systems of education: the teacher training, the arrangement of furniture, the shape of the curriculum, the pedagogic tools, the technologies such as the brushes, powder paints, easels, computers, looms and so on. 'Child-centred art' as discourse, for instance, is represented in artistic practices that use specific formal techniques, and the deployment of specific personal behaviours. It has institutions established to promote its ideals of freedom and liberation, textbooks are written which explain its practice based in child psychology, and individuals are dedicated to maintaining its correct implementation in the classroom through peda- gogic practices of care and love. Within the discourse of child-centred art is a particular notion of the child as free and creative, a particular notion of 'child art' and a specific idea of the teacher–pupil relationship. All these dis- cursive practices together go to make up the discourse that is 'child-centred art education'.

Art education as a whole has been constructed within many such dis- courses – romanticism, vocationalism, systems approaches and classical ideals – each having their own institutional practices, associated materials and personal performative behaviours.

Discourses (as Foucault explained) are always interacting; they modify each other and borrow power from each other's practices.[53]

> Power arrangements shift and new social patterns emerge through dis- course. Groups are excluded or included through discursive practices and those with little power are given new legitimacy by adopting a 'legitimate' discourse.[54]

Discourses are not in themselves inherently liberating or essentially oppres- sive. Some, like the paternal discourses of the law, responsibility, repression and rationality, are more powerful, but they are not necessarily pernicious: they can be borrowed, recombined and redeployed to support and legitimize any emergent new strategic aims, including those of feminism or education. On the other hand, feminine discourses of care, love and empowerment are not always positive and, as in the examples I give in Chapter 5, can be used manipulatively in management practices.[55] Discourses are always available to be called on and their practices can be adopted to add their established meanings to any partisan argument.

Discourses, I suggest, are gendered. The notion of art education as a field of interacting and competing discourses, each having their own gendered connotations of power and their historical antecedents, has been central to the structuring of this book.

Critical art practices

Art education has taken its meanings about art from the wider culture of modern art and design, but it has not merely reflected or represented the best or most progressive art of the day. When the whole range of modern- ist art practices are surveyed, it can be seen that art education has adopted a particularly narrow, perceptualist notion of modernist art, which I shall be expanding on in Chapter 3. What follows here is a brief introduction to radical and critical movements of modernism that have been omitted from art education and which, I suggest, could be revisited to provide examples and models for practice in a critical postmodern art education.

Modernist art practices

In continental Europe in the first few decades of the twentieth century, influenced by the same social and economic upheavals of modernization that had been shaping the concerns of the Frankfurt School, new art practices emerged. Radical arts challenged the Classic and Romantic dominance of oil painting and its traditional themes of history painting, portrait, landscape and still life. Modernist practices disturbed not only the themes of traditional bourgeois art, but also the conventions of art-making itself. They fractured the mode of viewing of perspectival realism and the unitary identity of the viewing subject. Some practices explicitly set out to challenge capitalism's art markets and gallery systems and others – such as the Bauhaus School of Art – implicitly disturbed the traditions of art education that had prevailed since the Renaissance.[56] The radical art forms that emerged across continental Europe had no unifying aims: Dada's non-logical and bizarre practices challenged the rationality and order of Enlightenment subjectivity. Surrealism and Expressionism in France, whilst being subversive of the logic of realism, continued in the conservative discourses of painting and gallery art; however, others like Constructivism in Russia employed new industrial practices and completely different modes of artistic production. Radical modernist art took on new technologies in new formal and interdisciplinary practices: installation, concrete poetry, collage and performance. Artists embraced popular discursive forms such as cabaret, print culture – photography and typography – cinema and dance, and combined them with traditional art practices.

Feminist art of the early 1970s revisited many of continental radical modernism's early themes. One of the practices of feminist scholarship has been to bring to light the work of women artists of continental modernism: the Productivist artists, Varvara Stepanova and Liubov Popova, the filmmaker, Maya Dering, the Mexican photographer, Tina Modotti and the painter, Frida Kahlo, have been reappraised. Surrealist artists such as Leonore Fini and Claude Cahun were researched.[57] Women whose contributions to modernism had been neglected became subjects of study and inspiration to feminist art.[58]

In recent years, the discourses of radical art practice and those of academic critical theory have overlapped. They have borrowed from each other's discursive practices and now represent a broad field of critical aesthetic debate. Art practice is now accepted as a form of theorizing, and contemporary artists include writing, teaching and theorizing as part of their art practice.[59] It is this field of research and practice – found in journals such as *October, Screen, Ideology and Consciousness, Block* – that have provided the critical background and social context of this book.

Cultural studies

A more recently established field of debate, which informs this book and which could also be of value for theorizing change in art education, is that of *cultural studies*. Cultural studies emerged as an interdisciplinary field of research in English Literature departments in universities in post-war Britain and found its focus in the work of the Birmingham Centre for Contemporary Cultural Studies. It had been shaped initially by German critical theory and sociological debate, and was further developed by debates on Althusserian ideology.[60]

Like the Frankfurt School, in its early days cultural studies was centred on Marxist, masculine themes and working class men's identities established in manufacture and heavy industry. In the early 1970s, with the emergence of 'Women's Liberation', feminists insisted on incorporating 'the personal', the private and unpaid domestic and women's labour into cultural studies. They interrupted the privileging of economic rationales as determining identity, and began to weave into political theorizing issues of the family, sexuality, housework, pleasure and consumption, and the social production of art.[61]

Cultural studies is an important field of debate for art education because it attempts to understand culture – which includes but does not privilege fine art, painting and drawing, architecture and sculpture – and the way it is viewed, produced and disseminated. Cultural studies has analysed the institutions that transmit culture – the family, religion, education and the media (television, advertising, magazines and newspapers) – and how they work as ideology and become part of people's everyday common-sense thinking. It has made specific studies of the young, of the effects of popular culture, film consumption and fashion and has critiqued the ideological effects of education.

In the early 1970s a new genre of British 'community arts' practice emerged, loosely influenced by the discourses of cultural studies but also as a separate reaction to the formalism and abstraction of dominant American modernist art and the elitism of the gallery system at that time. Politically contextualized art practices began to represent the lives and voices of the 'subcultures' identified by cultural research: those voices that had been suppressed or ignored by mainstream art and its markets such as young people, British blacks and Asians, women, lesbians and gay men and the rural working classes. Critical community arts practice not only accepted and celebrated working class culture, but also examined the processes by which the 'working class', 'blacks' and 'women' and so on as categories are produced. Lorraine Leeson and Peter Dunn, for instance, worked with London's

Docklands communities threatened by redevelopment.[62] Conrad Atkinson documented and represented the lives and work of the coal miners in Cumbria and the communities of Northern Ireland.[63] Margaret Harrison, Kay Hunt and Mary Kelly produced film work as a result of collaboration with a night cleaners' campaign for better working conditions and pay. Community arts workshops, arts resource centres, new socially contextualized degree courses, student placements, artist run journals and studios, public art, non–gallery arts in factories and shopping malls created new areas of praxis for critical community arts in the 1970s and early 1980s.

Feminist art practice was at the forefront of this contextualized art and it privileged the hitherto 'trivial' and private economic and aesthetic issues of domestic labour – menstruation, childbirth, childcare – and introduced a subversive, feminine symbolic difference to artistic practice. Feminist artists broke down media barriers prevalent in art criticism and education, and employed interdisciplinary techniques with 'content'. They asserted the functions of the body in performance. Using strategies of embarrassment and shame, they disturbed and exposed the modernist claims of autonomy, objectivity and implicitly questioned the privileging of the Cartesian subject underpinning the priorities of abstract and conceptual art. They brought new issues, often in the face of institutional opposition and ridicule, into the mainstream of aesthetic debate in events such as Judy Chicago's *Dinner Party*, Suzanne Lacey's Quilt performance, Kate Walker's *Feministo*, and Tricia Davis and Phil Goodall's *Mother's Pride, Mother's Ruin*.[64] They brought new, feminine genres and skills to bear on critical art practice: sewing, cooking, minor crafts, knitting, upholstery, leisure crafts and 'kitsch'. Feminist art began to change contemporary art practice.

Cultural studies and its associated artistic genre had a later and renewed existence in multicultural and postcolonial contexts in the United States. Mierle Laderman Ukeles, for instance, documented the work of waste disposal workers in New York City.[65] Krzysztof Wodiczko produced projects on homelessness, and Dominique Mazaud curated work on environmental issues. Exhibitions such as *La Frontera* represented the contemporary experience of Mexican and Chicano workers. 'Folk art' and indigenous cultural crafts were colourfully incorporated into American Modernism. In the United States cultural studies is growing and – not unproblematically – is becoming increasingly 'professionalized and institutionalized' and is having a direct influence on critical pedagogy.[66]

In both Britain and the United States, cultural studies and its associated artistic genre represent an established field of praxis. It provides a rich source of contextual information about art and the media, their functions and meanings in post-industrial society in a global context and continues to interrogate comprehensively the nature of multicultural and gendered identities.

Today, cultural studies and critical theory – which have embraced Lacanian and Foucauldian psychoanalytic and poststructural theory – and critical art practice are hardly distinguishable as separate fields. They overlap, they borrow from each other, they share common platforms and theoretical models and give support and strength as well as critical challenge to each other's discourses. But together they represent a wide field critical debate within which art education could locate itself. These traditions represent a field of discourse, a huge resource from which British art education can begin to re-examine critically its own histories and fundamental assumptions and locate itself as an active, meaning-making practice.

Radical education

Radical education is another discourse that informs this book and that has transformed some aspects of art education. It was a popular and informal movement among teachers and educators in the early 1970s; an attempt to theorize cultural studies specifically in relation to ideology, and the reproduction of class structures in education. It brought together a complex of liberatory ideas from cultural studies, academic sociology of education, influenced by the liberatory politics of empowerment from theorists such as Antonio Gramsci, Ivan Illich and Paulo Freire.[67] It analysed education's role in reproducing class hierarchies and investigated and revealed the processes of schooling that predisposed children to enter prescribed positions in an hierarchical labour force. Sociologists of education, most notably Pierre Bourdieu, recognized the importance of fine art in this process and began to pinpoint the social role of art – museums, galleries and the values of 'high art' in the reproduction of dominant ideologies and marginalizing cultural forms.[68]

Unlike critical theory and recent cultural studies, however, its assumptions about the child and the arts have mainly been traditionally humanist and masculine. Bourdieu, for instance, managed to identify a subordinate field of domestic art and craft without any reference to gender, and Ivan Illich, the popular 'de-schooler', argued that art education is becoming 'emasculated': 'men just can't do women's work, nor can they use women's tools. Each gender has its own grasp on reality'. Illich argued for a return to a different education for boys and girls.[69]

Radical education's writings were very much concerned with the subject of the rebellious working class 'lad' and his future employment in productive, paid work. It implicitly constructed an image of the girl as passive, conservative and obedient.[70] It virtually ignored any reference to the ideological function of art education. In the influential texts of radical education, such as *Knowledge and Control* and *Schooling in Capitalist America*,[71] and in journals which captured the spirit of libertarian thinking in education at that time, such as *Radical Education* and *Children's Rights*, and in the debates on 'Free Schooling and De-schooling', the arts – that is the technologies and formal concerns of drawing, painting, crafts, stories, poetry and so on – were unproblematically assumed as transparent media. The arts were seen as having no structural meanings of their own, but serving merely as vehicles to convey the authentic expression of working class children's thoughts, feelings and experiences. Art itself was assumed as innocent in the process of what was then described as the 'factory' process of forcing working class children into working class jobs.[72] The 'fine arts' – painting, drawing and the visiting of galleries and museums – were rejected out of hand as the elitist imposition of despised bourgeois feminine values on authentic working class, usually masculine, culture.[73]

Radical education adopted a form of reductive Marxist aesthetics where art was seen unproblematically to 'reflect', 'mirror' or 'represent' the economic values and interests of the existing social order and dominant culture. Black and white documentary photography, film and realism in painting were its favoured aesthetic and technological modes, regarded as more 'truthful' in their depiction of the reality of working class lives.

The continuing importance of radical pedagogy for contemporary education lies in this promotion of film, and television and media studies. It has been within subsequent debates about aesthetics, authorship and media that issues of culture, racial and gendered identities and critiques of modernist regimes of viewing and perception began to enter schools. It was through film and media studies that the methods of semiology began to enter education, which involved questioning the traditional 'literary' modes of analysis of images and texts that had been prevalent in schools – albeit at the very fringes.[74] Radical pedagogic discourse, although it often negated the feminine, and the lived experiences of girls, in its contemporary manifestations in the pages of journals such as *Screen Education*, offered models of theory and practice and strategies of intervention which question the traditional, Eurocentric norms and narratives of bourgeois art which sanctioned gender difference.

Critical pedagogy

Both cultural studies and radical pedagogy were initially British phenomena. A version of critical education has emerged in recent years in North America and Australia in their different and specific contexts of multiculturalism and postcolonialism. *Critical pedagogy*, as it is called, has explicitly returned to early modern German critical theory, particularly with reference to the writings of later European critical thinkers, Antonio Gramsci, Jürgen Habermas and Foucault, as well as the liberatory postcolonial work of Paulo Freire.

Critical pedagogy shows education to be 'deeply implicated in the construction of knowledge, subjectivities, and social relations'.[75] It has attempted to provide explanations for how the social world, mediated through education, is produced in the identity of the individual child, and how children in their turn can actively make meanings to empower themselves and transform the wider social world. One of critical pedagogy's strengths in thinking about issues of gender is that it produces a notion of the child as an active and creative agent in the educational process, not just as a passive receiver, 'subjected' to pedagogic power.

Once again, however, as feminist educational theorists have demonstrated, fine art and the feminine and the specific realities of girl's education have been omitted from its discourse.[76] There are some recent texts from the discourse of critical pedagogy, however, which have been significant in supporting the arguments in this book. They address the collusion of arts education with late capitalism's modes of consumer culture. These texts, together with the discourse of feminist critical pedagogy, provide a way of bringing women back into the picture and throw light on the gendered role of art in the construction of feminine identities in constructing the cultural values of a feminized consumer society.[77]

Deconstruction

The critical discourses I have outlined above all form the background to *The Gendering of Art Education*, and I have borrowed from each of them in constructing the arguments in this book. As I have indicated, all have fallen short of or have omitted to mention the political, economic and social effects of the gendered art curriculum. To help to uncover the particular role that art education has played in the construction of gender, I am drawing on a form of *deconstruction* to trace and to reveal the gendered themes that have been hidden or are implicit in the narratives of Art education in the secondary school.[78]

Christopher Norris has described deconstruction as

a hybrid between 'destruction' and 'construction', conveying the idea that the old and obsolete concepts have to be demolished for new ones to be erected . . . as . . . the vigilant seeking-out of those 'aporias' contradictory, blind-spots or moments of self-contradiction where a text involuntarily betrays the tension between rhetoric and logic, between what it manifestly means to say and what it is nonetheless constrained to mean.[79]

There is a great deal of difficult theory written about deconstructive methods, but feminists have always, at an everyday, grassroots sense, been engaged in deconstructive processes by being suspicious of all existing male defined knowledge. They have asked reasonable questions about the languages, the self-interested desires and conceptual models that male theorists have employed, and have followed the answers through to their logical conclusions. Asking a simple question like 'Why have there been no great women artists?' – which is what a series of essays did in 1974 and which Germaine Greer addressed again in the 1980s in *The Obstacle Race* – opened up a Pandora's box of suppressed discourses and a chain reaction of new questions: who makes the definitions of art? What criteria establish 'greatness'? Who pays for the art? Who is the audience? It raised questions about the omission of women's art from art history: the subordination of women into domestic arts, the lack of training of women, women's lack of confidence, women's role as mothers, the omission of women's contributions to art. It reveals hidden male interests at work, unconscious misogyny, bad faith and evidence of imagined fears of feminine disruption and disorder to carefully but precariously constructed systems of masculine power and meaning.[80]

Jacques Derrida's concept of deconstruction has been of particular significance to feminist inquiry because it has provided a way of revealing and understanding the power of the imaginary and of rhetorical processes: the creative, 'story telling' techniques that have been involved in the narrating of exclusive histories. Deconstruction operates 'necessarily from the inside, borrowing all the strategic and economic resources of subversion from the old structure, borrowing them structurally' and questioning the phallocentric languages with which stories are told.[81] Deconstruction involves an examination of the use of metaphors and analogies and the unconscious use of imaginary hierarchical binary concepts: the discursive dividing of concepts into science/art, culture/nature, classic/romantic, art/craft and so on into naturalizing masculine and feminine relations of power. Deconstruction does not suggest that there any 'real' truth hidden behind 'false' appearances, but instead it is a process of revealing the operations of power of the imaginary symbolic order in language. The binary of 'form' and 'content' become problematic as deconstruction makes clear that 'forms', structures and systems that supposedly just 'carry' meanings, have meanings in themselves, often more potent because they are invisible and non-consciously acquired. *The Gendering of Art Education* looks at the non-explicit structures of art education and in particular at the invisible structures and systems and procedures that deliver art pedagogy, arguing that they are productive of gender identity just as much as art education's explicit subject matter.

Modernization, modernity and modernism

Debates on what constitutes the term modernity have been in progress for many decades now and have been subject to a variety of interpretations and defining characteristics.[82] Before going any further, I shall indicate the main themes of these debates, and the particular versions that are being employed in this book.

Modernization is generally agreed to refer to the economic and social changes brought about by the Enlightenment's dominant rational and scientific modes of thought. Modernization in Britain, which had been taking place from the late seventeenth century, produced technological and industrial changes as populations moved from relatively stable, rural communities to urban centres to find work. Production processes changed from slower hand-crafted skills to speeded up and intensified forms of regulated mass production. Development of transport and communications systems made possible new interactions between hitherto separate communities and ways of life. In the process of modernization, social life became increasingly organized, bureaucratized and controlled. Although the processes of modernization have been taking place over a long period, it has been generally regarded by cultural theorists to have been at its most dynamic and intense in the West during the hundred years or so between the mid-nineteenth century up to the late 1960s. It is within this period of intense modernization that the state became involved in the bureaucratic organization, administration and education of the urban working class.

The term *modernity* can be understood as the ideology of modernization. It is used to represent the way that people believed, understood and imagined their relation to the dynamic and transformative changes that were taking place. This experience has been described as a psychological revolution in human consciousness and behaviour, a fundamental uprooting of traditional beliefs, values and even intimate social relations.[83] Modernity has historically been identified with the Enlightenment's dominant project, as a continuation of progress towards a rationally ordered and civilized world. It has been experienced and understood in the 'grand narratives' of freedom, reason and progress achieved through progressive institutions of law, democratic politics, medicine and education. Modernity has always been primarily represented as being self-conscious and self-critical, of having a scientific attitude that continually allows for adjustment and forward moving progress.

Postmodern critics such as Jean-François Lyotard, however, have questioned an uncritical belief in Enlightenment modernity's narratives of freedom and progress, and others such as Zygmunt Bauman have revealed a 'dark side' to modernity's democratizing and civilizing processes.[84] Modernity's faith in the rational, it has been observed, has led to increased bureaucratization, surveillance and social control and to personal alienation and isolation. Modernization may have brought about progressive changes, but its technologies and values have also been responsible for mass annihilation, culminating in the horrors of the Holocaust and environmental destruction.[85] Peter Berger has described modernity as always having had a contradictory 'underside', always threatening to break through the fantasy of reason and the logic of social control. Modernity has always been a 'seesaw dynamic', of opposing forces of modernization and counter-modernization.[86] The dominant discourse of civilization and rationality remains stable only by keeping the countermodern, the 'abject, the despised, the obscene, the hybrid and the monstrous' under control.

Andreas Huyssens has shown how the threat of the countermodern has always been imagined as feminine. Culture and civilization, he has argued, have been gendered as masculine, whilst the feminine is ascribed to all that is feared as illogical, troublesome, destructive of reason and backward looking.[87] Julia Kristeva has described this feminine 'other' in culture as 'what disturbs identity, system, order. What does not respect borders, positions, rules', always lying in wait to disturb, engulf masculine logic and dissolve fantasies of freedom.[88] So the term modernity itself emerges as split: as a predominantly masculine concept, but always having within it the threat of a dark, feminine 'other'.

Modernism and *modernist* are terms which refer specifically to modernization's cultural and artistic forms and have been used descriptively to convey a cluster of values and attitudes that are critical of older artistic paradigms. Raymond Williams, in discussing the problematic terms, identified the beginnings of modernism in art as a radical break from traditional forms of painting found first in the work of the French Impressionists in the 1860s.[89] Perry Anderson and others argued that since French Impressionism, not one, but 'a multiplicity of modernisms' have emerged in art:

> With Symbolism, expressionism, cubism, futurism or constructivism, surrealism – there were perhaps five or six decisive currents of 'modernism' from which nearly everything thereafter was a derivation or mutant.[90]

But as Griselda Pollock has argued, only one dominant account of modernism in art has survived in traditional art historical accounts. She described this as the culmination of 'a narrow selective tradition', narrated as a linear progression of Great Male Artists, stretching in an unbroken line of inheritance from Impressionism, through Cézanne and Cubism to its final apogee in high modernist abstract painting of North America in the 1940s to the 1960s.[91] This is often referred to as 'American Modernism'. This version has eclipsed most other early radical modernist as well as later avant garde practices such as conceptual art, the art of Fluxus, the Situationists.[92] It also negated practices which it positioned as outside definitions of art altogether: feminine crafts in textiles, indigenous rural and domestic arts, non-Western arts, popular arts. These neglected heterogeneous art forms represented the counter-modernist traditions of art: 'the popular, the low, the regional and the impure', which, for the survival of the purity and integrity of traditional modernist art, have to be kept at bay.[93]

Postmodernity

Postmodernity in this book is given an imaginary starting point of 1968 – the year of student cultural 'revolution' – and represents the beginnings of a cultural distancing from Enlightenment thinking. Like *modernity, postmodernity* is a complex of competing, often contradictory definitions. One version, summarized by the literary theorist Terry Eagleton, suggests that postmodernism

> is suspicious of classical notions of truth, reason, identity and objectivity, of the idea of universal progress or emancipation, of single frameworks, grand narratives or ultimate grounds of explanation. Against these Enlightenment norms it sees the world as contingent, ungrounded, diverse, unstable, indeterminate, a set of disunified cultures or interpretations which breed a degree of scepticism about the objectivity of truth, history and norms, the givenness of natures and the coherence of identities.[94]

This version of postmodernism has been of intense concern to practising artists and cultural theoreticians today. But it contradicts the very foundations on which education is made possible. Education was founded in Enlightened principles and without belief in reason, progress and shared values (or 'truths') it is hard to see how education can exist at all.[95] Art teachers are in a particularly paradoxical position: whilst art itself – poetry, painting, dance and so on – can function outside and undermine and disturb Enlightenment classical notions of objectivity, identity, truth and reason, the practices of art education are firmly entrenched within them.

But there are other versions of postmodernism that are available for art education which, whilst they are always sceptical of the claims of reason, objectivity, truth, science and so on, do not reject the possibility of their usefulness altogether.[96]

A *critical postmodernism* is the concept employed in this book, rather than an artistic or stylistic postmodernism. Critical postmodernism is seen as a continuation of a kind of modernist thinking, which looks back and reasserts the hidden discourses of counter-modernism. It critically reflects on modernism, but is not a complete break with it.[97] For education, and for this book, postmodernity could best be understood as

> a self-critical – a sceptical, ironic, but nevertheless unrelenting form of modernism . . . it would still preserve the rational, subversive and experimental spirit of modern democracy, modern art, modern science and modern individualism. In its moral and intellectual substance it would be the heir and not the end of the great tradition of European Enlightenment.[98]

The feminine postmodern

For some postmodern theorists, notably Derrida and Baudrillard, 'the feminine', the 'countermodern' values of modernity, and the taking on of the voice of 'the other' have become the privileged mode of postmodern identification.[99] But feminist theorists, while they engage with Derridean thought, have been sceptical of this privileging of the feminine:

> Is this merely a question of a new ruse of reason, a kind of 'seducing' of feminist discourse; an attempt to render feminist discourse seductive (to men)? Might there be a new kind of desire on the part of (Modern) Man to occupy all positions at once (among women, among texts?) Are we here only brushing up against a new version of an old male fantasy?[100]

For many male artists today, 'the feminine', represented in formal concerns of trivia, the domestic, the sexual, the intimate, the indeterminate and so on, is now seen as a potentially powerful site of disruption, subversion and a way of speaking of the body, the unconscious, a disturbing of the dominant paternal symbolic order.[101]

Deconstruction and the privileging of 'the feminine' are tactics, but their stress on rhetoric and the discursive has led to a neglect of the material reality of women's lives. The feminine subversive is not the preserve of women and gender codes shift with shifts in social power. Postmodernism, as feminist critics have observed, has been in the process of claiming for itself a masculine identity. In its theories 'the absence or disappearance of concrete women and gender relations suggests the possibility that postmodernism is not only or simply opposed to phallocentrism but may be "its latest ruse" '.[102] Henry Giroux, writing from the context of critical pedagogy, has identified re-appropriation at work in the 'new patriarchy of the sensitive man' and in the re-emergence of traditional family values. The power of real women, he argues, can be undermined by a male deployment of femininity.[103]

So, whilst adopting deconstruction as a process, and arguing for a strategic re-evaluation of 'the feminine' in postmodern art and education, this book also keeps in view the traditions of Enlightenment feminism, maintaining a 'modernist' interrogating, rational and critical vigilance towards shifting codes of masculinity, and the exploitation of 'the subversive feminine' to the disadvantage of real women. It remains necessary to keep track of regenerative patriarchal patterns of authority, and the movements of real men into postmodern positions of economic and meaning-making power in gendered divisions of labour in the arts and in the art educational world.

2   Nineteenth century contexts

The late nineteenth century in England was the founding moment for many of the practices that are visible in art education today. Academic life drawing, objective drawing, still life and portrait traditions all owe their place in art education to what were dominant practices in the nineteenth century. Romantic and Classic values can still be found in art education, as can the vestiges of a gender divided system of Art and Design based in gendered divisions of labour and distinctions between male public and female private realms that were prevalent in the nineteenth century.

Understanding art education as a gendered discourse necessitates tracing back the genealogy of its discourses to their significant moment embedded in industrial modernization.

Enlightenment, modernity and education

Mass education as it emerged in the last quarter of the nineteenth century took its founding values from the project of Enlightened modernity. Robin Usher and Richard Edwards have argued in their book *Postmodernism and Education* that the Enlightenment ideal of the rational, fully self-aware, civilized individual provided the background against which the very notion of the modern educational process was made possible.

> Historically, education can be seen as the vehicle by which modernity's 'grand narratives', the Enlightenment ideals of critical reason, individual freedom, progress and benevolent change, are substantiated and realised. The very rationale of the educational process and the role of the educator is founded on modernity's self-motivated, self-directing rational subject.[1]

Critical feminist sociologists, notably Barbara Marshall and Alison Assiter, have argued that the ideal of Enlightenment's liberalism has been essentially male.[2] The idea of modern man, they argue, has been constructed within legal definitions of freedoms, rights and responsibilities of a male public citizen:

> There is no question that the individual of liberalism was male; women were excluded from the public in both its political and economic senses, being subsumed under the authority of their husbands and fathers.[3]

Liberalism was premised upon a distinction between public and private life: on two distinct realms separating out the public citizen as male and the domestic, the concerns of the body as particularly private and feminine.[4]

The social divisions between the two gendered realms of public and private provided a fundamentally gendered structure on which Western education was established. The discourse of education has primarily had as its subject the boy, as the inheritor of culture and civilization, whilst girls were largely educated at home for a role in preparation for private and domestic life.[5]

The discourse of public education

Much has been written of the role of public schools in forming the character of the boy as the ideal English man:

> their capacity to govern others and control themselves, their aptitude for combining freedom with order, their public spirit, their vigour and manliness of character, their strong but not slavish respect for public opinion, their love of healthy sports and exercise. These schools have been the chief nurseries of our statesmen; in them, and in schools modelled after the . . . have perhaps the largest share in moulding the character of an English Gentleman.[6]

English public school education has never been confined solely to the passing on of skills and vocational knowledges, but has always had an explicit role in 'moulding characters', shaping ideal identities which, in the nineteenth century, corresponded to the interests of a patriarchal and imperialist nation. The curriculum for boys in public schools broadly consisted of classical subjects – Ancient Latin and Greek, History, Geography, English Language and Literature, and later Science. Apart from conventional moralities imposed by religion, and fraternal masculine bonds acquired by organized team games, there was no concept of educating the 'personal' or domestic: a boy's private life was his own business and any concern with emotions or fantasies, or the workings or appearance of his body was designated embarrassing, weak or effeminate. There was certainly no instruction in domestic or textile skills, sex or childcare or lessons in how to conduct relationships. Christine Heward, in her study of boarding schools as late as the 1960s, has shown how boys were explicitly weaned away from the softening and subversive influences of the home, embodied in the influence of women. Loyalty to the mother was 'purposefully eliminated' and they were shielded from her 'doting permissiveness' which, it was said, 'menaced the development' of their characters.[7]

Boys' own stories

Freud had established that for full adult maturity and the maintaining of stable ego boundaries, it is necessary for a child to repudiate the maternal. As Kristeva put it: 'Matricide is our vital necessity, the *sine qua non* condition of our individuation'.[8]

This process is more urgent for boys who, in order to achieve a masculine identity, need to establish a visible difference from the feminine. The image and the body of the mother must be repressed for she represents the undifferentiated sexuality of early childhood which threatens the fantasy of a unified ego and the shaky boundaries of the emerging rational male identity. This process of separation, however, is always unstable and never completely assured; emotional 'weaknesses' and sexual desires, easy pleasures and domestic comforts – identified as feminine – are imagined as always lying in wait to disrupt and corrupt. Masculine identities and ego boundaries have constantly to be reaffirmed throughout life.

Contemporary film theorists and art historians have shown how popular stories, myths and images in art provide reassuring and comforting narratives for negotiating the processes of separation and identification.[9] Nineteenth century stories for boys consisted of ideal images of masculine identity in 'ripping yarns', rite-of-passage narratives, stories of adventure away from the home and family, and stoicism and heroism, and emotional self-control. Biblical lineages of patriarchal inheritance, stories of Jesus and the prodigal son and models of opportunist heroes from classical myth, provided examples of different masculine plots and heroes with which they could imaginatively identify and become men.

Schools as patriarchal institutions

Authority in nineteenth century boys' public schools was constructed in an Oedipal model through the passing on of knowledges from older men to younger boys. Pierre Bourdieu and Jean-Claude Passeron, in their analysis of education as late as the 1970s, demonstrated how patriarchal family relations are deployed in the school and exploited in pedagogic relations. They cite Freud, who wrote:

> We understand now our relations with our teachers. These men who were not even fathers themselves, became for us paternal substitutes . . .

we transferred onto them the respect and hopes the omniscient father of our childhood inspired in us and we started to treat them as we used to treat our father at home.[10]

Paternal pedagogy can be recognized in a cluster of practices and personal behaviours. Its style is academic, formal and authoritarian. In its worst aspects, paternal pedagogy is pictured in Dickensian terms as domineering, bullying, undemocratic and controlling; underpinned by threats of punishment and physical violence. The painful separation of the little boy was assured through the oft recounted public school stories of punishments, ritual bullyings and humiliations by older men.[11] But paternal pedagogy can also appear as beneficent: in it there is a putative appeal to justice, to law and reason. Its rule is explicit and socially sanctioned and through it, boys gain in self-control, mastery and in turn rule over others.

Many women adopt paternal signifiers to support their authority. They lower their voices – as Margaret Thatcher learned to do – they 'power dress' by wearing suits, and they can adopt punitive, harsh and authoritarian attitudes. But their performance of power, their authority, however expertly deployed, are understood differently and not supported by children's experience at home and in the culture at large. Women's power, usually experienced in the domestic context, has no legitimacy in public display and is often interpreted as 'strident', 'shrill' or merely ridiculous. Children take a woman teacher's authority less seriously.[12]

Bourdieu and Passeron have argued that personal authority can be assured only if it is backed up by symbolic, social and economic power in the culture at large.[13]

Paternal pedagogy in the nineteenth century was indeed symbolically and socially sanctioned. In representations in popular cultural forms – in the novels of Dickens, Trollope, James and Mrs Gaskell, in plays, melodrama and Victorian narrative paintings and prints, and in the newly emergent entertainments of photography and film – the figure of the father is usually pictured as dominant and women and girls as submissive and docile, or as in the case of many adventure stories, invisible altogether. Patriarchal authority embodied in older men was juridically maintained through laws of inheritance and the father as head of the family. Family relations were transposed to work relations, where male power was exerted through bosses, foremen and directors. Masculine values were assured through the establishment of legitimate histories of a succession of men's achievements, and the suppression of women's; the passing on of exclusive male knowledges and the professionalization and masculinization of the military, religion, medicine, law, politics and education. Law and custom supported the real authority and power of men, and women and girls in the nineteenth century were absent in the dominant economic and symbolic discourses of power. It was in this patriarchal society and pedagogy that state interest in art education first emerged.

Classical art

Art was sometimes taught in the English public school, but it did not appear as an imaginative, personal or self-expressive activity; it was taught in a Classical genre that privileged the Enlightenment's public, patriarchal and imperialist values, as an amateur activity, a 'rounding off' of the character of the English gentleman as a marker of his taste and discernment.

Classical education had always been a means of passing on exclusive knowledges denied to women and the working classes. At the same time its ideological values represented desirable attitudes of mind and body seen as appropriate in forming the character of the gentleman.[14] Antique histories of culture and art spoke of Great Men, heroic achievements and civic values. Its monosexual, masculine themes and romances, its myths of honour, bravery, love and loyalty, brotherhood and friendship provided patterns for conducting public behaviour, and models of conducting personal relations between men.

The discourse of the classical spoke of measurement, classification and proportion, on rational organization of space, and harmonious balance. Its themes were of imperialism and civic purpose. Its theatricality and statuary provided an ideological model of art that was both public and individually heroic. The formal emphasis in Classical art was on purity, hardness and clarity of outline. Visible mark-making and colour were suppressed. Moderation was privileged; fantasy and the imagination were controlled through techniques which emphasized realism and the exact copying of ideal models. Excess, intensity, emotion, flamboyance, decoration, extravagance: all the personal, imaginative attributes associated with artistic genre such as the Baroque, the primitive, the feminine or the uncontrolled extremes of Romanticism were not selected as appropriate values and practices for an English gentleman's education.

Culture was understood as a personal attribute, rather than a learned skill. Evidence of work or the hard labour involved in making art, sustained study, or signs of effort or passion were treated with embarrassment, suspicion and ridicule as the uncontrolled, slightly ridiculous, earnest activity of artisans, the eccentric, the effeminate, Jews, 'foreigners' or younger impecunious sons.

Public school attitudes to art were absorbed into later models of state-maintained boys' school education, where art was not taken seriously. Robert Carline, in his history of the teaching of drawing, summed up the attitudes with this example:

> If the drawing class was regarded by the staff with kindly contempt, it was scarcely to be expected that the pupils would treat it with any higher degree of respect. This was particularly apparent in boys' schools, where art, flowers and needlework were regarded as the concern of their sisters.

Any evidence of taste or love of beauty was frowned upon as 'effeminate', and the story is recorded that when a horticultural enthusiast at one of our public schools ventured to cultivate a pot of hyacinths in his study, the house captain, catching sight of it, swept it to the ground with the warning: 'there is no room for this rotten effeminate stuff here'.[15]

Classical discourse

The discourse of the Classical is not essentially aristocratic or masculine, and it clearly is not English. But it has had, for hundreds of years, imaginary associations with patriarchal authority, imperialism and the values and interests of the male ruling classes. It has been deployed to support different contexts of power in civic architecture and public monuments – in fascist Italy and Germany, in imperial India – and has been a favoured form in establishing a stable image of civilization, strength and security for banks, town halls and universities throughout the Western influenced world.

Although Classical culture was constructed within the values of Liberalism – individual citizenship, freedom and rights – it also had within it a hidden history. Classical values privileged the life-world and fantasies of men. It subordinated and silenced women, it denigrated the feminine, and was built on a slave culture that rejected the primitive, the foreign and the plebeian. 'The Classic' is always equivocal in its meanings; it remains a difficult (although not impossible) artistic genre to introduce in a contemporary context as progressive or transformative for women.

Classical art, with its masculine associations, was the preferred mode of artistic practice that was imported into emergent forms of state education to be taught through drawing and painting, to both boys and girls in the late nineteenth century. Its academic, formal and civilizing associations provided a foundation of seemingly natural, fixed and unchanging principles upon which a national identity could be shaped, and the elevated values of a 'pure, elegant and refined' and restrained taste transmitted to working class children.[16]

Scientific drawing discourse

A different art educational discourse had existed at the same time, taught to boys from 'humbler walks of life'.[17] This mode of art education, a 'scientific' and observational form of drawing which had been taught since the late seventeenth century, was based in classical values, but it was couched in more modern, Enlightened, vocational and empirical terms.

The Enlightenment vision

Postmodern theorists of vision have shown that the late seventeenth and eighteenth centuries had been characterized in Europe by an explosion of scientific investigation and exploratory activity.[18] Enlightened man's identity had been privileged as observing, curious, analytic and creative. Through newly developed visual technologies – lenses, microscopes, telescopes – and through detailed techniques of drawing using accurate methods of perspective and proportion, disseminated through new engraving and printing processes, Western man's capacity to see, to dissect, examine, analyse, assess and his power to record his observations had increased. The conventions and techniques of realism – shading, stippling, perspective, modelling – were developed to an exacting pitch which rendered optical truth to Western men's observations.[19] Western man travelled the globe, closely observed, pictured, named, categorized, classified and regulated what he saw. The truths that this empirical mode of observation 'discovered' were spread in new forms of publication: atlases, encyclopedias, pattern-books, drawing manuals, anatomies, dictionaries and educational textbooks. Definitive illustrations of the world and its inhabitants were seen and drawn realistically as 'facts' by the Western, white, male, middle class, empirical gaze, and formed the possibility for repeatable, consistent mass educational systems.

As Ludmilla Jordanova and others have argued, this 'Enlightenment gaze' of knowledge and mastery was essentially masculine. Nature, which in the eighteenth century included non-Western 'natives', 'primitives' and women, were the objects of its study:

> the Enlightenment vision explicitly denied that women possessed the reason and powers of dispassionate, objective observation required by scientific thinking. Women could be objects of reason and observation but never the subjects, never the reflecting and universalising human minds.[20]

Observational and mechanical drawing was taught to boys in the eighteenth and nineteenth centuries, as a result of the demand for accurate documentors, illustrators, engravers and technicians capable of making up architectural plans, scaled drawings, geometric preparatory models and working designs. It was taught to boys destined to become military engineers, shipbuilders, mapmakers, navigators and architects in England's colonial enterprises. Topographical copy books showed boys how to draw figures in relation to harbours, fortifications and rivers. The aim of this vocational discourse of drawing was optical correspondence to images received by the eye: realism. Its governing values were scientific, objective and empirical. It required close observation of structure and form, accuracy and mechanical rigour; there was no room for sentiment, emotions or graphic expressions of the self.[21] Observation, measurement, realism in drawing, engraving and publishing were part of the technologies of power of this colonizing male gaze.

It was the ideology of this Classical/mechanical model of vocational drawing for boys which formed the basis for Art in schools for working class boys and girls in the late nineteenth century.

Schooling and regulation

Scientific, techno-mechanical systems of drawing were introduced at a particular moment in English history, amidst middle class fears of urban unrest and profound social upheaval and change.[22] The mass of the population, it was thought, were involved in licentiousness, prostitution, irreligion, depravity, thriftlessness, criminality and drunkenness. It was believed by some that the corruption and disorderliness of the masses 'must eventually terminate in the destruction of order and the dissolution of government'.[23]

John Tagg has shown how in the mid-nineteenth century, photography gradually replaced drawing as a tool of organization and control which led to habits of orderliness and self-control among the urban population. The investigative and intrusive methods of observation and surveillance that had categorized and subdued indigenous peoples of British colonies had been turned on the working classes. The English urban poor became accustomed to being surveyed, measured, photographed and questioned 'for their own good' and submitted themselves to systems of welfare, policing, medical, psychological and educational regulation.

John Swift, in his article 'Controlling the masses', has traced the same functional and positivist practices of organization and social power at work in the establishment of a regulated system of drawing in state schools. The National Course of Instruction (as it was called), designed and promoted by Henry Cole, consisted of a process of teaching and learning drawing that was fragmented into rigid hierarchical and sequential stages with precise regulations about achievements at each stage. 'Each stage and its sub stages were self-contained packages; each stage had clear criteria concerning accuracy, precision and type of marks allowed; each stage had to be completed before a more "advanced" stage could be studied', and so on. These stages were based on a simple to complex theory of learning where outline preceded shade, which preceded monochrome, which preceded colour. Flat examples preceded round, which were followed by living examples. Drawing geometric forms came before historical models, which preceded actual examples from everyday life.[24]

The more complex forms consisted of drawing from casts of classical statuary or architecture; not whole objects, but copies of pre-classified engravings printed in books – an acanthus leaf, a foot from a classical sculpture, or an architectural detail. Children did not draw from life or from copies of the complete human figure. They did not learn the techniques of painting, nor use colour at all until the later stages of their education, a stage which many children never reached. Drawing had nothing do with creativity, self-expression or fine art. It taught Classical tastes and values but through its fragmented, hierarchical and systemitized procedures, children assimilated correct and orderly and organized ways of doing things.

> School drawing was not allowed to veer towards fine art – it had to remain firmly mechanical. It was intended to improve mechanical imitation, accuracy, hand and eye co-ordination, and above all, the ability to follow orders precisely and neatly.[25]

It found its logic and social relevance in the fragmented, mechanical and staged factory processes of mass production.

Arthur Efland and Peter Smith in their histories of American art education have both traced the influence of Cole's system of drawing, through Walter Smith, to the establishment of mechanical or industrial drawing in the United States in the second half of the nineteenth century.[26] Although Smith's classical content was eventually rejected as 'class based' and inappropriate for 'democratic American culture', its hierarchical and fragmented structures lent themselves to the delivery of later behavioural systems of art pedagogy. The same systems of classified and staged sequences of drawing could be easily transposed onto the psychologically informed developmental systems of behavioural models of art that became established in the twentieth century.

Mechanical drawing and girls

Contemporary psychologists and cultural analysts have argued that learning does not necessarily take place in the linear, progressive order designed by educationalists.[27] It does not always build up logically and sequentially, but sometimes moves 'sideways' and is repetitive or even retrogressive. What is learned in school is given (or not given) sanction and meaning by children's experience in the home, in the culture at large, by peer example, popular culture and their own personal desires and interests. Landon Beyer has argued that meanings about art education and how children learn are constructed through the interaction of 'private', already established beliefs acquired at home that children bring to school and then relate to the subjects on the school curricula. Without any social sanction or recognition of the place of school knowledges in their own system of desire and meaning, Beyer argued, children 'disengage' and remain disconnected from school values and activities: education ceases to be relevant and learning is impeded.[28]

As it was practised in the late nineteenth century, drawing was gendered as masculine, conceived and practised within Classical public values, and vocational practices in engineering and manufacture. Options were available for girls to draw flowers and natural forms, but these were structured within similar systematic methods. Drawing in logical, staged sequences is likely to have been understood differently by boys and girls who brought to bear on it different everyday experiences. The importance of Classical values, of systematization, the rational organization of space, of analytic, objective and orderly modes of procedure, whilst providing recognizable values and identifications that found their ultimate meanings in modern routinized modes of factory organization and mass production processes, could have found little resonance in working class girls' lives in the nineteenth century. Women worked in mass production but their lives were also bounded in the informal, heterogeneous and bodily tasks connected with domestic work. They were daily faced with the responsibilities of the affective labour of childcare, sickness, feeding, mending and washing clothes. Classical values of purity, distancing observational skills and analytic and objective, classifying and fragmented cognitive modes would have found little support or recognition in the realities of everyday working class girls' lives in the nineteenth century. It could be argued that girls would have shown less interest and been less absorbed in art education's classical and vocational procedures and practices. Girls would have been more likely, in Beyer's terms, to 'disengage' from school art and be less successful in its practices.

Romantic discourse

The Enlightenment's privileged model of a wholly restrained, techno-rational and objective identity for man as public citizen could not fully be sustained without some recognition of man's other capacities: his 'messier' emotional, private and aesthetic needs. Romanticism emerged as part of Enlightenment discourse, as the antithesis of the rational ideal, an acknowledgement of man's 'inner self' and his capacity for emotion, his capacity to reach the heights of the sublime as well as the depths of madness and cruelty. Romanticism was characterized by a more personal concept of creativity, one that followed natural rather than man-made laws.[29] It often signified 'tempestuous emotion and overwhelming events, lofty ambition and huge energy, whose central image is the eternal struggle of the human spirit, be it heroic or tragic, against the forces of fate'.[30] The extremes of nature – storms, vast vistas, deep chasms – provided its metaphoric themes. Formally it was characterized in visual art by use of intense and saturated colour, visible gestural and impasto brushmarks and dramatic tonal contrasts, dynamic and distorted lines. Visible evidence and expression of emotional or 'inner' truth were more important than any correspondence with optical reality. Themes were often of heroism and adventure, male sexual desire, exotic, occult and oriental scenes, 'foreignness' as imagined by the Western male gaze.[31] Romanticism in visual art was not identified with the feminine: it never concerned itself with the trivial aspects of domestic crafts, with women's skills in embroidery and textile arts. It eschewed the 'gross' aspects of private life and human reproduction. It did not stoop to interest itself in popular arts, carnival, print culture or the street entertainment of the working classes. For the English, Romanticism was represented in changes in the weather, in a culturally acceptable gallery art, an expression of middle class man's inner angst. It was not irrational or out of control, but the legitimate aesthetic safety valve for the most obvious contradictions of scientific and positivist thinking: a different path to Enlightenment.

Feminine Romantic discourse

Romantic discourses have been assigned a feminine identification in relation to the classic/scientific and women's relegation to the natural world and the world of the emotions would seem to give them privileged access to its forms.[32] Indeed, feminist literary theorists have shown how women were able to find an important place in Romantic discourse as novelists and poets. But in visual art, Romanticism remained a masculine preserve. Important art – which in the nineteenth century meant architecture, sculpture and painting – unlike literature, required formal training, the use of specialist spaces, tools, materials and technical procedures outside the home. It *appeared* untutored, wild and free, but actually required skill to hide its technical effort. The processes by which women were excluded from academies of art and from the necessary technical skills of drawing from the figure are now well documented.[33] Professional and legal exclusions were further legitimized by popular prejudices that women were too physically fragile to work out of doors; that intellectual and emotional effort was dangerous for their nervous systems.[34] 'Nature' for women did not include violent storms of emotion, but was limited to forms that could easily be brought into the drawing-room – leaves, fruit and flowers. Watercolour painting was privileged because of its clarity of colour and its ability to reflect the subtler and more spiritual emotions. Oil painting by comparison was regarded as gross and dirty. Added to these popular prejudices was the aesthetic notion of a masculine sublime which gave intellectual credence to a version of romanticism that could legitimately delegate women's natural dispositions within the inferior discourses of beauty and taste.[35] A specifically feminine discourse of the beautiful allowed the expression of tender and subtle emotion, of taste, elegance and smoothness. Enthusiasm, passion, excitement, emotion or sustained intellectual involvement was frowned upon as beyond the capacity of woman. Academic leanings or technical skill – all the basic requirements of being a significant artist in the nineteenth century – were represented as harmful, déclassé or unfeminine.

For women in the nineteenth century, art practice was mainly represented within the discourses of a feminine romanticism, in arts practised by middle and upper class women in leisure pastimes and accomplishments in the home.

It was to be this feminine version of romanticism, represented within the discourses of taste and the beautiful, and taught by bourgeois women teachers, which was imported into school as a counter-discourse to the dominance of rational models of drawing. Through the benevolence of the bourgeois woman art teacher, the taste and behaviour of working class children could be elevated and improved.

The art education of middle class girls

Although this book is centred on the education of working class girls, some understanding of middle class women's art education has to be considered because it was these women and their accomplishments, their values and skills that were to be deployed to teach romantic discourses of art, to refine and subdue the vulgar habits and degraded tastes of working class girls.

Middle and upper class girls in the eighteenth century and for most of the nineteenth century had been excluded from formal classical knowledges, scientific culture and vocational training in drawing or painting.[36] Their education through most of the century had been carried out haphazardly in the home or in private seminaries where they were prepared for marriage and taught accomplishments: varied combinations of 'English composition, geography and the use of dumb-bells . . . writing, arithmetic, dancing, music and general fascination . . . the art of needlework, marking and samplery'.[37]

Skill and hard work were positively discouraged:

> Comparative excellence is all to which gentlewoman artists usually pre-
> tend, all to which they expect to attain. The wishes of obliging friends
> are satisfied with a few drawings in handsome frames to be hung up for
> the young ladies' credit; and when it is allowed amongst their acquaint-
> ance that she draws in a superior style then the purpose of this part of
> her education is satisfactorily answered.[38]

Some of the better private schools had been aware of Enlightened ideas and aimed for a more liberalized education for girls. Rousseau's *Emile* is gener-ally regarded as the clearest expression of a Romantic, liberal education, but it was the education of the often forgotten Sophy that was to influence the teaching of girls. Rousseau had advocated a liberal curriculum for both girls and boys that was to be rational, civilized, progressive and useful. But for girls he outlined an additional educational burden, a contradictory curricu-lum that was to run alongside the main 'gender neutral' strand, based on needlework and a feminine, romantic version of art.[39] He did not encourage professionalism, rigour or commitment for girls but suggested that drawing be taught as a domestic leisure art, as an art which is 'closely connected with taste in dress'. He did not recommend landscape, objective or figure drawing as he had for boys, but suggested that girls could draw 'Leaves, flowers, draperies, such things as enliven dress'.[40]

The legitimate appeal of a powerful liberal influence such as Rousseau's, combined with a bourgeois fantasy of the English 'Lady', provided a model for the education of the English middle class girl. The image of the domestic arrangements of an imagined rural aristocracy, and the efficient management of servants of the Lady of a country house, her character of restraint, good breeding and moderation and her charitable pastimes provided the educator with an ideal of English womanhood.[41]

Leisure activities

Aspiring middle class girls adopted the same drawing-room pastimes, the accomplishments and the charitable pursuits that were understood to be those of a more elevated class. Embroidery and decorative arts were practised in the home, but the production of useful items such as clothes, upholstery or domestic textiles was strictly demarcated as servants' work. One contemporary commentator sums up the popular ideology of women's bourgeois arts when she stated: 'There are many methods for young men to acquire a genteel maintenance; but for a girl I know not one way of support that does not by the esteem of the world throw her beneath the rank of a gentlewoman'.[42] Payment meant loss of middle class status. The drawingroom crafts practised mainly consisted of sewing and embroidery but also included the making of small furniture items, such as boxes, tables, cushions and screens to decorate the home and to exhibit signs of taste and domestic fidelity. The popular *Woman's Art Journal* listed in the mid-nineteenth century the most popular range of women's leisure crafts:

> crochet and netting, tatting and tambouring, patchwork, featherwork, straw-work, artificial flower making, bread seal making, filigree work, black and white work, potichomane, oriental tinting, japanning and Berlin wool work as well as embroidery.[43]

New leisure craft industries

The nineteenth century has been described as a period of social mobility and change. Catherine Hall and Leonore Davidoff suggested that by the end of the nineteenth century '20–25% of the total population could be described in some way as middle class'.[44] For working class families 'leisure' was the performance of a new class status. Housewives and daughters in aspiring working class families took up leisure pursuits. Supported and promoted by a growing consumer leisure industry, by the end of the nineteenth century, bourgeois leisure crafts constructed in imitation and representations of natural forms had become a major popular craze.[45] New manufacturing interests supplied catalogues where women could order the beads, trimmings, paintboxes, drawing pencils, threads, buttons, fringes for amateur arts and crafts that were clean, simple and decorative and could easily be carried out in the home by unskilled women. Women's magazines gave instructions on designs and patterns, and provided exemplars of taste on interior decoration. They advertised and supplied patterns, tools and advice on art and craft skills. Cut off by class aspirations from traditional English artisanal skills and designs, having no formal art education, and being insecure in their social position, middle class girls learned about art within the discourses of a new leisure consumer culture. Their tastes and pleasures were passively formed within a design industry that rendered them dependent on pre-produced patterns and materials specially designed for non-useful leisure hobbies. Women consumed large amounts of materials, and inevitably produced items that were derided in the press and art criticism as feeble in execution and of questionable aesthetic and functional value.

Ideologies of feminine leisure arts

Discourses on 'the lady artist' have proliferated in the modern period and are continually being reactivated. The ideology of 'the lady amateur' has been synonymous with bad art; art that is unprofessional, weak, unskilled, trivial, bourgeois, merely decorative and so on:

> Even today . . . It is not easy . . . for women to escape the influence of the common notions of 'amateur', as contrasted with 'professional' work, by which, in a strange confusion of meaning, we have come to understand that to do a thing 'for love of it' is really equivalent to doing it imperfectly.[46]

The notion of the bourgeois lady amateur has come to be an ideological construct applied to all women's productive activity, regardless of class, ability or the quality of the product. It has functioned to valorize men's work and lower value and status of all women's work. Lisa Tickner described, for instance, how in the rhetoric of British modernism, critics saw in women, regardless of their different abilities, a disturbance of the rigour and purity of modernist art. Women artists, they feared, threatened 'to become a veritable plague, a fearful confusion, and a terrifying stream of mediocrity'.[47] Even in these postmodern, pluralist and eclectic times, the bourgeois feminine image of 'the blue rinse brigade' – a taunt recently levelled at an amateur art exhibition – still disturbs the unstable boundaries of identity of the professional postmodern artist.[48]

The ideology of feminine art carries with it a cluster of identifications which have their bases in nineteenth century patriarchal family relations and divisions of labour, when women were legally dependent on men and had no access to art education.

This quote from one skilled craftsman sums up the ideology of the lady amateur:

> In the guilds workshops our fellows are rightly nervous of the lady amateur . . . I have seen a great deal of her work in the last ten years, she is very versatile, she makes jewellery, she binds books, she enamels, she carves, she does leather work, a hundred different graceful and delicate crafts. She is very modest and does not profess to any high standard nor does she compete in any lines of work where physique or experience are desired, but she is perpetually tingling to sell her work before she half knows how to make it, and she does compete because her name is legion and because, being supported by her parents she is prepared to sell her labour for 2d an hour where the skilled workman has to sell his for 1s in order to keep up standards and support his family.[49]

Leisure discourse has constructed an image of women as docile, modest, domestic, patient, good at tedious and repetitive work such as embroidery, which requires manual dexterity and fine detail. In feminist literary studies, Tania Modelski has argued that:

> The image of countless Victorian women who spent much of their middle-class girlhoods prostrate on chaise longues with their heads buried in worthless novels provided historical preparation for the practice of countless critics who persist in equating femininity, consumption, and reading on one hand, and masculinity, production and writing on the other.[50]

The same prejudices inform much of contemporary art criticism.

Although progress in equal pay and equal education and evidences produced by psychologists and feminists have removed the material basis for stigmatizing women's art, the cluster of feminine ideological identifications of leisure and amateurism lives on. It has proved to be powerful and persistent, and has been constantly reactivated throughout the twentieth century to support low pay for women's skills, and the inferiority of women's art.

The arts management as 'service'

Charitable work had always been one of the few ways that middle class English woman could, in the nineteenth century, enter the public realm and do useful work independently of men. The main access that women as artists had to a public was through the charitable sale and organization of crafts and embroidery and the organization of arts events: hosting cultural events, supporting artists, entertaining, 'networking' and fundraising for charity. They revived women's rural handicrafts, they organized art meetings and established evening classes, founding organizations such as the Home Arts and Industries Association.[51]

Mary Garrard explored this continuing association of bourgeois women with patronage, art collecting and with amateur, volunteer and support roles. She concluded that they have

> virtually cornered the market in art activity . . . women presently make up a majority in most art schools, a trend initiated in the later 19th century; have played a significant role as patrons of the arts and fill nearly all the army of volunteers who offer their services to museums.[52]

'Knowing about art' is a feminine and a female activity. Art history is an area of study in universities that is dominated by middle class girls from fee paying schools. Elizabeth McGregor, writing about the contemporary practice of curating, described how curators are expected to behave like bourgeois mothers. They 'soothe the tantrums' of artists, act as social hostesses, wheedling money out of patrons with charm and smiles.[53] Women's work in fundraising, managing, sponsoring and collecting of art continues to support many contemporary art institutions as it did in the nineteenth century.

Through these spaces in modernity – in art history, writing, curating and art criticism – middle class women have been able to exert power in the fine arts. But only a few have extended their critical gaze to include meanings about fine art produced by working class women.

Crafts education for working class children

Until the beginnings of state-maintained education, working class girls were not taught fine art at all. Most of their art-making activities centred around the production and care of domestic textiles: in sewing, laundry work, mending and knitting. These handicrafts always had a place in the Dame schools, in the factory and private schools that preceded state education and it was common practice for girls to do handicrafts and sewing whilst boys did reading, writing and arithmetic.[54] The same pattern was continued in state education, legitimized by the liberal ideology of separate spheres. It was common for boys to do technical drawing, mathematics, science, rural, wood and metal crafts,[55] while the same time in the curriculum for girls was spent on childcare, laundrywork, sewing, embroidery and light crafts. As feminist researchers have made clear, it was explicit in girls' education that they were being educated to become better wives and mothers. Girls, as potential guardians of the home, were to be deployed in the service of the state to combat the crime, dirt, immorality and bad habits of their menfolk and children. As one contemporary educator expressed it: 'The infant cannot indeed be saved by the state. It can only be saved by the mother. But the mother can be helped and can be taught by the state'.[56]

Needlework was a compulsory examination subject for all elementary school teachers; girls from the age of 5 upwards were taught elementary sewing procedures. Girls of 12 or upwards learned to sew accurately, quickly and neatly. They did long seams, basic fastenings and mending techniques. Housewifery included such things as washing, starching, pressing clothes and the skills required for service in middle class homes: the care of embroidery and lace, and pressing ruffles and frills.

The same orderly methods and habit forming practices of stages and systematization that characterized drawing were repeated in sewing:

> The children learn their stitches according to time, naming in unison each movement as they make it. Sixty little girls chant thus in a monotonous sing-song over their knitting: 'Needle through, thread taken, bring it back, take it off.' It is claimed for this method that it prevents the formation of slovenly habits of work and keeps the class together.[57]

Craft ideologies

Boys and girls absorbed and became familiar with the ideological assumptions within which gendered technologies and skills were taught. Boys' crafts assumed a future of self-help, financial independence in rhetorics of the dignity of labour, manual skill, pride in workmanship, and working for 'a man's wage'. The discourses of girls' handicrafts were couched in terms of acquiring personal attributes of patience, modesty, neatness, orderliness and cleanliness. Their ideological values, constructed in the domestic setting, stressed service to others. Textile work in sewing, embroidery, dressmaking, fabric care and light crafts were represented as pleasant tasks, compared to the evils and horrors of factory work, to be carried out by women for love, unpaid, for the family in the home, or for personal improvement or adornment. Whilst boys putatively learned skills for future employment, payment or professionalism, for girls, paid employment was hardly, if ever, mentioned as an aim towards which girls should aspire.[58] Yet throughout the nineteenth century and beyond, women were dependent on employment in textile related industries.

Textile production in the nineteenth century

Throughout the nineteenth century, most working women spent their daily lives in some kind of textile related activity. Women in the Midlands and North of England worked in cotton and woollen mills, whilst those in urban centres, particularly in London, were active in light craft production: the making of items for retail and wholesale. Mervyn Romans has traced the increasing importance of this kind of craft work towards the end of the nineteenth century as part of the expansion of consumer activity.[59]

Slopwork

Sally Alexander has described 'slopwork', as it was called, as an invisible part of 'the industrial revolution'. Slopwork included the making of small consumer goods: furniture, upholstery, boxes, parasols, bags, artificial flowers, decorative ornaments, shoes, millinery, haberdashery, gloves, ribbons, hats and so on. It employed large numbers of women and young girls, often immigrants. It was characterized as work that required a variety of different skills to produce large numbers of identical items for retail and wholesale which was carried out in small, patriarchally organized workshops. It was seasonal work that had to respond quickly to fashion, characterized by long hours, piecework, irregular employment and wages often below subsistence level. The textile crafts industries introduced new and cheaper work methods, such as subcontracting and undercutting, 'sweating' and 'scamping', thereby shortening the amount of time to make articles and cutting down on unnecessary 'quality' procedures.

Working women's identities had been bound up in textiles. Young girls learned to sew and launder in the home and they saw their mothers do the same. They learned at school the skills of sewing, cutting and constructing with cloth. They were familiar with handling soft textile materials and found pleasure in their leisure hours working in feathers, ribbons and trimmings to decorate their clothes. They did not need to be coerced or forced into textile employments, in textile mills or in slopwork, but family patterns, custom, habit and years of training had, by the time they left school, made textile practices an almost inevitable choice. At the same time, exclusive labour laws and working class men's resistance kept them out of better paid work. The ideologies of leisure crafts and bourgeois social ideal of the lady amateur supported a view of women's work as essentially easy, pleasurable and unpaid, requiring 'nimble fingers' and superficially acquired skills. The ideological discourse of the patriarchal family with the male as the breadwinner combined with the feminine virtues of modesty and self-sacrifice learned at school were in happy coincidence with a need for a constant cheap supply of a large skilled labour force. The ideological values of the school, the dominant discourses of art, and the economic requirements of the labour force all supported each other.

The discourse of service

The feminine identifications that handicrafts in schools encouraged for work in production – docility, dependence, cleanliness and 'taste' – also produced in working class girls identities that fitted them for employment as servants: the maids, cooks, charladies, laundry workers and childcarers that were employed in vast numbers throughout the nineteenth century and into the twentieth in middle class homes. What appeared as middle class ladies' charitable and philanthropic concern with the health, welfare, honesty and cleanliness of the working class girl also benefited their own interests in producing a constant supply of presentable, clean and well-behaved servants.

To succeed in service, working class girls had to be trained into middle class habits, taste and behaviours. Servants needed to be loyal and discreet, to identify their own interests with those of the family in which they worked. 'Refinement', a good personal presentation, cleanliness, neatness and social discernment were required to do the work of a maid, dressmaker or domestic in close bodily proximity with the middle classes. Through domestic service, working class girls, not always successfully, took on middle class identifications, habits, tastes and pleasures.

Modernity and identity

The contemporary cultural theorists, Peter Berger and Anthony Giddens, have both argued in different contexts that changes of modernization, such as urbanization and mechanization, produced typically 'modern' identities. The modern identity, they suggest, has been characterized by an increasing ability for abstract thought, rationality, risk-taking and an interrogating and observing curiosity.[60] Much has been written of modern man constructed as alienated, individualistic, competitive, rational and aggressive, the flâneur as a leisurely observer of modern urban life. This particular cluster of modern identifications – while it was increasingly becoming available to modern woman – primarily formed the identity of the modern, middle class male.[61] Most working class women's identities would have been constructed within different discursive experiences. Working class women in service were dependent on the family who employed them, rather than wholly on their male providers. Their class loyalties were equivocal. In service, they experienced at first hand a taste, smell and feel of luxury and different modes of behaviour to which their menfolk had no access. Having a job as a higher servant was a fantasy of ease for a working class girl and such desirable work could be attained only by changes of manner, appearance, voice and style. Working class 'vulgarity', 'loudness', 'stridency' and 'showiness' had to be repressed. Acquiring knowledges about art, beauty and culture throughout education were means of performing elevated behaviours and provided fantasies of achieving higher social status and easier employment.

The literature and social relations of the English are steeped in the ridicule of the snobbish working class woman – and the immigrant – who 'apes her betters' and attempts to elevate herself

> by tastelessly attiring [her]self with the fashions and designations which have become unalterably associated with a wealthy and refined class, and which, tricking out those who have neither wealth nor refinement, are ridiculous.[62]

The experiences of modernization changed intimate behaviours, but it changed men and women of different classes in different ways. Snobbery and the display of 'elevated taste', for instance, are characteristics acquired through negotiating the changing class structures of modernity; they are, as Chaney has observed, 'reactions to the collapse of "naturally" ordered distinctions and the attempts to form new identities and social networks'.[63]

Vulgarity, snobbery, bad taste and 'showiness' are personal identifications pejoratively associated with urban women. Images of the loud and 'refined' factory girl or of the vulgar and overdressed urban woman – with its undertones of sexual immorality – were often compared in novels to the simplicity and purity of the country girl. These images find their examples in narratives in modern melodrama, romance and film: in the novels of Thomas Hardy, for instance, or in the depiction of Mrs Bast as the uneducated foil to her aspiring and earnest husband and sensitive middle class artistic women in E. M. Forster's *Howards End*. Today, the vulgar and unfeeling working class mother can be seen represented in the film *Little Voice*, and the popular ideology of 'Essex Girl' is a recurring joke about affluent working class girls as stupid, 'loud-mouthed', 'over-sexed' and 'showy'.

These feminine, working class identifications operate as a means of ridicule, shame and control of women and are just as much productions of modernity and modernization as are the better known modern identities of detective, the scientist, the flâneur or the urban man about town.[64]

Working class women and modern art

Fine art education had been considered pointless for working class children, particularly those girls who were destined to be domestic servants. Yet the image of working class women was highly visible in nineteenth century painting, particularly in French Impressionism and realism. Whilst they went about their business earning money, their activities caught the visual imagination and fantasies of the modern middle class male artist. As models, seamstresses, servants, prostitutes, dancers and entertainers, working in laundries, ironing, washing, selling clothes and breastfeeding, working class women are identifiable as the silent objects of paintings and photographs produced by middle class men for other men to enjoy.[65] Working class women have no acknowledged role in the story of modern art, but it was no doubt they as a class who mothered, cleaned, nursed, cooked for, modelled, made and washed the clothes, sexually serviced and made possible the work of modern artists. They supported and looked after the children of art historians, the critics and the connoisseurs: male and female. The bodies and the labour of working class women are invisible but present in modernity's artistic forms.

These are the images and implicit meanings that are present in reproductions of paintings that children are now being given to appreciate, copy and observe in art education. In a recent art educational text the example is given of 'washerwomen pushing old prams' who assume a 'peacefully moving grandeur and nobility, opening up a new world of compositional possibilities and subject matter'.[66] Images like this, which are familiar subjects of French Impressionist paintings, are underscored by the realities of domestic work that working class girls' mothers actually do today as cleaners, carers, waitresses and cooks in the home, in schools and art institutions. We have to question what meanings and identifications today's working class girls are taking on as they negotiate these romanticized fine art images of women, alongside real women who are their friends and relatives.

Nineteenth-century identities

New roles and opportunities had opened up for the more prosperous section of working class women in the second half of the nineteenth century. The growth of manufacturing and industry meant that an increasing sector of the urban working class had money and were responding to new ways of spending it in newly developed modern pleasures of shopping, gallery going, magazine reading, music hall and theatre entertainment. Expanding consumer activities of domestic crafts, interior decoration, hobbies and fashion became available to more working class women as the nineteenth century progressed. The image of the bourgeois 'Leisured Lady' was reactivated by advertisers and appeared in novels and songs as the ideal aspirational model of womanhood. The country house and rural image of squirearchy was held out as a 'beau ideal' for urban living.[67] People aspired to a new status, and reproduced (on a small scale in their homes) the interiors, furniture and stuffed comforts and chintzes of the country houses of an imagined rural aristocracy.

Changing class identities

Changing class identity required a whole new set of skills and attributes, a taking on of the behaviours, culture, networks, lifestyle and speech patterns and dress of another class. Penny Sparke, analysing the feminine culture of modernity, has written at length of processes by which shopping, dress, interior display and other modes of consumption were used to perform new class status and create a new identity. The home itself became one of the ways in which status could be displayed and new class position consolidated and communicated. Sparke describes how a room in lower middle class homes was set aside as a way of displaying subtle differences of meaning in status through objects and their juxtaposition:

> The parlour communicated through a visual language which consisted of a set of standard artefacts . . . The subtleties of variation mirrored the dialects of a language which gave away, at first hearing, the social and cultural position of the speaker. The way in which knick-knacks were arranged, combined with the elaborateness or otherwise of a particular parlour, was an immediate sign to a visitor of its inhabitants' actual, or aspired to, social status.[68]

Consumption

Consumption is not just about buying things, but also a meaning-making practice carried out in the work of choosing and redeploying objects, acquiring new knowledges about taste, decoration, etiquette and dress and knowing when and how to use them creatively to achieve desired effects. Consumption is the visual performance of taste, it consolidates identity and communicates through objects, acts, performances and display. As Baudrillard observed, it operates like a language:

> Consumption is a system which assures the regulation of signs and the integration of the group: it is simultaneously a morality (a system of ideological values) and a system of communication, a structure of exchange . . . a system of meanings, like language or like the kinship system in primitive societies.[69]

Women had to *work* at consumption. Information had to be acquired about available products, on how to use and maintain them. It required attention to detail, observation and imitation. The performance of new class identities required new skills: a good eye for workmanship, judgement and discrimination developed to select and prioritize purchases and an unerring and accurate judgement of value, fashion and performance. A slip of accent, a mistake in dress, a lack of knowledge of appropriate manners would reveal undesirable old class behaviours.[70] Newly opened galleries, department stores and museums worked in conjunction with advice in women's and art magazines to provide information on etiquette, taste and the correct deployment of new purchases.

The performance of consumption was not so much an expression of an already existing class identity, but was class identity 'in-the-making', achieved through everyday practices and performances.

Art education, through the romanticized and elevated tastes of bourgeois women teachers, and their leisure values of beauty, refinement was recognized as the place where the skills of consumption could be passed on.

Middle class women as teachers

Anthea Callen has traced the struggle of women in Britain and the United States to gain entry to a professional education in art and has documented the gradual opening of art schools to women students from the early nineteenth century.[71] There was a rapid growth in art schools after 1880, ostensibly to provide employment in design for what was constructed as the new 'artisan' classes, male and female.[72] In many of these art schools, however, the demand for 'ladies' lessons' for 'the better and educated classes' was great. Accusations that middle and upper class women were taking up charitable places that had been intended for girls 'of humbler origin' were not uncommon.[73] It was the ability of middle class women to pay, to exercise their talents in fundraising and their ability and willingness to do the social 'hostessing' work of the institution, that made them popular as students:

> It was said that at York 'the school was greatly strengthened by the accession of these ladies'. The ladies not only paid full fees but busied themselves organising bazaars which produced for some Schools more than half their annual income. For instance, at Warrington in 1854 the Christmas Bazaar and Tree brought in £138 out of a total income of £265. Some large occasions such as a ball for the Spitalfields School of Design or the Bloomsbury Female School could bring in a thousand pounds or more.[74]

The crafts practised by women in art schools built on already existing feminine leisure discourses of art, combined with the useful and 'respectable' trades that had been working class women's work, for example illustration, embroidery, bookbinding, cabinet making, millinery, dressmaking and jewellery making, which were promoted by the Arts and Crafts Movement.[75] The discourse of the accomplishments was reactivated in the teaching of the drawing natural forms: flowers, birds and fruit, and pattern design. Art school training itself, as Sara Dodd and Anthea Callen have both argued, provided few opportunities or skills for women to be the equals of men in product or industrial design, in architecture or in professional art practice. Misogyny, restrictive unions and ideological pressures continued to restrict women's opportunities.[76] Most newly art-educated women were encouraged and indeed welcomed the opportunities to use their skills and accomplishments in the newly available profession of elementary school teaching.

From the authoritarian to the caring teacher

Pedagogy that had relied on classical and vocational ideologies and overt paternal systems of authority, which had been the prerogative of school masters in public education, had been introduced into state education.[77] But systematizing, regulating 'drilling' and strict regimes for the very young child were soon to be challenged by approaches derived from psychology based on what was believed to be the nature of the child. Such approaches were promoted in the work of Froebel and Pestalozzi in Europe, Robert Owen and his school in the New Lanark Mills, and Itard and Seguin in France, whom Maria Montessori followed. At the moment when 'nature' was introduced into pedagogy, as Walkerdine has argued, there came a shift from overt paternal authority to covert control of the growing child through a more child-centred and caring model of pedagogy. This shift was co-terminous with the entry of women into teaching. 'Through the figure of the maternal teacher, the harsh power of the authoritarian father [was] converted into the soft benevolence of the bourgeois mother'.[78]

Women were entering the teaching profession in large numbers not to replace authoritarian pedagogy – which continued in the teaching of older children – but explicitly to add a quasi-maternal nurturance to the teaching of the elementary school child. The teaching of arts and crafts was seen as an ideal means of enabling the child to learn and develop naturally through play, spontaneity and colour, and free manipulation of materials. Liberalized, child-centred education rejected the passing on of established knowledges, and the horrors of and tedium of 'child labour' in school. Play was seen as the proper medium of learning for children.

The hidden control of progressive pedagogy

Valerie Walkerdine and Nikolas Rose have both emphasized that the ultimate aims of child-centred education were the same as those of traditional Classical and vocational modes of education, that is to turn the uncontrolled, uncoordinated young child into a self-disciplined, self-regulating, docile and rational being. The training of women teachers to manage young children was part of this process:

The freedom of children is suggested by teachers who are not the Oedipal father, but the pre-Oedipal mother, whose attachment to the children in her care, together with her total presence, ensures their psychic health.[79]

The difference was that bourgeois women teachers could, with love, care, 'fun' and freedom, work together with children, to empower and enable, and make the civilizing process more pleasurable. Self-control would then be 'second nature', to become part of the child's identity, part of their own values, preferences and habitual behaviour.[80] The patriarchal authority of the father was hidden and the labour of socializing the child fell on the executive, management and maternal skills of the bourgeois woman teacher.

Middle class women as art teachers

The leisure skills and liberal romantic leisure attitudes of bourgeois women of this period lent themselves to the values of progressive pedagogy. Whilst a minority of women found ways of practising as professional artists and educators, most were neither as highly trained in art nor as well educated as their male counterparts.[81] They may have had some drawing, design and craft education in an art school and been introduced to wider forms of artistic practice in Romantic and Classical/vocational art techniques, but most had opted for the traditional feminine arts subjects in their training, and had achieved at home, in school and in their compulsory teacher training, considerable skills in needlecrafts. They had less attention paid in their education to physical sciences, to product design or architecture, nor had they usually worked in heavy and hard materials in general. Objective and analytic drawing, anatomy, perspective, geometry and other technical aspects of image-making had not been readily available in a middle class girls' education. Girls' drawing skills had been shaped within pattern design, decoration, the drawing of the draped figure and natural forms such as flowers and leaves that could be used in the decoration of fabrics and ceramics.

The amateur crafts that many middle class women practised in the drawing-room, and which appeared in women's magazines as leisure pastimes, soon began to appear in the elementary classroom.

As late as 1926, the Hadow Report recommended in the Art lesson for adolescents the teaching of

decoration for lamp shades, wall papers, title pages of books, posters, embroidery, lettering and book decorations . . . leather work, book-binding, stencilling and where conditions are suitable, pottery, enamelling and weaving.[82]

The same manufacturers who had supplied straws, beads, threads and papers for women's amateur arts began to turn their attention to education and provided a new market in art educational supplies. Drawing-room leisure crafts were adapted to fit child art programmes.[83] Consumer leisure practices in felt, silver paper, straws, soft toy making, embroidery, cut paper work, printing, appliqué, bead work and so on emerged through the myriad traits of bourgeois women teachers into elementary art and handicraft teaching. Whilst the rhetoric of crafts was often concerned with the educational purposes of the development of manual abilities, the instilling of the 'dignity of labour', the importance of the use of tools and technologies and providing children with simple skills in design, in practice the activities in the artroom were often led by the discourses of leisure through the consumption of craft supplies from manufacturers in the context of a growing leisure and hobby industry.[84]

A gender divided curriculum

The profession and practice of art education at the beginning of the twentieth century was divided into two major discursive modes: Classical, vocational modes based on observational and mechanical drawing and child-centred, progressive modes which were less concerned with standards in art and more with the health development of the child. David Thistlewood summarized this division:

> There was a tacit distinction between the 'higher' discipline of teaching drawing and design and the 'lower' discipline of teaching art. The former was associated with national economic purposes and aspired to academic respectability; the latter connoted 'play' and rather modest learning. The National Society of Art Masters encouraged its members to pursue high levels of technical accomplishment as measured by its own examination system . . . The Art Teachers Guild on the other hand was much more concerned with tactical approaches necessary for encouraging an essential creativity . . . in children not specifically destined for an aesthetic way of life . . . art as an aspect of human development.[85]

What Thistlewood did not make explicit was that this division of teaching Art was clearly gendered: the National Society of Schoolmasters, as its name suggests, was a male institution, while the Art Teachers Guild recruited women of 'modest learning'.

Handicrafts at that time were taught quite separately from Art. The exact pattern of the Art and Craft curriculum at the end of the nineteenth century varied between different schools and regions and was often influenced by gendered employment practices in different parts of the country. Syllabuses for the younger and the less able child usually had larger amounts of hand-icrafts, which for girls often meant more needlework.[86] The ideologies and aims, and the unproblematically gender divided nature of crafts education can be summed up in this proposal for an ideal curriculum for working class children in the early part of the twentieth century:

> In boys' central schools with an industrial bias, special attention is devoted to practical mathematics, practical science, and handwork. Stress is laid on technical drawing, which includes designing, scale drawing, tracing and the making of blueprints . . . and in girls' schools in the last year of schooling, housecraft in its various branches, to book-keeping based on household accounts, to needlework, to sick nursing, and an elementary hygiene based on a science syllabus which comprises the necessary foundations of elementary chemistry and biology . . . and courses with an industrial bias generally comprise instruction in dress-making, millinery and the like.[87]

Even in its most idealized form, crafts education for working class children was unproblematically gendered and divided into 'public and private' activi-ties. The discourses that made up the field of art education for the older child – classical values, vocational drawing, design, technical and objective draw-ing – were gendered as masculine.

The place where the vast majority of girls received their information about art would more likely to have been in the growing consumer discourses of leisure, fashion, interior design, which were increasingly being targeted towards the desires and fantasies of working class girls, through shopping, advertising and in new women's magazines. Whilst girls at school were being taught the values of clarity, rationality, objectivity, proportion, perspective and realism through drawing and were beginning to be included in the pro-fessional discourses of vocational design, they had also to take into account contradictory meanings about taste, surface decoration, neatness, cleanli-ness and altruism that were heavily promoted through textiles discourses, and through the romantic leisure practices in schools, biased towards the home and domesticity.

Modernization and working class girls

The available employment and the everyday life of working class women had not fundamentally changed during the nineteenth century. Fast moving technological developments of modernization in heavy industry, and manu-facture building and engineering mainly affected men's work. Although there were a few jobs available in design, in the pottery and fashion indus-tries, in clerical work, communications and art teaching, these were mainly taken up by middle class women. The vast majority of working class women continued as low paid workers as servants, cleaners, cooks and child-rearers, and were increasingly found in extensions of feminized work in sales and catering work. The need for large numbers of immigrant and female labour in slopwork and light crafts continued to increase and the need for the cheap labour of women in the textile industry had not diminished. This conservatism in modern employment was mirrored in schools where the art curriculum for girls remained, in technological terms, unprogressive and domestic. At the end of the nineteenth century, girls were still doing large amounts of sewing, laundry work, mending and textile crafts and decorative arts.

Art education, no doubt, did not actively conspire to subordinate working class girls but it offered few alternatives. The more potentially transformative discourses of the Socialist Arts and Crafts Movement,[88] the influences of feminist educators who argued against the necessity for a gender divided curriculum,[89] and the discourses of radical and challenging forms of modernist art were promoted by a minority, and they were available as alternatives. But they were overlooked, ignored or swamped by the gender divided discourses that could conveniently be adapted to fit more powerful economic rationales.

3 Psychology in art education

After the Second World War and with the expansion of education for working class children, the progressive discourses of art, based on new knowledges about the child, began to replace the authoritarian conventional pedagogies of instrumental/vocational models of art education.

No account of twentieth-century 'high modernist' art education would be complete without acknowledging the central position of psychology in establishing its founding assumptions about art, the child, creativity and perception. Psychology and modernist art education have been saturated in each other's practices, both emerging as new institutions towards the end of the nineteenth century in the context of urban modernization.

Walkerdine has argued that: 'Schooling and psychology have a joint and twin history . . . when we look at schools we are not seeing a place where psychology is applied so much as a place where certain truths about children are continually produced.' What I want to describe in this section is the extent to which psychology is embedded in art educational discourse, and the extent to which the truths it produces about children are gendered.[1]

Psychology had provided education with scientifically legitimized knowledges about the normal child since the late nineteenth century in the context of the Child Study Movement. Experimental work right through the twentieth century measured young people's behaviour, their manual abilities, their perceptual abilities, their intellectual and cognitive abilities, as well as abilities differentiated by age, culture, race and gender. Psychological studies provided classifications of children into different types, personalities, tastes and talents. The norms – as well as the categories of 'subnormal', 'deviant' and 'abnormal' – produced about the average child provided a scientific authority on which different educational curricula could be planned and projected.

Psychology was built on to the two major discourses of art education. Behavioural psychology (which I shall return to in Chapter 4) based on observations of 'normal' child behaviours and responses to stimuli, strengthened and legitimized the evolutionary stages and classifications that were already present in sequenced drawing schemes. The same experimental work underpinned child-centred, progressive models of art education. These were later combined with psychoanalytically informed models. In the early twentieth century, theories of early childhood provided progressive art education with its rationales for the importance of play and self-directed activity in fostering creativity and the healthy development of the average child.

What follows is a brief outline of the two models, which in practice often combined and overlapped, but together formed dynamically interacting discourses within which the child of modernist art education was constructed.

'Rational' art education and psychometric testing

Psychometric testing – that is, the testing and measurement of mental qualities – was carried out in schools from the late nineteenth century up to the mid-twentieth century.[2] Psychometric testers were not concerned with drawing as art, but with the 'window' it provided onto the child's mind: it was a means of interpreting the cognitive development of the average child. Drawing was understood to be a universal and spontaneous practice of young children, which seemed to change in consistent ways as the child got older. The regular changes in children's drawing were seen to reflect regular changes taking place in cognitive development. From the results of experiments based on observations of children's drawing, vast amounts of information, about the development of intelligence,[3] of emotional states, of personality,[4] and general mental abilities,[5] and of sexual difference,[6] were amassed.

Experiments in drawing were extrapolated to apply to all art and craft practices in the classroom, and the fragmentation of art-making into stages and differences, which appeared to correspond with natural human development, meant that art education could be delivered in progressively organized systems of teaching and learning that would apply to all children, whatever their background and differences. All children could first be introduced to simple forms and basic mark-making, progress to two-dimensional forms, and then to three-dimensional forms and more complex interactions with social meanings about art. Empirical research in the psychology of human behaviour provided scientific legitimacy for systematized and sequentially delivered modes of art pedagogy.

Child-centred psychological models

Systematic and mechanistic models of art education always had their critics. Progressive educators such as Froebel and Montessori, in the early part of the twentieth century, had rejected the notions of drilling and training evident in systems such as the National Course of Instruction in favour of a Rousseauian approach allowing for the natural growth of the child 'not as a mind to be instructed and a body to be drilled, but a growing organism'.[7]

Rational and organized modes of delivering art education were criticized as having too much emphasis on the measurable and quantifiable to be useful in fully understanding the complexities, the imaginative and affective processes of making and understanding art.[8] Progressive art education appeared to be in opposition to 'scientific' approaches, it placed more stress on emotions, feelings and unconscious processes, on the inner life and what has been perceived to be the nature of the child. Progressive art pedagogy seemed less coercive, and gave a more active role to the child, valuing exploration, inquiry, creativity and discovery encouraged and supported by a non-interventionist teacher. Rachel MacMillan wrote:

> take the little girl as she is – with her long sighted eye, her hunger for bright colour, her small undeveloped hand, her wandering desires . . . they do not ask from her what she cannot give – Imagination without memories, fine or complex work ere yet any real power for fine co-ordination has been won. From the first, the child works with psychologists, who know where she is, physically, and also with artists, in short with teachers who can understand her naive efforts.[9]

In progressive art education the child-like quality of art is cherished, what is valued and evaluated is the child's normal and healthy growth through the process of art-making, rather than competitive judgements of a final art product.

Psychoanalytic and therapeutic models of art pedagogy

In their critique of the behavioural emphasis of systems models, progressive art educators turned to psychologies which attempt to deal with the origins of emotions, anxieties and non-visible, otherwise unaccountable behaviours. Psychoanalytic models were drawn into what was called a 'new psychology' in the early decades of the twentieth century, largely based in versions of object-relations theories from Melanie Klein and Donald Winnicott, whose accounts of human development emphasized the significance of human communication and interrelationships – particularly the child–mother relationship.[10] They laid stress on the importance, in early childhood, of establishing a safe, secure and non-threatening environment for play, the imagination and fantasy as a basis for establishing an individual that is confident, creative and trusting. Klein's work was popularized in educational circles by Susan Isaacs and promoted in art education through the writings of Marion Milner and Carl Rogers.[11] Rogers used Kleinian notions of trust in therapeutic models of artistic activity, based on clinical experience of encounter groups in psychoanalysis. He suggested that

> psychological safety, psychological freedom, the acceptance of the individual as of unconditional worth; the absence of external evaluation; empathetic understanding; and the permission of complete freedom of symbolic expression are all preconditions to creativity.[12]

In the 1970s the art educator Malcolm Ross drew on this concept of nurturing creativity and argued that the art teacher, both male and female, should provide an uncritical and supportive environment in the classroom that fosters creativity and trust; that the teacher should become in Kleinian terms a 'good-enough' teacher.[13]

Psychoanalytic theories allowed for a more fluid and reflexive approach to understanding art and the child. They allowed more room for interpretation and response, and stressed the influence of non-productive play, dreams and fantasies in art-making, the sharing of experience and activities, and they began to provide explanations for the meaning-making function of objects. Progressive art pedagogy was, in conventional terms, more feminine, concerned as it was with the privacy of emotions, feelings and experience. It was taught by teachers using more maternal, caring styles of pedagogy. Its discursive themes were often the traditional humanist subjects of bourgeois feminine arts – portrait painting, landscape, the figure and natural objects that were brought into the classroom, leaves, seed heads, flowers, patterns, and so on. It was couched in romantic formal genres of mark-making, impasto techniques, use of colour and semi-representational themes that did not emphasize realism, accuracy or detail, but concentrated more on the visible expression of emotion and child-like qualities.

Progressive pedagogy as repressive

Nonetheless, the concept of the normal creative child who is imagined as the subject of progressive education, owes its existence to the same scientific, empirical and evolutionary models as systems approaches. Psychoanalytically informed models also produced a largely developmental version of the child: a healthy ego gradually evolving from complete narcissistic identification with the mother, to gradual experience of separation, and identification with the father, towards an interest in people and later adolescent struggles around final assertive independence in relation to the outer world, ultimately achieving a stable and unified identity. The same experimental work on child development and the classifying psychological types and age differences are there, but are less visible, concealed within the rhetorics of play, spontaneity, self-expression, liberation and creativity.[14] Child-centred pedagogy, as Walkerdine suggested, rendered the presence of psychology invisible.

> whisper its name, but whisper it almost inaudibly, so that you might be led to believe that these pragmatic devices, these common-sense and obvious assumptions about what children are, and what good learning and teaching are, have little to do with psychology.[15]

The child and the teacher were so positioned within progressive practices as not to see the systems and structures to which they are subjected. They have become so successfully internalized and are so invisible, that teachers believe themselves to be acting spontaneously and freely choosing their own actions.[16]

The production of child art in progressive art pedagogy

Although the rhetoric of progressive pedagogy was tied in notions of freedom and self-agency, choice and self-expression, it was in progressive pedagogies that some of the most rigid, formulaic and static systems of art teaching have been established. Children were putatively free to choose their own activity and materials, but the classroom was so organized that only certain materials were available; materials that were perceived to fit stages of development or manual ability as determined by developmental psychology. Paints available were often in primary colours. Black or brown paint, industrial materials, smooth white paper and fine fibre-tipped pens were often forbidden. It seemed natural to give small children large paint-brushes, large sheets of tinted 'sugar paper' to meet their simple perceptual abilities and crude wax crayons for 'little hands to hold'. They had available special pre-cut simple shapes and forms to match their early perceptual and manual skills. Copying, attempts at fine detail or realism and the use of drawing instruments, rulers or optical devices were not encouraged. Gentle persuasion was employed to approve appropriate child art practice and discourage undesirable art – cartoon drawings, drawings of sex or copying commercial illustrations of fashion or war – that children, left to their own devices, were apt to 'fall into'. Such work was removed, it received little praise or simply was not put on the classroom walls. A genre of school art emerged that had a specific 'look': a gender neutral 'Child Art'. The innocence and simplicity, the developmental stages and the a-sexuality of the modern child were *produced* in these feminine, romantic, progressive art educational discourses. A narrative of art having an 'earlier stage of development' as child-like and feminine, progressing to later, rational, realistic and masculine representations, was constructed through the discourses of both behavioural and progressive pedagogy.

'Old Paradigm' psychology

The behavioural and therapeutic psychologies on which both scientific and progressive models of art pedagogy have been established are based on the progressive development of a unified and purely cognitive notion of identity, constructed in what are now being called 'Old Paradigm' psychologies.

> Traditional experimental psychology – the Old Paradigm . . . was based not only on an outdated philosophical theory of science but also on a much criticized metaphysical thesis regarding human beings. It assumed mind–body dualism, sometimes called Cartesianism after René Descartes, the most famous exponent of the idea that human beings are composed of two systems, one mental and one material . . . the idea that the mental life was 'inner', as distinct from behaviour which was 'outer' lingered on.[17]

Art education's dominant assumptions about the child and about art have been structured within this Cartesian model. Most educational textbooks have some version of an inner self that is either expressed, represented or communicated to an outside world through 'art', and that the outside world, in turn, acts upon the inner self. The model most commonly employed today is that of cognitive psychology which describes an adaptive interaction between inner and outer worlds similar to computer models. This model is most clearly explained in the words of the contemporary art educational psychologist Elliot Eisner:

> the operations of our mental life are essentially private in character. What we think, feel, or imagine is located in our psyche and can be enjoyed, used, or criticized only by ourselves. If what we create in our mental life is to be made social, we must find some means to make it public. It is this realm, the realm through which the private is made public, that we come to the visible and sharable products of our culture. These products are made public in the forms through which we represent what we have conceived. The arts constitute one of the important forms of representation through which humans share what they have thought, felt or believed.[18]

Art – its materials and technologies – in this model is merely the transparent medium through which ideas and emotions are made manifest and shared with others.

Feminist psychologists and cultural critics have argued that the Cartesian mind that Old Paradigm psychologists studied has been essentially male. They have shown how science, technology and psychology itself have been constructed discursively as part of the Cartesian masculine identity that has effectively excluded women as a thinking and rational subject. Since the

Enlightenment, the gradually developing intellect has been imagined and constructed as a paternal entity ruling over 'wayward and feminine', natural, desiring uncontrollable and material body, in the same way that the father rules in the family.[19]

Two sides of modernity

Both psychological discourses in art education in the scientific and the progressive modes relied on empirical evidences collected by scientific methods of observation, both models were based on a Cartesian male subject, and are focused on mental activity, and neither take into account the senses and the body.[20] Both were structured within discourses of progressive, non-repeatable, developmental sequences in growth. Both modes of art education construct portraits of the mind and artistic activity which suggest that individual growth and learning and mental phenomena are separate from social interactions, that individuals exist in a kind of historical vacuum, influenced by external events, but fundamentally developing according to an inner logic and natural laws. Both have a notion of the child that, while it allows for certain specific deviations or differences in female behaviour, is fundamentally gender neutral. Both behaviourist and progressive pedagogies were based on two sides of the same coin of modernist psychology's Cartesian subject.

Evolutionary narratives

Old Paradigm psychology has been visible in the structuring of modernist art education. It constructs a notion of the feminine as an earlier, primitive stage of development, moving towards rational, abstract and more masculine cognitive styles as its end aim. This gendered narrative of simple to complex change inhabits the fundamental structuring forms of modernist art education, and constructs the feminine as subordinate, in the discourses of play, spontaneity, and earlier concrete modes of cognition typical of progressive pedagogy.

Evolutionary narratives in art education

Schooling is a long term experience and because it is evident that young people's cognitive abilities change so much in early life, some predictable account of how they change has to be useful in structuring a progressive path through the different years of the educational process. Evolutionary narratives have provided powerful metaphors accounting for change in fields that have nothing to do with biology, and narratives of evolution be seen throughout the practices of art education.[21]

Art historians used evolutionary logic to explain different artistic styles, with one style reacting to and developing out of another: traditional histories of art have been structured as a 'Story of Art' stretching in an unbroken line from the primitive 'cave man' to a 'flowering in the Renaissance, to an abstract, spiritual apogee in modernist abstraction'.[22] Culture has been subjected to the same evolutionary story: non-Western peoples have been assumed to be in primitive or 'earlier stages of development' whilst industrialized societies are in their more mature stages of civilization. These evolutionary and teleological models are now being critiqued as part of a narrativization of modernity itself.[23]

Evolutionary models were imported into education, specifically influenced by the British philosopher Herbert Spencer and promoted in North American education by the psychologist Granville Stanley Hall.[24] In the Darwinian model of educational progress, children's cognitive abilities were seen to pass through all the evolutionary stages from simple savagery to complex civilization. A theory of recapitulation, in which the growth of the individual (ontology) was seen to parallel the development of the human species (phylogeny) seemed to provide an explanation for gradual change, growth and developmental progress. Education was structured in stages to guide children through what was thought to be their natural ontology. In art education specifically, these developmental approaches can be seen in the influence of modernist art educators such as Franz Cizek, Roger Fry and Marion Richardson and have persisted well into the twentieth century.

Paul Klee, Herbert Read and Ernst Gombrich – each one of whom had a significant influence on modern art education – all adopted versions of recapitulation theory, each believing that children's art paralleled the development of art in man's childhood. Recapitulationary ideas can be seen as late as 1989 in Robert Witkin's influential writings, where he bases his ideas about progress in art education on 'a parallel between the theory of progress in child development and the theory of progress in the development of society'.[25] Although recapitulatory theories have been discredited, Sue Malvern has demonstrated how their evolutionary rhetorics and structures continue vigorously to inhabit art education's pedagogic practices as well as the languages of contemporary art criticism and assessment.[26]

The work of Jean Piaget is significant in this context because it was his well-defined account of cognitive development in the twentieth century that brought Darwinian developmentalism up to date and offered modernist education its clearest scientifically legitimized sequential structuring paradigm. Piaget's work was produced in the context of evolutionary biology and in a concept of nature which presents an object world as an environment to which organisms successively adapt towards a higher stages. It was a

.tesian model, with rationality cast as the pinnacle of
owards which the subject evolves.[27]

: Lowenfeld devised a Piagetian staged system for art edu-
ɩn what he concluded were parallel themes of creative
ɩ the child which was to be influential in art education
ɩe English speaking world.[28] As Lambert Brittain wrote in
ɩ. oreword to a reprint of Lowenfeld's successful book *Creative
and Menɩɑ. Growth*, 'It is with a great deal of satisfaction that I can look
back over the past several years and note that the original philosophy of
Viktor Lowenfeld is still fundamental in the field of art education', an observation recognized in Peter Smith's history of American art education,
in his assessment of the crucial part that Lowenfeld's ideas continue to play
in art education's contemporary structuring forms.[29]

The psychologist, Howard Gardner, also produced a model of aesthetic
development in music, literature and painting which, although more fluid
and complex in its analysis, nonetheless owed an explicit debt to evolutionary models of stage and sequence based in the work of Piaget, Freud
and the behavioural psychologist, Konrad Lorenz.[30] Gardner describes the
'free years of creativity in the child', from the ages of 4 to 7, a latency period
from 7 to 11 as a critical time when the child's personality is coalescing and
when children are able to incorporate other conventions into their own
work, and the adolescent period after 12, 'a period of danger when the less
committed or less supported child may withdraw from participation in art
as their rational and self-critical faculties come into play'.[31] These stages
correspond in type and sequence to the Piagetian model of cognitive
development.

Evolutionary narratives can still be seen at work in the fundamental structuring forms of the contemporary English National Curriculum document.
Its key stages of art education are premised on hierarchical, sequential, progressive modes of thinking, where one stage has to be completed before the
next can be attempted, and its examples become increasingly complex.
Robert Clement, who has provided an exemplary handbook for negotiating
the national curriculum, puts it thus:

> In their years of schooling, between the ages of five to sixteen, children
> go through three different stages in their perception and understand-
> ing of the world. These transitions have a profound influence upon
> their visual perception of the world and need to be understood in
> order that teachers can properly match their work to the needs of the
> children.

Clement emphasizes the importance of 'good progression' from stage to
stage and the necessity for teachers to understand the transitions from one
stage to the next.[32]

Today, in art education, Piaget's formulations are rarely explicitly taught to trainee art teachers, but developmental narratives, based on evolutionary narratives nonetheless, are uncritically accepted as the normal way of delivering art education in sequences from early simple to later complex stages.

Whether or not these stages actually match Piaget's original formulations is not really at issue, although questions have been asked as to how far it has been appropriate to transpose Piaget's model of cognitive growth onto changes in creative and artistic ability. Cross-cultural studies have suggested that the stages of artistic development based on the classic studies of Piaget and Inhelder, upon which so many drawing systems and notions of Child Art are based, are not universal or fixed. Erica Burman suggests that developmental psychology has to be regarded now as an historically and socially specific practice as 'a paradigmatically modern discipline, arising at a time of commitment to narratives of truth, objectivity, science and reason.' Evolutionary models of development begin to appear as a Western and historically recent and specific practice.[33]

Critiques of evolutionary development

There does need to be some account of changes that take place as children grow, but what is at issue here are the meanings, values and gendered hierarchical associations that have become connected with the evolutionary narrative. Some feminist psychologists, most notably Carol Gilligan, continue to work within a developmental approach, but question a Piagetian hierarchy that privileges reason and intellect as the summit of human attainment.[34] Gilligan suggests that women's psychosexual development may be differently organized, and that there is no reason why cooperation and care rather than abstraction and intellect should be the desired aim of human development. The Russian psychologist Lev Vygotsky, who was working at about the same time as Piaget, also produced a developmental scheme but he questioned its forward moving and biologistic metaphors. He suggested that cognitive growth is sometimes retrogressive, it can stand still or move backwards and repeat some events. Cognitive development does not occur as an unfolding of a pre-existing inner nature, but grows as a result of social interactions, with the body, with languages, tools and technologies.[35]

Progressive and behavioural psychologies in art education have the same narrative in that they both start with the early years of 'inner' life in play, fantasy, colour, creativity, spontaneity and closeness to the mother, and gradually progress. They adapt gradually to greater interaction with the social world to a final aim of a mature adult adopting cultural conventions of realism, objective drawing, design and control of media. Rationality and masculinity as the mature conclusion of a linear development is built into art education's sequential stages and creative processes.

The mastery of reason

Psychologist Valerie Walkerdine, who worked within Lacanian and Vygot-skian theories, has questioned the psychological practices through which the rational is produced as masculine in her study of mathematics education. She demonstrated, in her detailed and convincing studies, that the meanings and pleasures of the intellect and rationality are continually constructed through discursive narratives of pedagogy, through the things that children and teachers do and say and the symbolic materials they use. Reason, she argues – its superiority, its social status, the potential pleasures and its rewards of control and mastery – is not *in* the child to be drawn out and nurtured, but is *produced* as the climax of a narrative of mathematical discourse which involves a consequent denial of the feminine:

> this so-called natural process of mastery entails considerable and complex suppression. That suppression is both painful and extremely powerful. That power is pleasurable. It is the power of the triumph of reason over emotion . . . the power afforded by the mastery of reason is fictional, but its effects are real and material.[36]

Walkerdine described how, as girls negotiate the formalities, the linear narratives, the abstract aims, the classifications and hierarchies, the everyday practices, the snubs and disappointments of rational pedagogic practice, they learn that 'the feminine' is equated with failure and best left behind as an earlier and more child-like stage of development.

Walkerdine's arguments point to the possibility that the same rationalizing and masculinizing narratives at work in mathematics education may also be working in modernist art and design education's evolutionary narratives, and that they too are productive of rational identities as masculine with a consequent suppression of 'the feminine'.

Evolutionary narrative in discourses of creativity

Creativity has a privileged place in art education, and like other discourses, has gendered connotations.[37] Psychology in art education has constructed a major discourse of creativity which, following on the experimental work of the psychologists Sherrie Turkle and Seymour Papert, I shall refer to as the 'planning' mode.

The modernist, 'planning' model

Turkle and Papert, in their investigation of the different ways that children engage with computers, have described a specific and culturally dominant model of creativity which involves linear, developmental and sequential thinking. In this model of creativity, basic rules and existing precedents are mastered through research, and innovative thinking proceeds through logically ordered processes of adjustment and empirical testing. Prototypes are constructed and if not successful are discarded on the way as 'natural wastage'. The final outcome is a new and original idea or a product which has developed out of, but is different from the old. These 'planners', Turkle and Papert suggest, enjoy a high level of abstraction, hierarchy and structure and they have found that boys and scientists are often, but not always, most successful as planners.[38] This description of creativity is similar to the logical, deductive and sequential thinking processes that Liam Hudson produced in his notion of 'convergent' thinkers.[39]

The same 'planning' mode of creativity has been identified in the processes of producing modernist art. Norman Bryson gives an account of painting as an evolutionary problem-solving practice. The artist responds and builds on to existing visual problems on the canvas in the same way as the scientists respond to problems in science:

> The pattern for art is the same as that for science. First there is an initial problem . . . tradition suggests a particular formula or schema for its transcription onto canvas . . . Observation reveals that the . . . schema is inadequate to the empirical findings, and that the schema must be modified in accordance with the discrepant data. The modified schema in turn enters the repertoire of schemata and will in due course be subjected to similar tests and elaboration as its predecessor . . . What the painter does, what the scientist does is to test these schemata against experimental observation.[40]

The narrative of the creative process in modernist art education was similarly represented: first children observed, examined and drew the growth and structure of natural forms, noting accurately how different elements were constructed. Then they freely played with different ideas, colours and materials, if possible making prototypes; they then tried out different samples, adapting and modifying them in relation to other external factors such as the nature of materials, the target audience and the time available. They then selected the best idea from the options they made, treating the rejected models as 'natural wastage' and bringing the final product (the painting, the pot, the embroidery) to a finished state, testing and evaluating it against the original aims. This creative process is the process of evolution, scaled down and encoded in processes for producing art.

Donna Haraway's concept of 'natural encoding' has suggested how narratives of natural evolution have provided legitimizing models for imagining all kinds of productivity in the modern world.[41] The processes of mass production, as Evan Watkins pointed out, have been similarly 'techno-ideologically coded': creative product innovation, adaptation (modification) of prototypes, research and development involving 'natural wastage', production in sequential, progressive linear stages. Product evaluation and testing of the final new product is the paradigm of 'the survival of the fittest', in a process that mimics the narratives of evolution.[42]

It is not that art and art education have consciously and rigorously adopted evolutionary methodologies, but the evolutionary narrative is a powerful story of natural change and growth that lends its legitimacy to explanations of any process of change. Misia Landau, in her analysis of the way scientists work, has demonstrated how unconscious evolutionary narratives actually shape the way that knowledges and other creative outcomes are constructed:

> The growth of a plant, the progress of a disease, the formation of a beach, the evolution of an organism – any set of events which can be arranged in a sequence and related can also be narrated . . . Whether or not scientists follow such a narrative structure in their work, they do not often recognise the extent to which they use narrative in their thinking and in communicating their ideas. Consequently, they may be unaware of the narrative presuppositions which inform their science.[43]

What is significant in this context is that Piaget's evolutionary models of cognitive development provide a *rhetoric* of growth and creativity that always has the same trajectory, moving from inferior, simple, uncoordinated and feminine tasks towards mature, masculine, logical and rational ends. It is a narrative that privileges the experience and the life-world of modern man.

The design process

The natural encodings of evolution were, in the mid-twentieth century in Britain, transposed to the new subject of Design in schools, which was taught through an evolutionary 'Design Process', a system to rationalize and organize the teaching of what had been old Handicraft subjects.

In the Design Process

> The student identifies a problem, explores its requirements, executes possible solutions, evaluates them and eventually reaches an acceptable well verified answer to the problem with which he began . . . Both start with a situation (the consumer), progress through investigation (research), specification and production to assessment and feedback.[44]

Children produced 'worksheets' which were documentations of the process, and demonstrated logical development from exploratory drawing through to the final product. It has been argued that the techno-rational codings of the design and creative processes did not find their justification in the psychological needs of the individual child. Nor did they find their logic in aesthetics or art history. Amanda Weate in her analysis of the discourses of creativity has argued that this particular form of creativity has been a positivist, instrumental model, bound up with the solving of technical problems in a post-war economic context. Its sequences reproduced efficient Fordist production processes, mainly encountered in productive work carried out by men in solving problems in engineering, technology and manufacture.[45] 'Planning' modes of creativity represent a method of production that, in the post-war economy, privileged the work and vocational expectations of boys.

Bricolage

Traditional psychology has produced other models of creativity which appear to be in opposition and subordinate to the planning mode, associated with play, with 'concrete' thinking and earlier modes of learning. These models have been called 'combinatory' or 'bricolage' creative modes.[46] Combinatory creativity is recognized as a form of creativity that involves a broader, eclectic approach rather than a linear approach. It collects and gathers heterogeneous information and ignores boundaries. It recombines existing ideas and genres in unorthodox ways. It corresponds to Hudson's notions of 'divergent' thinkers.[47] Divergent thinkers, traditional psychology suggests, are less original and less creative than 'convergent' planners. It appears to allow individuals to become 'too creative', to bring in 'irrelevant' or trivial concerns:

> In terms of requirements for an act of originality, the divergent thinking tests leave a lot to be desired ... The responses frequently serve no useful purpose and often display flights of fancy bordering on the grotesque, the sadistic and trivial. What we have are two operational definitions of short term thinking styles: one, the divergent kind relying on ideational fluency in open ended problems; the other, convergent thinking favouring those who like homing in on one solution.[48]

The anthropologist Claude Lévi-Strauss recognized divergent combinatory thinking in 'simple' cultures, where people were apparently engaged in 'primitive' and 'concrete', rather than abstract modes of creative activity. He referred to this style of creativity as 'bricolage', a term which has seen a revival of interest through the writings of Lyotard.[49] Turkle and Papert in recent years have argued for the privileging of this notion of divergent/ bricolage thinking:

> The bricoleur resembles the painter who stands back between brushstrokes, looks at the canvas, and only after this contemplation, decides what to do next. For planners, mistakes are missteps; for bricoleurs they are the essence of a navigation by mid-course corrections. For planners,

a program is an instrument for premeditated control; bricoleurs have no goals, but set out to realise them in the spirit of a collaborative venture with the machine . . . While hierarchy and abstraction are valued by the structured programmers' planners aesthetic, bricoleur programmers prefer negotiation and rearrangement of their materials.[50]

They suggest that the skills and values of bricolage – cooperation, play, concrete application of ideas, negotiation, the breaking of boundaries – have been neglected in education and are today as, if not more, important than older planning modes. Bricolage as a feminine form of creativity has, as Turkle and Papert suggest, been unappreciated, and it has been more successfully practised by girls. It is associated with earlier stages of cognition and is gendered as feminine.

Feminine, combinatory modes of creativity such as bricolage – although they are not usually termed as such – appear to be enjoying a new role as part of pluralist, multicultural and eclectic art-making in schools today. The multiplicity of choices on the curriculum, the packaging of knowledges and artistic genres into consumable forms, the fragmentation of time and the breaking down of discipline barriers in Art lend themselves to acts of bricolage where children can choose, collect and visually combine heterogeneous elements from different sources. Historical and globally diverse artistic genres, contemporary, popular and 'high' art and cultural practices can be collaged and juxtaposed to create new configurations.

In contemporary art these acts of bricolage have been related to transgressive and 'feminine' acts of appropriation in which anything can be redeployed and recombined to make art. Abject and despised 'non-art' materials such as bodily waste, children's toys and do-it-yourself (DIY) materials are combined with artistic genres such as academic realism, classical art, Indonesian textiles, pornography and religious artefacts which are all legitimately reused, rearranged and reworked to challenge existing boundaries in art criticism and produce new visual configurations.

Feminine bricolage

While it has to be fully explored as a creative process to be taught in schools, there is nothing *essentially* positive about feminine modes of bricolage that is progressive for women and girls.

Acts of bricolage in art and art education do not, on the whole take into account social and historical values and meanings about genres, products and technologies it redeploys, nor has it any moral or ethical responsibility for plagiarizing and plundering other people's ideas. It relies on the existence of a resource of original work and the highly developed skills of scientists, artists and craftspeople. It takes traditionally developed patterns, materials and objects from other cultures, and the results of skills developed in other artistic genre and marginal arts, taken out of their original contexts, reworked, playfully appropriated, re-presented in new aesthetic configurations. Bricolage finds its logic in consumer skills and bourgeois leisure ideologies: it requires visual choice and discrimination and a fine judgement of the meanings of objects and their potential signification when juxtaposed. The talents of bricoleurs find their most potent expression in fashion and in media journalism of television: in the fragmented, colourful, gossipy, eclectic, multidisciplinary, pleasurable and immediately accessible styles that 'eat up' and consume information, images and knowledges.

That said, 'planning modes' are not in themselves either positive or negative in their effects or essentially tied to male or female cognitive modes either. Planning modes of creativity can be effective in any context. Their methodologies, involving in-depth research, building on established knowledges and historical precedents, their rational and logically forward moving procedures and their values of planning, evaluation and new products in the form of ideas as well as objects, are practices that can be deployed to forward the aims of any project, including those of feminism. The 'planning' mode of creativity may be modernist, and it may have operated in collusion with the dominant ideologies of modernist productivity and masculinity, but it is not necessarily redundant as a creative and knowledge producing practice.

The planning modes have their logic in the technoideological codes of modernist production, and the methodologies of science. Bricolage modes find their logic and value system in modern discourses of consumption and in the methodologies of the postmodern artist. Girls' identities and creative skills have emphasized 'bricolage', concrete thinking, play, and the value of fashion and visual arrangement in consuming modes of creative activity. Perhaps at this moment in contemporary art and employment, girls may more profitably be introduced to the modernist values of 'planning modes', which could lead to more emphasis on research, acquisition of useful knowledges and criticism.

Modernity and the visual

Psychology provided art education with its dominant concept of the developing subject, and with creativity. It has also provided art education with a particular notion of perception and visual art. Modernist art education has always privileged the visual sense: teaching art has been synonymous with the 'educating of artistic vision' and 'visual literacy'.[51]

Experimental psychology, in central Europe in the late nineteenth century and North America in particular in the early twentieth century, amassed a quantity of empirical data on perception. Theories of vision were based on observations of how the eye and body reacts to external visual stimuli: to tonal differences, to colour, space, vertical and horizontal movements, dark and light, solids and transparencies, optical illusions and so on.[52] Roger Fry in his book *Vision and Design* in 1920 suggested that rhythm, line, mass, space, light and shade and colour each had a direct correlation with a specific bodily experience. 'He [the artist] presents these forms in such a manner that the forms themselves generate in us emotional states, based upon the fundamental necessities of our physical and physiological nature'. These he referred to in scientistic terms as 'the elements of art'.[53] Versions of the 'elements of art' are now standard knowledges which are taught in art education in the secondary school, their basis in early experimental psychology forgotten.[54]

Following on from theories in Kantian aesthetics, Fry offered what seemed like scientific verification for the belief that appreciation in art is an immanent and visual experience, and that the act of pure vision could be abstracted from association with any other sensory or affective influence. The appreciation of art, Fry suggested, was a 'disinterested intensity of contemplation' in which the viewer 'can both feel the emotion and watch it'.[55] The inner emotions of the artist are expressed in formal configurations on the canvas, and the sensitive viewer receives the corresponding emotions and bodily reactions to that expression through the elements of art via the organ of the eye, direct and unmediated. Too much knowledge about the art work was seen to interfere with direct visual response. The experience of art was represented as a private event of communication between the outer image on the canvas and the inner mind of the spectator. As the modernist art critic Clement Greenberg put it: 'When it comes to aesthetic experience you're all alone to start and end with'.[56]

This perceptualist account of art constructs a particular notion of the viewer. The assumption is that because all humans have the same visual apparatus, they all see the same and receive the same physiological responses. Children, men, women, Africans and Asians and people of all historical epochs will all see the same and have the same experience. As Bryson argues, this stress on the psychology of perception, which he exemplifies in the accounts of Ernst Gombrich, 'has in effect dehistoricised the relation of the viewer to the painting'.[57] It also renders the viewer neutral in terms of gender, race and class and makes any discussion of gender for instance, beside the point in any evaluation process. A perceptual concept of art based in the individual Cartesian and masculine psychology of the viewer, closes off questions of differences. It does not regard art as a symbolic, social and meaning making practice but, as Victor Burgin wryly expressed it, is a fundamentally Pavlovian response to art.[58]

This psychological version of art, however, seemed in the early part of the twentieth century to offer a new and exciting break from old bourgeois and elitist forms of 'high art' for education. It appeared more democratic in that all people, even very young children, could understand and enjoy art immediately, through the eye, without knowing anything about it. In modernist art education, the need for art historical and aesthetic knowledges declined and were no longer taught to teachers. Art it was assumed was an immanent experience, direct and unmediated by knowledge and prejudice. Children needed only to be trained to 'see'. In art school art education, and supported by the influential writings of art historians such as Ernst Gombrich, psychological explanations took the place of art's traditional legitimizing practices of art history and aesthetics.

Educating artistic vision

Throughout the twentieth century, formalist abstract modernism was never really accepted for teaching older children. Art education continued on in the traditional subjects of portrait, landscape, still life and figure drawing. Assessment and evaluation, however, were 'modernized' through formal immanent analysis of line, tone and so on, and formal 'elements of art' were introduced to be taught as simpler basic stages towards the final achievement of mature realism.[59]

The language of observational drawing continued as a separate practice (and continues to this day) to bear the marks of the predatory nineteenth century adventurer when approaching a 'primitive' tribe. First, children are required to adopt an objective, non-involved stance, then 'explore' and 'closely observe', then 'analyse, experiment, monitor and select'. Objects/people are classified into formal elements of size, shape, colour, and so on and then make 'carefully observed drawings' or 'detailed studies' and accurate records and documentations.[60]

The emphasis on the purely visual, and the consequent negation of knowledges about art, produced a belief that something can be known and understood just by looking carefully, by simply making visual judgements. If something *looks* and feels right, then it *is* right. Children have not been taught not to go far beyond the surface of the visible. Nick Stanley has critiqued this attitude that is prevalent in museum study. He suggests that caution needs to taken in 'the enthusiasm for the look of things'. Instead of plundering and bricolaging artefacts from other cultures for their immediate visual appeal, children should be encouraged to situate them historically and culturally.[61] The performance artist Andrea Fraser has taken this idea further; she challenges the way that viewing itself is constructed by the gallery. In her performance as a 'gallery guide' she gradually reveals herself as a critical interrogator and questions the audience, jolting them out of an accepting, observing and passive mode.[62]

Perceptual accounts of vision have been mainly concerned with static images, a contemplative mode and a fixed viewpoint.[63] Assessment and evaluation of images based on immanent perceptual psychological accounts have not been able to provide ways of theorizing complex, global, repetitive and intrusive social and gendered visual practices such as advertising and pornographic violence, nor have they been able to incorporate 'other' perspectives and points of view. Immanent assessment of art work and the formal analysis of static visual elements are in any case irrelevant and in most instances inadequate when dealing with non-visual and time-based art, performance, site specific and installation arts. They find little resonance in the fast moving, quickly edited, repetitive images that are characteristic of today's club and magazine culture, television, computers and film.

Postmodern accounts of vision

Martin Jay has identified different modes of viewing in modernity, and referred to the dominant traditions of realism as 'Cartesian perspectivalism'. In this tradition the viewer must adopt the same static, monocular position as the painter. It is a mode of viewing that individualizes and reduces identity to a viewing eye and brain, denying the body and other possible viewpoints.[64] Christian Metz writes of this specific mode of organizing the visual as the 'scopic regime of modernity'.[65] The notion of the 'scopic regime' has become metaphorically and metonymically associated with the 'Male Gaze', the 'I' (eye) of the modernist visual artist and scientist. Enlightenment man, with technologically devised apparatuses, historically observed, named and categorized other people into races, genders and hierarchies; as women, as black, as working class, as 'oriental' and so on. This scopic regime makes the concept of a 'female gaze' and 'pluralism' problematic; for 'allowing' women or non-Westerners or children to have 'their' say or represent 'their' point of view, only reinforces a point of view historically constructed and defined from a masculine, patriarchal and modernist perspective.

Pollock has demonstrated, for example, that is not possible to balance the inequality of men and women's modern art practice by just adding women artists' work to art history or by including a female point of view. Using as an example the work of artists such as Mary Cassatt and Berthe Morisot, she suggested that modernism has been constructed through a male gaze: they painted children and interiors not necessarily because it was their preferred subject matter, but because they were not allowed into bars, streets or brothels which formed the content of the truly 'creative' male artist. Their social limitations as women shaped what they were able to see. Women's eyes, their creative potential, their visual responses and their 'optical apparatus' may have been the same as men's, but the legal and conventional restrictions placed on what they were allowed to look at and where they could go meant that their art took on different, and in modernist terms, subordinate, subject matter.[66]

Laura Mulvey's famous essay on visual pleasure also genders the actual process of vision, suggesting that people with different experiences and different psychic organization take different meanings from the same visual experience. She provides an argument to show that cultural artefacts – in this case Hollywood films – are gendered in ways that attract and provide specifically gendered pleasures with which the viewer identifies. There is no possibility of separating eyes and brains from socially regulated gendered and raced bodies and experiences: Fry's 'disinterested contemplation of vision' exists an imaginary ideal. Gender differences are constructed and consolidated 'at the borders' in the very acts of watching films and seeing images.[67]

Realism, narrative and the self

Lacan's description of the mirror stage in infancy provided the psycho-analytic explanation for the process of imaginary identification and con-structing gender difference. Identity and gender are something we have to keep on adjusting as we encounter new circumstances, incorporate into stories that we create to make us feel *as if* we possess a developing self. Film theorists and art historians have taken this notion further in explaining some of the functions of art, suggesting that we produce optically realistic images such as those in film and art to reflect back a satisfactory image of self:

> It seems that the necessity of the work of art, like all other signifying systems is its double function as mirror and as screen for the fictitious unity of the subject's sense of self to parade before and hide behind. We produce these mirrors to show us who we are and who we would like to be, and screens onto which we endlessly project everything we reject and we endlessly repeat the games of stepping inside and outside the rules of what is and ought to be.[68]

Literary theorists suggest that it is through the realistic and optically con-vincing images of realism that a coherent sense of self is constructed. Pic-tures, stories and narratives provide reassuring unified and coherent mirror images, which are always, as Lacan suggests, mis-recognitions. They do not actually exist except in the imagination. Yet they are necessary fictions in that they 'hold together' otherwise fragmented, chaotic and undifferentiated states of being.

Vision and modernity

The modern world and the notion of the Cartesian identity privileged the eye as the most important human sense; it represented the window on the 'inner' realm of the mind, a clear link between 'inner' and 'outer' self.[69] The modern technologies developed in relation to vision have not been neutral in their object and purposes. It has been noted that the psychology of perception itself, along with optics, photography, video and computer-generated imagery, have been developed and sustained in the modern economic and social contexts of war, weaponry, public surveillance and espionage.[70] It is no accident that most video and computer games are about blasting something out of existence. Modernity has always valued the usual metaphors of 'probing intellects' and 'penetrating analyses'.

The emphasis on vision shapes the way we understand and relate to the world, as distant and observing. Haraway talks of the 'deeply predatory nature of a photographic consciousness'.[71] The intervention of technical apparatus – a camera obscura, telescope, the microscope and even the picture frame – separates out the viewer in time and place from what is going on, turns them into a kind of voyeur, a 'Peeping Tom'.[72] It makes the viewer feel superior to the world they view, controlling and distant, objectifying and reducing to an object the thing or the person looked at, and creates a masculine viewing identity. Jay identifies this position at work in Western realist tradition of painting:

> The abstract coldness of the perspectival gaze and the withdrawal of the painter's emotional entanglement with the objects depicted in geometricalized space. The participatory involvement of more absorptive visual modes has diminished, if not entirely suppressed, as the gap between spectator and spectacle widened . . . the bodies of the painter and viewer were forgotten in the name of an allegedly disincarnated, absolute eye.[73]

Feminists have also argued that the privileging of vision has negated the body and the emotions. Modernity has developed the technologies of the visual to a high degree and has been relatively backward in developing the other senses or technologies for enhancing bodily performance.

Some feminist theorists argue that the aesthetic discourses of the body – the senses of touch, taste and smell, of sexuality, of childbirth, of bodily health and dirt and disorder – historically assigned to the feminine, are not enjoyed by the eye. Looking itself is privileged as a masculine, intellectualizing practice. As Luce Irigaray has suggested: 'In our culture the predominance of the look over smell, taste, touch and hearing has brought about an impoverishment of bodily relations. The moment the look dominates, the body loses its materiality.'[74]

At the level of popular culture the body is always asserting itself. It speaks particularly in non-legitimate 'feminine' and 'lower class', popular activities: in anorexia, slimming, in body-shaping, make-up, body piercing and decoration, in carnival, dancing, street fashion, in sexual enjoyment, play and drug taking.

Feminist arts of the 1970s began to re-engage in bodily art practices partly as a reaction to the mental, abstract, visual and intellectual privileging of formalist modernist art, minimalism and conceptual art. Artists such as Helen Chadwick revisited the fine art genres of the Baroque and Rococo with their emphasis on sensual, melodramatic and bodily subject matter. Susan Hiller and Beth Edleson focused on the maternal body, and performance artists Judy Chicago and Cate Elwes used their own menstrual blood. Feminists re-established artistic discourses of dance, performance and body art.[75] They used soft sculptural materials of textiles reminiscent of flesh and the often despised emotionally suffused objects of crafts, toys, food and domestic objects to make art and they brought the body into the political arena in documentations of rape, sexual and domestic violence. In these practices, feminists re-engaged with the values that had been suppressed by the privileging of the visual in Enlightenment modernity's discourses.

The assessment of women's art in education

Many teachers are introducing contemporary women's art and multi-cultural practices into the classroom, and whilst some are critically informed and educationally strategic, more commonly they are arbitrarily chosen without any educational rationales, and are taken out of their contexts in contemporary aesthetic cultural and critical debate in areas of vision and identity.

The popular and widely used book *The Visual Arts in Education* offers an example.[76] One prominent case illustrates the work of an artist celebrating the mother–daughter relationship, and there is an uncritical endorsement of patriarchal motherhood, a reassertion of the natural role of woman in a celebration of normalizing childcare. In another case, the work of the feminist artist Rose Garrard – in which she depicts the fragmentations and social contingency of identity – is reinserted into modernism's unifying psychological themes of autobiography, motivation and art as expression of inner experience. Feminist and postcolonial art practices are just seen as new topics and new materials, cut off from their situated meanings. Without a contextual understanding of what these artists are trying to do or any understanding of the cultural and aesthetic debates within which such work is created, evaluation inevitably is reabsorbed into established modernist visual practices, and robs the work of its critical potential.[77] As Griselda Pollock has indicated, in the case of the introduction of women's art:

> there is still in education, hostility to the political culture of feminism from which these works come, what they address and why they might have something to offer that realigns our understanding of the world in general.[78]

Postmodern notions of subjectivity

Psychology has claimed to be a 'science of the person'. Inevitably its focus has been on the individual, and that individual has been shown to be the male, Cartesian *cogito*: an intellectualizing, observing, fully conscious self.

Newer approaches from constructionist psychologies are challenging the Cartesian binary model of the self, and have shifted psychology's empirical gaze away from an objective, distancing experimental mode which constructs the human as an isolated and individual entity. Instead they attempt to interpret human behaviour and growth by looking at human interactions and social institutions and at the things people make: objects, institutions, relationships, languages, images and art.

Constructionist psychologies assert that no useful sense can be gained by imagining an 'inner' and 'outer' self; they propose, instead, a notion of the self that is 'social through and through'.[79] Drawing on the work of Lacan, who developed some of the ideas of Winnicott, they suggest, in different ways that human identity – including differences of gender – is made up of conscious and unconscious interactions with the everyday world. The work of Vygotsky and Bakhtin has been significant in this context. John Shotter, drawing on the insights of Mikhail Bakhtin, has developed Vygotsky's notion of the 'internalization' of culture.[80] Shotter argues that the 'inner life' of the mind reflects in its functioning the same ethical and rhetorical considerations that people employ in everyday transactions and personal interactions. Instead of the 'inner life' being understood as the 'core' of the self, it exists, as it were, on the borders – on the periphery, between the self and negotiations with the world. Our thoughts do not have orderly form existing 'inside our heads', but are produced in the making of social speech using socially agreed conventions and symbol systems – such as art. It is in practices – 'doing', using tools and technologies – that our selves are realized *to* ourselves. Bakhtin said: 'I am conscious of myself and become myself only while revealing myself for another . . . every internal experience ends up on the boundary.'[81]

Art and languages act as the tools by which we reciprocally construct our own and other people's identities: 'the speaker speaks with an expectation of the listener preparing a response, agreement, sympathy, objection, execution and so forth.[82] The speaker always assumes they are addressing a gendered individual and in the process of communicating with that individual, acts to confirm and reconstruct their own and the other's gender identity.[83]

Old paradigm notions of self-expression rely on a pre-existing, fixed notion of a gendered self 'already there' to be intentionally expressed and represented or communicated 'through' transparent media such as art. Postmodern psychologies suggest, on the other hand, that representation, and making art, is more a process through which identity and meaning are produced and made real. Gender, for instance, does not exist *in* a person, but is continually being produced and confirmed in everyday acts. As Judith Butler has put it: 'there need not be a "doer behind the deed," but that the "doer" is variably constructed in and through the deed'. Visual art, writing and music are not expressions or representations of an existing self, but rather are elements of the continuing *formation* of the identity through the practice of consuming and making.[84]

Other theorists, working from a perspective of culture and consumer studies, see the self as non-consciously and consciously 'designed' in aesthetic acts. David Chaney, for example, uses the concept of the 'designing self' and argues that, to a certain extent, identity is a creative act involving some choice and self-positioning.[85] Evan Watkins and Paul Willis have both argued in a similar vein but in different contexts, that identities are produced and consolidated in everyday lifestyle choices and acts of consumption.[86] In this sense, identity does not 'develop' according to some inner logic, or have an inner core, nor does it necessarily move from evolutionary simple to complex configurations, but is saturated through with arbitrary and contingent social meanings, produced in 'performances' and enactments using displays of objects, dress and behaviour.

Psychologists Candace West and Don Zimmerman theorize this creative construction of self in relation to gender:

> We contend that the 'doing' of gender is undertaken by women and men whose competence as members of society is hostage to its production. Doing gender involves a complex of socially guided perceptual interactional and micropolitical activities that cast particular pursuits as expressions of masculine and feminine 'natures' . . . we conceive of gender as an emergent feature of social situations: both as an outcome of and rationale for various social arrangements and as a means of legitimating one of the most fundamental divisions in society.[87]

By taking on and engaging with masculine and feminine ideological discourses, people continually strengthen, perform and communicate their sense of who they are as well as confirming in others their own sense of identity. Wearing a dress, being 'hopeless at using technology' and getting boys to help, engaging in art as a leisure pursuit and not competing with men, speaking softly, changing nappies, and so on are all everyday acts.[88] These are all *practices*, some of which are performed in schools, which are ideologically gendered as feminine and their performance enacts and continually construct a feminine identity.

There are, of course, limits to the performance and choice of identity.[89] We are restricted to a certain extent by our bodies, our geographical location, the times we live in and our personal experiences and histories. We can work only with available symbolic material and within existing discourses at hand. Too many contradictions between material realities over which we have no control and our imaginative beliefs can cause a disruption of the necessary cohering narratives of the self, a 'breakdown', or an inability to cope with everyday interactions and relationships. We have to construct privileged narratives of the self to function and act as healthy people.

These notions of the performance of identity, or the 'socially saturated self', represent a shift away from biological determinism of gender, and binary oppositions, as well as undermining the notion of the unfolding, developing ideal masculine Cartesian self that underpins notions of art and notions of the child in art education.

In conclusion

It has been possible to critique only briefly old paradigms of psychology that inhabit art education and to introduce some of the newer ideas about identity that are current from a range of heterogeneous contemporary discourse, and which are changing the shape of psychology. What I do want to stress, however, is the continuing importance of a discourse of psychology for constructing change in art education. What distinguishes psychology from many other discourses on identity is that it is a modernist practice and claims to maintain a broadly scientific attitude – albeit with a different understanding of what 'science' is – in understanding the self. That is, it attempts to provide evidences for its assertions and it continues in the modernist habits of research, building on knowledges, self-criticism and self-renewal. Psychology is changing and incorporating many of these psychoanalytically informed concepts of the self into its theorizing and, with all its shortcomings, can still provide a basis for the critique and understanding of the gendered concepts we already hold. It provides the possibility of having some shared concept of the child – however imaginary we accept it to be – on which to plan an art education that is repeatable and relatively consistent and accountable.

4 Modernist art and design education

Psychology as a new and modern discourse was built on to and legitimized existing art pedagogies. Up to the 1930s, the art curriculum had consisted of the two discrete modes of rational and progressive pedagogy, with progressive art education mainly confined to the teaching of the very young. But Marion Richardson, supported by the psychological influences in child development, and formalist art from Roger Fry, provided evidences that the freer, creative and imaginative thinking, typical of progressive pedagogy, could be protracted beneficially beyond early childhood years. Herbert Read has been credited as a major influence in establishing a model for secondary school art education which combined the two aspects of the rational and the progressive modes into a new and modern, unified, but dynamically interacting form, to be taught to all children up to the ages of 14 or so.[1] Towards the mid-twentieth century, Art in secondary schools became more 'progressive'. The formal traditions of objective and academic drawing and realism continued, but were 'softened' and romanticized. The modernist art practice of expressionism, itself forged within modern discourses of humanist psychology, lent its romantic and 'modern' legitimacy to self-expression in the classroom. Older children were encouraged to experiment, to bring spontaneity, gestural 'mark-making' and a freer imagination to their landscape, still life and portraiture or to combine it with a modernistic, semi-surreal and organic abstraction. Romantic techniques of free brushwork, distortion of forms and saturated colour as an expression of inner emotion was encouraged. Less emphasis was placed on visual realism, copying, accuracy, proportion, perspective or measurement. The art environment in the secondary school, particularly for the 'less able' child, began to take on a more relaxed, creative and colourful appearance similar to the environment of the elementary classroom and more women began to be employed as art teachers of older children. Art became more feminine in its gender identifications.

Towards the end of the 1960s and throughout the 1970s, and in the context of the ideology of the 'white heat of technology' of the British economy, more 'scientific', rationalized modes of delivering art and design were introduced to the curriculum. Although the 'content' of Art remained traditional and feminine, and painting, drawing and minor crafts continued, the structures and systems within which it was taught were tightened up and systematized with the introduction of behavioural systems of art education, originating from North America.

Systems structures for art education

'Systems' had originally been designed for the bureaucratic organization of businesses and the personnel management of large multinational corporations, but they were seen to have an ideal application in large comprehensive schools and in the delivery of centrally organized curricula.[2] Systems of art pedagogy, based on meanings about art and the child established in behavioural and cognitive psychologies, had always been adaptable to 'packaging'. The advantage of systems models has been that large numbers of children can be taught the same curriculum, since all children are seen to have the same developmental progression, the same perceptual organization and the same basic human traits. The delivery of art based on a system allows for a universal 'wholistic' curriculum, but also can be adapted for specific differences and diversity: for differences established by psychology, between boys and girls, between different personality and creative types, between different ethnic groups and differing age abilities. Centrally conceived philosophies of art designed by experts and specialists, with an understanding of child psychology, can be modularized and packaged, to be taught by teachers, who need not themselves have a professional training in art or psychology. Once established, systems allow for the maintaining of standards, quality assessment and the delivery of nationally organized curricula based on the psychologically established attainments of the 'average child' which can be objectively monitored against national norms.

A systems model has been most clearly described in the work of Mary Rouse and Guy Hubbard, who in the early 1970s devised an art education, based on behavioural objectives, that could be delivered by teachers in elementary schools to the 20 million children across North America, 'who otherwise would have no hope for anything approximating a real art education program'.[3] In this system, they first identified appropriate empirical research areas, using what they described as 'the best information available' at that time. They gleaned evidences about normal children from psychological tests of

> graphic behaviour, aesthetic choice behaviour, perceptual development, creative behaviour, and cognitive and physical development . . .

Sequencing also was based on an analysis of which behaviours logically precede other more complex behaviours.

Appropriate subject matter, choice of materials, suitable tools and technologies were introduced at different stages to meet the psychologically informed needs of the child at different stages in their growth. To structure the delivery of art curricula they outlined six complete years of objectives, corresponding to the child's years of schooling, which were broken down into annual behavioural aims and objectives. These were further fragmented into individual learning modules, 'and finally into weeks and days'. Evaluation was centrally moderated and could be consistent.

To deliver systems models fairly and to establish standards of quality, intensive training and uniformity among the principal authors and evaluators have to be set in place. Teachers have to be trained in the basic delivery of the programme and to be aware of attainment targets. Methods of schematically delivering material in the form of teaching aids, textbooks, easily assimilated charts, diagrams and sequential procedures have to be designed and disseminated. Systems models allow for freedom about 'content', that is what the teacher chooses to teach; but overall aims and evaluative standards have to adhere to externally and expertly agreed criteria. Although the 'content' or subject matter of the 'packages' could be liberal, romantic, feminine or expressionistic, traditional or modern, they were delivered in a totalizing, rationalizing, scientist language of aims, objectives, outcomes and quality assessment.

While the content and the teaching styles of the modernist artroom were becoming increasingly feminized in progressive pedagogy, what was taught and how it was taught were both subject to the masculine and invisible styles of an increasingly rationalized and invisible system.

Design discourses

In the mid-twentieth century, boys' handicrafts were updated and modernized to form the new subject of Design. Design education continued as closely linked to Art and was often taught by the same teacher, sometimes in the same classroom, in large 'Art and Design' or, later, 'Craft, Design and Technology' (CDT) departments. The methods and productive values of observational drawing, technical drawing, wood, metal, ceramics: the masculine, 'productive' and scientific art practices provided the basis for this new school subject. Girls' handicrafts in the four key areas of Domestic Science, Childcare, Cookery and Textiles were also subsumed under the umbrella of Design. What brought these heterogeneous and unrelated practices into a spurious unity was the translation of all their processes into a system, the Design Process, and natural encoding of a planning creative mode. The Design Process could be adapted to fit any Art and Design problem:

> in these terms a culinary recipe is a design, so is a musical or chronological score. These together with flow charts, computer programs and knitting patterns are a special kind of design called algorithms . . . the production of a meal for a special occasion with its demanding restraints of quantity, cost, nutrition and above all time, is a classic design brief. The planning of work which includes such diverse activities as shopping, housework, cookery and needlecrafts demands a high level of systems organisation.[4]

With the Sex Equality Act in 1975 it became mandatory for boys and girls to have the same opportunities. With so many subjects in Art, Design and Home Economics on offer, children typically took a turn – which often meant between seven and twelve hours or so a week – in six different Art, Craft, Design and HE subjects. One child of 13 or 14, for instance, could spend a year on what was called the 'Roundabout' or 'Carousel' system, learning about textiles, ceramics, two-dimensional art, three-dimensional design, domestic studies or graphic design in turn.

In spite of efforts to 'evaluate the different cries of a baby' or to find a place for the traditional emphasis in girls' education on feminine values of altruism and care, and personal development, domestic and textile subjects did not fit easily into new Design processes and systems models. The subject of textiles continued, however, to be a crucial part of working class girls' education. It was broken up and taught across the new Art and Design discourses. Weaving, fabric printing and pattern design were subsumed under Design and Technology; Creative Embroidery became a new 'art' subject for public examination, whilst 'light crafts' continued in unexamined practices as part of the everyday art lesson. Dressmaking and sewing along with consumer studies continued in Domestic Science or (as it later became known) Home Economics, to be taught to the less able, working class girl. So although there was not a separate and visible subject called 'Textiles', girls found that, as in the nineteenth century, they were still doing large amounts of textile related practices in school.[5]

Dena Attar, in her book *Wasting Girls' Time*, focused her arguments on the amount of time spent by girls on trivial and unnecessary domestic subjects in schools, instead of on more useful subjects such as Languages, Science, Technology, History and Geography. She has pointed out that no empirical studies have been carried out to show that domestic subjects in schools produce any improvement in women's everyday lives, arguing that boys and brighter girls, who do no domestic subjects, seem to manage as adults very well without them.[6]

Boys' craft ideologies

It has been retrospectively revealed that the teaching of Design and Technology in the 1960s was, even at its best, held back by the continuation of entrenched and redundant gendered attitudes and by nineteenth century masculine notions of 'work', craft and manual skills.[7] What was actually taught varied from school to school, and was dependent on existing contingencies: resources and machinery, rooms and equipment, the training, interests and sex of the staff, and the sex and class of the children.[8]

Each area on the Roundabout maintained their own trained staff. Boys' craft teachers – who were sometimes ex-servicemen or former industrial foremen – often found themselves ill equipped for the teaching of girls. 'Frankly', as one metalwork teacher stated, 'if girls come into metalwork, we're lumbered'.[9] Boys' handicrafts were taught in the physical contexts of mini-industrial workshops with their noise, smells and dirt, using hard materials and power tools. A boy's bodily and cognitive relation to materials was constructed in the educational literature as active, productivist, interventionist and controlling, employing knowledgeable and skilled use of tools and techniques. Textbooks emphasized the importance of 'manipulating', 'shaping', 'construction' and 'building'.[10] Classroom practices regularly employed process such as moulding, casting and forging. Boys were expected to manage and overcome their apprehension of the unfamiliar and potentially dangerous machines of the workshop; to handle and manipulate resistant and heavy materials with specialist tools in a craftsmanlike atmosphere. They learned to achieve confidence in tackling large or heavy projects, to exert imaginative force, physical strength and mastery over inert materials in the languages and contexts of future work in engineering and industrial production. Technical drawing – often taught to the 'brighter' working class boy – required the use of mathematical instruments: dividers, compasses, rulers and the use of drawing tables, plans, blueprints. Through the language of the draughtsman, boys came to appreciate the skills of accurate observation, precision, measurement and clarity. As in the nineteenth century, boys were taught basic perspective and projections and became familiarized with the idea of imagining and representing three-dimensional forms, structure and mass and visualizing hypothetical solid objects, skills that were useful in art, which working class girls had no chance to acquire.

Masculine, working class identities were produced through these discourses and in a context of male friendship and working class solidarity. Difference from and imagined superiority in strength and skill over girls and women were part of the necessary process of identification for the boy and supported his psychological separation from home and mother. As Paul Willis has argued, the promise of sexual rewards and mastery over women was implicit in these discourses and compensated for the absence of real economic power available for working class men.[11]

Girls' craft ideologies

Whilst boys were readied for the public world of manual work, a family wage, and work in modern technology and production, girls were learning their crafts in very different ideological contexts. There was the unproblematic assumption that girls' craft skills were for eventual use in a non-productive, domestic context. The Newsom Report stated unequivocally:

> With the less able girls we think that the schools can and should make more adjustments to the fact that marriage now looms much larger and nearer in the pupils' eyes than it has ever done before . . . at this time therefore the prospect of courtship and marriage should rightly influence the education of the adolescent girl . . . her direct interest in dress, personal appearance and the problems of human relations should be given a central place in her education.[12]

Teaching aids and textbook narratives were constructed within the ideological images of the heterosexual housewife. Girls' adult lives were imagined as mothers, responsible for the moral and physical well-being of adult men and children. In 1971 the Schools Council stated that HE teaching should 'encourage in pupils a sense of values; to encourage unselfishness, co-operation, self-control . . . to learn to know and understand their place in the family and community'.[13] Education was not for girls themselves, but in the service of others.

Domestic subjects, particularly in girls' schools, were often taught in clean, quiet, safe, colourful settings, with specially constructed 'flats', mini-kitchens and bedrooms. They were often carpeted, curtained and quiet. Domestic crafts such as dressmaking were 'another kind of afternoon out, a pleasant oasis of girls-only time in a mixed school'.[14] One student remarked on the calm that used to fall in that classroom in needlework and domestic science. 'I remember thinking that it was good to be away from the boys in these lessons'.[15] Compared with the clean and brightly decorated kitchens of HE, boys' craft areas must have been a challenge to the senses. Many girls expressed fears of dirty, heavy work, noisy and potentially dangerous workshops. They worried about lack of help and isolation.[16] Girls could be welcomed with elaborate courtesy, expected to tie their hair back and don oversized protective gear designed for larger boys. They learned a different vocabulary of technical terms, to accept different, more formal rules of behaviour and cope with and negotiate the anxiety of unfamiliar masculine territory. They adopted coping strategies that could disarm criticism and diminish the threat of punishment or ridicule – reciprocal strategies that confirmed masculine and feminine identity. Paul Willis described these kind of behaviours: 'Wheedling around male teachers, or challenging both them and female teachers with a direct sexuality'.[17] Being 'hopeless' or 'feigning inadequacy with machines' and courting assistance of boys and male teachers. These were subordinate behaviours produced within unfamiliar contexts.

Six weeks, which often amounted to six hours, in the woodwork and metalwork rooms with boys could have been enough to convince girls that they were not suited to Design and Technology and that they were 'no good' at using tools or machines.

Textiles

Girls' relation to materials was constructed differently from that of boys. The language of girls' crafts in textbooks constantly repeated the words 'responsiveness', 'appreciation', 'feel' and 'texture', 'discrimination', 'judgement' and 'evaluation'. In fashion and interior design, girls were advised to avoid 'showiness', 'flashiness', 'vulgarity' or 'looking cheap'.[18] Their relation to materials was constructed as passive and consuming. The materials that girls used were soft and flexible, two dimensional and, unlike metal and wood, were transient, cheaper and impermanent.[19] Girls' drawing skills in the nineteenth century had been constructed within textile requirements: they learned two-dimensional design, surface texture, pattern, colour and flower and nature drawing as potential decoration for fabric. The drawing of the draped figure was often to help in fashion, dress and design. In the twentieth century, although detached from explicit mention of textiles, these practices continued to be taught to girls and were chosen as options by them in examinations. They had become established as 'girls' subjects'.[20]

As well as doing two-dimensional drawing and design in Art, girls learned light crafts such as weaving and batik, embroidery and dyeing, fabric printing and collage. In HE and Design they learned how to cut and sew a garment from a prepared pattern, to make soft toys, children's clothes and small crafts, Christmas presents, domestic objects, pot-holders, bags, needle-cases, place-mats, napkins and aprons. They learned in consumer studies how to test 'scientifically' for fabric wear and washability, and identify fabric by feel and texture. They did comparative observational tests and applied taste and discrimination to detect the 'shoddy' from the well made. They found out how to clean and care for fabrics using the correct techniques and detergent products. They learned, by walking round department stores with a clipboard, how to select for quality and value for money.[21] Their work often involved a particular application of concrete 'science' or mathematics; in order to calculate and compare costs, analyse the properties of materials, or the square yardage of cloth. They learned the modern values and meanings about science, analysis, criticism and judgement in the everyday contexts of home management, home finances, shopping, dress and consumption.

The economic context of textiles

The self-expressive and domestic school subjects of two-dimensional Art and Textiles were taught to girls in an economic context in which textile related industries were vital to the British economy and were the largest employers of girls leaving school.[22] There was a continuing and increasing need for skilled workers in consumer craftwork (the old 'slopwork') trades: the making of millinery, shoes, artificial flowers, boxes, ornaments and soft toys, personal accessories such as bags, beadwork, badges and embroidered items, scarves, and domestic textiles such as cushions, lampshades and curtains, as well as modern leisure products, for example car seats, tents, sports equipment and so on. As the twentieth century progressed these jobs were being taken up by large numbers of immigrant women, in particular Asian women, who had come from cultures where fine textile work and decoration, and patriarchally organized family traditions and authority were culturally still strong.

Small craftwork relied on quickly changing fashion influences. It required a flexible workforce, prepared to do repetitive and detailed work, often requiring taste and judgement, a myriad of skills, and hand finishing techniques. It thrived on a workforce prepared to accept low wages, and slopwork practices such as homeworking, piecework and short term and casual employment.

Textiles education in schools, and as it appeared in popular textbooks, had never been taught in relation to mass production, engineering or technology as a career, or as a means of financial independence. For girls, production meant making small items, for charity, love or service to the family. The nineteenth century bourgeois leisure ideologies continued. Crafts and Art in progressive discourses emphasized art and textiles as leisure activities, in the context of fashion, dress, self-expression, intrinsic pleasure, self-adornment, or for display. Girls were taught to be responsive and appreciative of products made by others, but were not expected to understand their own work in terms of 'value for money'. Skill was not a high priority for girls. 'In-depth' projects where one piece of work was researched and made over a long period of time was not the object:

> in selecting such work it is necessary to make sure that it is not of the type that can be judged too easily by adult standards. 'Fun' things like . . . decorative beach bags, hair bands and cushions using embroidery or tie-dye fabrics for girls can be made. Pupils will be glad to use these without worrying if they match up to professional standards.[23]

Progressive art educational discourses of creativity and self-development never gave information about the value and meanings of art in a wider social context, and were not concerned with the contribution of textile production and manufacture and consumption to the economy.

The textile industries and girls' education

The careers information that was distributed to schools gave no indications of rates of pay, or promises of promotion, training, apprenticeships or a professional future in the industry to girls as they did to boys. The textile industry, instead of advertising its rates of pay, promised female school leavers 'a homely atmosphere, good personnel relations and friendliness', 'an exciting, fashionable and friendly atmosphere'. 'There are no unpleasant smells or disturbing noises . . . you will never soil your hands or your clothes – you can always go straight to a date from work' and 'workrooms are particularly attractive with a great variety of hat styles and hundreds of ribbons, flowers and other trimmings'.[24]

The growing fashion and retail industries and the new large post-war multinational textile corporations had expanded their interests and influence to Art, HE and Design departments in the post-war period, particularly for the 'less able' girl as defined by psychologists and intelligence tests. The Needlework Development Scheme, for instance, was adopted by the Ministry of Education as a means of improving the taste and aesthetic appreciation of the average working class schoolgirl.[25] To teachers in Art and HE, the scheme supplied paper patterns, fashion magazines, teaching aids and curriculum projects. Books, wall charts, visual aids and pamphlets with related catalogues supplied materials and patterns in the new Scandinavian 'modern' style. The scheme liaised with schools' suppliers, selling ready made lesson plans and craft kits which, neglected by Design educational discourse and male heads of Art departments, domestic craft teachers were often happy to use. Indeed as one report expressed it:

> it is particularly encouraging to see industries requesting the expertise of the Association [of Teachers of Domestic Science] for the resources and knowledge of industry can play an important part in the development of the subject in schools.[26]

From school, working class girls moved on to find the same patterns, processes, languages and brand names in women's magazines, to be obtained from craft outlets and department stores.[27] As in the nineteenth century, girls continued to practise leisure crafts at home: painting on velvet, stained glass, stencilling, weaving, knitting and dressmaking. Through these hobbies and through romantic, leisure discourses in Art and Design at school, girls learned useful skills for future employment in 'the rag trade'. They learned where to buy textile products and acquired skills of machining, cutting, seaming and sewing. They picked up artistic discourses of taste, discrimination and knowledges about, and languages and 'feel' for handling fabrics and materials. These attributes, although systematically taught to girls, were often regarded as natural and part of a 'woman's touch', rather than understood as systematically taught and laboriously acquired skills.

Identity, work and schooling

Moving from the home, the family and school to the values of competitive work is a time of potential insecurity and anxiety for young people. As they enter the adult world they need to learn a whole array of new attitudes and behaviours. This period of change is often a time of anxiety and insecurity. Dorrine Kondo in *Crafting Selves* showed how, in situations of change, people tend to conform to their peer group. They look for friends and allies in a new situation. They are eager to please, they want to fit in and are reluctant to complain, stand out or be different. They opt for what is known, familiar and friendly when faced with an alien situation.[28]

The working class girl, in seeking employment when she left school, entered textile related jobs, it could be argued, because they were familiar. It is what her friends did, it is maybe what her mother and sisters did, and she already possesses the confidence in her skills. In the 1960s and 1970s, by the time girls had left school at 15, they had mastered a variety of technical operational procedures without realizing it. Making clothes, fashion and shopping were things that girls read about in their magazines, which they did in their leisure time, so doing the same things for pay seemed less like real work. Girls were not physically forced or 'moulded' by education to fit into low paid and menial jobs. But the availability of expanding postwar employment requiring cutting, stitching, seaming, embroidering and machining is what girls would have felt confident in after years of schooling and their skills were needed. Their training in bourgeois leisure ideologies of altruism, taste, good manners and putting other people first, and the modest evaluation of their own abilities, would have been likely to produce a docile and uncomplaining workforce. The feminine values that girls were absorbing in progressive Art and Design education, it could be argued, predisposed them to accept to the feminized values and attitudes required of modern textile workers.

Consumer discourses

The period after the Second World War and up to the early 1970s was a time of economic growth and productivity in Britain. Home ownership increased, and standards of living improved, and there was a boost in investment in art and design education. This growth was primarily explained in the need for larger numbers of trained manual and technical operatives in engineering, technology and manufacture and the necessity to provide school leavers with appropriate skills to enter new areas of employment in design, fashion and advertising. It was less manifestly a means of educating children, especially girls, with the socially convenient skills and attitudes that predisposed them to work in expanding areas of consumer activity.[29]

People were being encouraged to spend. Through more aggressive media and advertising activities and newly available leisure industries, they were buying new kinds of clothes for new leisure opportunities, new kinds of food, furniture, electrical appliances, and were spending more time on holidaying, home decorating, on crafts, hobbies and gardening. The tasks of this increased consumer activity were, as in the nineteenth century, allotted to the housewife, or as she became known, 'The Lady of the Home'.

Betty Friedan in the late 1960s described the increasingly complex and arduous management tasks that were being undertaken by the housewife.[30] It was she who did most of the choosing and buying of food, clothes, domestic goods and furniture. It was the housewife who bought, cleaned and maintained household products, who selected and organized the decoration and maintaining of home interiors and gardens. The housewife saw to the purchase, maintenance and repair of clothing and domestic textiles, their cleaning, storage and replacement. Increasing domestic consumption also required management of the contexts in which consumption takes place: women supervised children's purchases, and managed the family's social and leisure activities. They kept an observant eye on the welfare of family members and friends, they remembered birthday presents, and the children's medical visits. Through women's work at weddings and funerals, holidays and dinners, the social networks of the family as a consumer unit were ritualized, performed and consolidated. It was women who followed advice in magazines about maintaining personal relationships; they did what feminists were to call 'the emotional housework', work that was performed unpaid as acts of service, love and care.[31] The hundreds of tasks and skills that Friedan identified in the late 1960s, that in the nineteenth century had been done for the middle classes by paid servants, was now performed unpaid by a 'crypto-servant' class of housewives. As the social historian Thorsten Veblen had pointed out: 'The Lady of the House became its chief menial'.[32]

Psychological research was mobilized, often funded by industrialists, manufacturers and advertisers to investigate the family and its needs, its leisure activities and behaviours. It was women's taste in particular that had to be understood, addressed and influenced. Research on child-rearing habits, on women's aspirations, preferences, sexual habits, tastes, fantasies and desires was carried out through profiling, surveys and questionnaires. Women's innermost thoughts and needs became of economic interest as market interests penetrated the privacy of the home, family and personal relationships.[33] The same research on behaviour and the same scientific knowledges that had been available for education, on motivation, perception, personality, creativity, intelligence and so on, were redeployed in the capitalist domain to promote female consumption. The feminine individual constructed by psychology for art education was the same feminine individual hailed as the ideological subject of consumption.

The discourses of consumer education

The potential of working class girls as future consumers was being fully realized. They had been identified as an important sector of consumer activity 'because of their fashion consciousness, their spending power – until marriage and the birth of their first child – and the need to build up their wardrobes after leaving school'.[34] The Newsom Report stated:

> Even those girls who do little sewing themselves will spend a sizeable amount of money on clothes, and as young married women they will soon be responsible for buying clothes for the family and furnishings for the home . . . they will need some foundation of taste, an eye for finished workmanship and quality in materials, fashion and design.[35]

Although consumption and the performance of services in the home required physical labour, drudgery, complex management and organizational skills, the rhetoric of the housewife's work, as Friedan demonstrated, was forged in terms of leisure, pleasure and love. The bourgeois leisure discourses of art and the terms 'creativity', 'self-expression' and 'imagination' were borrowed from fine art discourse to elevate domestic labour into an artistic activity, to make it seem less like work and more like fun, pleasure or another leisure 'hobby'. Cooking, cleaning, scrubbing, mending and so on were transformed rhetorically into 'domestic arts'. Friedan observed and described this change of popular discourses from drudgery to creativity in the 1950s and 1960s in the United States, exemplified in this advertising copy:

> Creativeness is the modern woman's answer to her changed position in the household. Thesis: I'm a housewife. Antithesis: I hate drudgery. Synthesis: I'm creative! . . . this feeling of creativeness also serves another purpose. It is an outlet for the liberated talents, the better taste, the freer imagination, the greater initiative of the modern woman. It permits her to use in the home all the faculties she would display in an outside career.[36]

'Convenient Social Virtues'

Galbraith described in the early 1970s how the success of consumer capitalism relies on the concealment of women's work as work, and how schools have been complicit in this concealment:

> the labour of women to facilitate consumption is not valued in national income or product. This is of some importance for its disguise; what is not counted is often not noticed. For this reason, and aided by conventional pedagogy as presently observed, it becomes possible for

women to study economics without becoming aware of their precise role in the economy. This in turn facilitates the acceptance of their role. Were their economic function more explicitly delineated in the current pedagogy, it might invite inconvenient rejection.[37]

He further argues that certain personal characteristic and pleasures have economic consequences. He called these personal identifications 'Convenient Social Virtues'.

> The Convenient Social Virtue ascribes merit to any pattern of behaviour, however uncomfortable or unnatural for the individual involved, that serves the comfort or well being of, or is otherwise advantageous for, the more powerful members of the community. The moral commendation of the community for convenient and therefore virtuous behaviour then serves as a substitute for pecuniary compensation. Inconvenient behaviour becomes deviant behaviour and is subject to righteous disapproval or sanction of the community.[38]

Convenient social virtues are important in any society in that they induce people to do the otherwise unpleasant, low status or unpaid tasks, vital for the economy, willingly and cheerfully as part of their own perceived preferences and in line with their own sense of who they are. The personal aims, preferences and tastes of the individual are at one with the aims and interests of 'the more powerful members of community'. Personal feminine values of altruism, love of family, interest in personal relationships, modesty and lack of ambition, as well as silliness, triviality, vanity and pleasures in shopping and self-adornment – 'femininity' itself can be seen as a socially convenient identity. People have personal characteristics which predispose them to enjoy consumption and housework. Working class girls' feminine identities were constructed in such a way that many were predisposed to identify with the unpaid, low status, low skilled roles in society and accept their role as housewives and mothers as natural.

Schools construct convenient femininity

Art and Craft discourse in schools in many ways colluded in this process of constructing subordinate feminine identities.

Girls were positively encouraged in arts and design to develop critical, analytical and moral faculties within feminized discourses of taste and beauty, rather than in the context of academic or intellectual activity. In one textbook they were encouraged to:

> *Discuss* outfits with friends . . . be *observant* of dress in all its aspects. *Study* fashion books very carefully. When a person impresses you as being charmingly dressed, *analyse* the reasons. *Criticise* constructively

the appearance of people whom one would expect to be well dressed.[39] (my italics)

Criticism, observation, study, discussion and analysis, all the discourses associated with modernist thinking, had different and specific meanings when applied to girls. It was unproblematically accepted to produce in working class girls cognitive habits that, in a modernist hierarchy of values, would be considered passive and trivial.

The close physical and historical connection of Art, Design and Home Economics meant a constant transferral of their discourses from one to the other. The formal elements of art, for instance – colour balance, proportion, line and composition – which had been initially constructed as psychological responses to individual visual phenomena – began to be applied to complex social forms of fashion, dress and interior decoration. Girls were encouraged for instance, to

> Watch the general tone of the skin against colours. Girls with rosy complexions may look hot and florid wearing warm tones of red, orange or wine, but look fresh and cool in cold blues and greens. Skins which are pale and colourless need the reflection of warm tones. Cold shades e.g. cold green or grey would increase the general cold effect.[40]

Conversely, it may be supposed the amateur, 'trivial', bourgeois leisure attitudes and technical practices from HE and textiles could be applied to the Art lesson. What girls had learned in Textiles about surface pattern, decoration and arrangement of materials, their acquired knowledges and experiences of texture, colour of soft materials and the skills of bricolage, could be deployed with a feeling of expertise and confidence in Design. Girls' familiarity with nature, with flowers, and arranging fruit in dressmaking and consumer education would have meant they were less likely to have reservations about choosing to draw and paint these topics in Art.

Boys were more likely to transfer their acquired skills of 'shaping, forging and manipulating' to painting and drawing in Art. Their skills in technical drawing, emphasizing mass, structure, accuracy and three-dimensional projections would be easily transferable into the drawing of man-made objects. In Art examinations, objective drawing was usually divided into a choice of 'man-made' or 'natural' objects and girls, not surprisingly, most often choose the options of drawing flowers, leaves, fruit and other natural forms, the kinds of subjects which as Rousseau had suggested 'enliven dress'.

Feminine modes of progressive art educational discourse did not of course aim to steer girls into low paid work, subordinate attitudes and convenient social virtues. However, its constitution within old paradigm psychological, individualist discourses meant that concerns with 'the social world' could be bracketed out, as outside the concerns of art education. The modernist notion of art as 'truth to materials' and as concerned with its own specific practices also legitimized a notion of art that was understood purely in psychological and visual terms.[41] It could be taught in a way that isolated it and created art education as separate from other gendered and social discourses of work, leisure, production and consumption.

Negotiating a modern identity

Not all modernist pedagogy produced socially convenient, trivial and conservative identities in working class girls. But it has to be wondered, given the prevailing cultural, economic, pre-feminist, post-war climate, how many teachers could actively and confidently act against the popular ideological tide. Before 1970 in Britain there was no visible discourse of feminism, of lesbian rights, or any cultural, ethnic or intellectual alternative for young girls. There were very few representations in film, novels, magazines or television at that time, which gave girls an image of pleasures outside the nuclear family life, popular heterosexual romance, or motherhood. Indeed, as cultural researchers have shown, the image of the patriarchal family was being aggressively marketed. There could have been few fantasies for girls, as there were for boys, of mastery, adventure, control, a public or politically active, academically or intellectually creative life. No role models were available in their art education of successful women artists, and few images of female intellectuals or scientists. The prevailing ideological attitudes encouraged the view that women's power and greatest chance of personal happiness were to be achieved through manipulating men, and using sexuality, personal attractiveness, dress and charm to achieve their aims. 'Wheedling' rather than reason, manipulation of emotions rather than assertion of rights, were assumed as women's route to power even in educational discourse. Ethical and moral identities were produced which, following the diktats of school Art lessons, had been diverted to exercise judgements on visual appearance. Girls were taught to respond to texture, colour, taste and beauty in art, rather than adopting a more aggressive stance of criticism, research or investigation, or a productive approach of moulding or forging. Modernist art values and modernist art education did not encourage the understanding of what lies behind visual appearances or to investigate issues such as class race or gender. Few, if any, girls would have been actively expected to understand the necessity in specific contexts for women to adopt masculine habits of bravery, aggression, ambition, competitiveness, or an intellectual or critical attitude.

Girls have often been criticized by teachers and educators, even in radical educational discourses, of being passive, conservative and accepting. The vigorous rebellion of boys is regarded as somehow 'more creative'.[42] Girls' art has been pejoratively compared to boys' art as being less innovative, less creative, weaker in structure, more decorative and 'pretty'. But girls had been excluded from the more rigorous forms of technical drawing. Their romantic and two-dimensional training in textile skills and leisure arts had constructed feminine skills in this form. Added to this was a culture of criticism and modernist aesthetic value that could find no way of appreciating and evaluating the skills that girls had acquired, and the potential of textiles as an artistic and critical medium. Their practice and taste was denigrated to the status of debased kitsch.

Working class women and modernist design

Modernism – with its clean lines, structural forms, absence of decoration, and minimal aesthetic – was the privileged cultural form in Fine Art and Design in Britain between the 1950s and 1970s. Modernist abstract painting, modernist architecture, as well as modernist forms of literature and music were influencing a minority of educated and intellectual tastes in high art, and architecture. Forms of American modernism were influencing further art education,[43] and towards the mid-twentieth century some selected ideas of the German Bauhaus School began to appear in Design education.[44]

But on the whole in Britain, foreignness, and particularly after the war, anything 'German' was popularly regarded with distrust. Continental ideas, modernist minimal architecture, formalist abstraction and interior decoration, art and culture were never fully accepted by the populace of post-war England. British culture was a version of what Stuart Hall has identified as 'regressive modernism'.[45] It was both a forward looking attempt to replace old values with those of science and social democracy whilst at the same time finding its cultural legitimacy in Victorian values. The image of 'America' held by the English, on the other hand, was of a country always in a state of change, open to foreign immigration and to new (often ' –fangled') ideas.

North America had been subject to radical cultural influences of European émigrés after the war, for example Theodor Adorno, Walter Benjamin, Max Horkheimer, Herbert Marcuse, Wilhelm Reich and Eric Fromm, and artists such as Bertolt Brecht, Arnold Schoenberg, Kurt Weill, Fritz Lang, Naum Gabo, Ludwig Mies van der Rohe, Annie Albers, Erwin Piscator, John Heartfield, Oska Kokoshka, Kurt Schwitters, Willem de Kooning and so on, all people who had been associated with the ideas of the Frankfurt School and radical art practices. They all worked or settled for a time in the United States and contributed to the shaping of its popular and high cultural forms.[46] The Black Mountain College was set up as an American form of the Bauhaus. It provided a point of contact between German traditions of critical and artistic thought and practice and emerging forms of American Modernist art and art education.[47] Modernist artists such as Robert Rauschenberg, musician John Cage, dancer Merce Cunningham and art educator John Dewey all at different times had contacts with the radical ideas of critical thinking and aesthetic issues discussed at the Black Mountain College. The influential Federal Art Project, for instance, set up in 1935, had been structured within early socialist and democratic ideals.[48] But these more radical forms of art were, at the time, unknown to English art education.

Perry Anderson, looking back from the vantage point of 1968, at the post-war migration of radical artists and mainly left-wing intellectuals from central Europe, argued that England – with its image of stable rural values, bourgeois comforts and class traditions – had attracted to it the less politically radical thinkers.[49] He suggested that it has been the undeserved influence of men such as Hans Eysenck in psychology, Ernst Gombrich in art history and Karl Popper in history that left a particular conservative intellectual stamp on English cultural life and had reduced aesthetics to versions of psychological interpretations of art. Anderson's critique, focused on the absence in England of any tradition of political and social analysis, described culture at that time as a 'deeply damaging and stifling force . . . which quite literally deprived the left of any source of concepts and categories with which to analyse its own society, and thereby attain a fundamental precondition for changing it'. Allowing for Anderson's polemical stance in what were troublesome times, and subsequent revisions of some of his themes, he and others have constructed a coherent picture of a culture of post-war Britain that was relatively static, class divided and conservative.[50]

It was within this cultural context and the discourses of the particularly conservative strands of modernism in art, and the absence of any critical or aesthetic traditions, that post-war modernist art education expanded.

Herbert Read, one of the most influential thinkers on post-war English art education, was a key figure in appreciating and promoting a version modernist art in secondary schools. But he challenged the more 'excessive' developments of modern art such as those found in Dada and Futurism, and later was to reject the work of American modernist artists such as Robert Rauschenberg, Jasper Johns, Roy Lichtenstein and Andy Warhol as 'eccentric'. He suggested that they failed because they 'fragmented art; instead of seeking for unity'. 'Op art', pop art and action painting and the more radical continental modernist art Read stigmatized as 'confused, spasmodic, fragmented, nihilistic, as constantly breaking off and disrupting unity', as always 'posing questions'. He argued against pure abstraction, formalism and minimalism in favour of a semi-abstract, organic, spiritual art: 'an alternation between abstraction and realism', an evolutionary doctrine of a gently unfolding and ultimately perfectible natural art of unity, nature and assimilation.[51] For the English, change was represented as progressive and above all 'natural', and culture was the 'slow product of the organic process we call history'.[52] 'Foreign' aesthetic notions of sudden revolution, discontinuity and subversion, which were strategic aesthetic practices favoured in the writings of Russian Formalism, Constructivism and Berlin Dada, and represented in the aesthetic debates of Viktor Shklovsky, Bertolt Brecht and Walter Benjamin and other radical continental artists, were omitted as too 'extreme' for schools.

Art as nature was seen by the English as the antidote to and the refuge from war and was visualized in the stability of unchanging values of England's landscapes. Reproductions of art sent round in the 'Picture for Schools' scheme, as examples of British contemporary art, celebrated the countryside, maternal images of nature and continuity and ideologies of a 'rural pastoralism'. A 'nest of gentle artists' working in organic, natural and semi-abstract forms, muted colours – and which included Barbara Hepworth, Paul Nash, Ben Nicholson and Henry Moore – were championed by Read's art criticism, their art serving as an exemplary model for English school art education.

English design

A compromised and cheaper modernist design emerged for the English domestic market, stylistically associated with revivals of Georgian classicism and the rural vernacular,[53] and based on politically less aggressive craft traditions in wood and textiles of Swedish and Danish design; a modernity inspired by nature, rather than the industrial, minimalist, machine aesthetic and the chrome and leather look of Russian and German modernisms which were regarded as 'un-English, hard and cold'. Modernism was gendered as hard, abstract, masculine and aggressive: in the broadest sense, the dominance of science, technology and rationality within the prevailing model of modernity meant the rule of a masculine cultural paradigm.[54] Male designers applied their fantasies and masculine versions of modernist design to new black and white 'streamlined' and minimally designed products – television sets, washing machines, vacuum cleaners, cars, radios, furniture and fabrics and so on.

The identity and the Oedipal fears of the modernist artist as detached, objective and autonomous meant that the affective, decorative and bodily concerns of women, particularly working class mothers with their uneducated tastes, were embarrassments to be kept out of sight. Working class women's taste was equated with bad taste, with low art and with 'kitsch'.[55] A modernist notion of an avant garde as urbane, metropolitan and cosmopolitan acted against the ideology of the housewife confined to an often suburban private life, surrounded by affective ties, children, family and untidiness. The 'white cube' of the gallery was as different as it was possible to be from a domestic interior. The masculine ideology of superior modernist 'high culture' was given credence by the fact that working class women were largely ignorant of its institutional practices. Most women had children. Galleries often banned children, thus effectively banning their mothers. Libraries, conferences, lectures, theatres, cinemas, art colleges and universities were (and are) all constructed for the independent, unencumbered individual and did not cater for children. Meeting places where ideas could be exchanged, such as cafés, tea-shops and pubs, excluded children and sometimes women altogether. On the other hand, aggressive consumer discourses of fashion, leisure and interior decoration reached out to young mothers, seemed to understand their intimate needs, made them feel important and directly designed their advertising to attract women's interests. Psychologically profiled campaigns based on the same theories that had been informing art education, hailed them directly and seemed to anticipate their desires and fantasies. Shops, department stores and supermarkets continued to develop as architecturally privileged women's spaces, welcoming working class women with their prams, their children and their elderly mothers with open tills. Bourgeois leisure arts and crafts in women's magazines continued the familiar themes of school arts and crafts and constructed an image of the normal white heterosexual mother-of-two in projects such as 'Make a Beanbag for Him', 'A Pretty Layette for Baby' or 'Cushions for the Home'. Home sewing, dressmaking and interior decoration leisure crafts were booming industries. Mail-order catalogues and new women's craft magazines dropped through their doors and daytime television entered women's homes, entered their lives, engaged their interests, wanted their opinions and catered for and constructed their pleasures and personal concerns.[56] The fragmented, chatty and colourful journalistic styles suited the busy and fragmented lifestyle of the homeworking woman, the home manager and her skills of bricolage and fragmented and contradictory identities.

Working class women's taste

Andreas Huyssens described how 'Modernism constituted itself through a conscious strategy of exclusion, an anxiety of contamination by its other, an increasingly consuming and engulfing mass culture' and how this 'engulfing mass culture' was personified as woman.[57] Feminist cultural theorists have explained this denial of the feminine as response to a social crisis in men's identity after the experiences of war, and a reaction to the fear of disorder, chaos and subversion represented by feminine popular culture and bad taste.[58] Mass culture had been represented by socialist critical theorists as 'seductions'; department stores were seen culturally by modernist critics as the 'cemeteries of culture'.[59]

Women's taste was represented in popular song, religious prints, melodrama, soap opera, romantic fiction, ballroom dancing, Hollywood film, mass produced paintings, cottage teapots, swirly carpets, ornaments on the mantelpiece. These consumer arts were combined with objects of personal meaning – family photographs, soft toys, amateur watercolours, souvenirs, children's gifts, memorabilia, family heirlooms, 'treasures' – which were all outside definitions of modernist art and regarded as bad taste. These were the tastes that the modernist art critic Clement Greenberg had designated 'kitsch'. In kitsch, he argued, 'there is no discontinuity between art and life' and in women's taste, this was certainly the case.[60]

Working class women had little access to critical modernist discourses and could work only from experience and knowledges learned in school and with the symbolic material and discursive modes available to them. They rearranged, repositioned and recombined 'modernistic' objects and incorporated them with their own familiar and traditional objects and domestic needs. Feminist cultural theorists have described this 'mis-use' of official style as a feminine site of refusal, a resistance to the imposition of a dominant masculine ideology of minimalism:

> Women played 'lip-service' to legitimate notions of 'good taste' (responsible consumption) while their pleasures in consumption were inevitably 'improper' . . . in failing to consume 'properly', working class women, in particular, resisted all this . . . Feminine taste remained hopelessly incompatible with the 'good taste' promoted by professional designers . . . it represented 'an inevitable failure of the dominant groups' ideal'.[61]

This rejection has not been recognized by art critics as a reasonable response to inadequate masculine design and the minimalist aesthetic, but a 'failure' on the part of women to appreciate the finer points of modernism. Women's 'improper' response in ironically rearranging and recombining consumer products, as Angela Partington has argued, could be seen as an assertion of creativity in constructing alternative meanings in a countermodern discourse, that male art critics and designers, trained with the notion of the pre-eminence of the visual and the utilitarian, have failed to appreciate.

Working class women's bricolaged identities

What modernist education, designers and advertisers planned for working class women, and what women themselves achieved, were not the same things. Although women had been subject to massive propaganda after the war to encourage them back into the home, and although the image of the housewife in the patriarchal nuclear family was aggressively asserted through education, advertising, by women's magazines and in popular films and television programmes, working class women were not simply passive creatures upon whom socially convenient feminine identities and patriarchal stereotypes could be imposed without contrary reactions and creative oppositions. Liberal education had two contradictory discourses: it constructed a notion of separate spheres for men and women, it privileged equality, freedom and liberation of the individual, but it also supported the romantic, domestic discourses of crafts. Although the rational discourses of modernist art, its abstraction, systems, scientism and techno-rational modes of practice privileged the life-world of the boy, they were, in modernist art education, beginning to be available for girls too, and could creatively integrated with feminine discourses of caring and altruism, fun and self-development.

Modernist education, constructed within liberal discourse, produced a generation of working class girls that, for the first time, had been able to choose boys' subjects at school. Girls, in the Roundabout system, had a taste of working in wood and metal and had begun to understand and appreciate the pleasures of mastery, of work, paid employment and careers. Fantasy and the imagination are not restricted by gender and they were able to read and enjoy their brothers' comics and story books. Although most plots had male protagonists, girls were able to identify imaginatively with discourses of the masculine. They could fantasize about bravery, fame, success and power. Towards the end of the 1970s, equal rights legislation was legitimizing, and making real, fantasies of equal pay, equal rights, equal responsibilities and opportunities in the workplace. Working class girls had personal experiences of the hard work of their own mothers in men's work in wartime. They had before them role models in female art teachers, who were increasingly to be seen in secondary schooling. Girls could see for themselves examples of active, independent women in paid professional employment.

The legislative power of the 1944 Education Act and the Welfare State had allowed, for the first time, the education to higher levels of a significant number of working class girls. 'Scholarship girls' were a distinct, post-war, modern phenomenon. It meant that a few had a chance for the first time to enter professional, meaning-making practices in the arts and in education. Carol Steedman relates this phenomenon to changes in the tenor of English cultural life. She suggests that the impact of a significant number of these women in academic and artistic life contributed to the new formal aesthetic genres of modernity.[62]

Liberal modernist art education made a *difference* to many working class women, and the emergence of the new wave of feminists and feminist art practices at the end of the 1960s is testament to the fact that in spite of the patriarchal family, the all pervasive consumer capitalist culture of advertising, of male dominance, and the feminizing process in domestic discourses in schools, that some did not buy it.

Power, as Foucault suggested, is not just exerted from above on hapless individuals, but individuals and groups together have power to refuse, resist and redeploy existing knowledges and practices in ways they were not designed to be used, to further their own interests and pleasures. Some women were able to resist the dominant ideologies of regressive femininity and assume identifications with masculinity and progress, rationality and science as part of their rightful human inheritance.

In numerical terms, only a minority of working class women identified as feminists. Others achieved an ironic detachment in relation to modernity's cultural forms and found pleasures and conscious and non-conscious resistance in kitsch, parody, decoration, frilliness, dumbness and pastiche. But this working class 'femininity' and bricolaging of identity became the material for the subversive and critical practice of feminist art practices, which in turn became the paradigm for the artistic critique of modernity.

5 The feminization of art education

Art education today appears to have taken on aspects of 'the feminine'. There are growing feminine rhetorics of empowerment, flexibility, creativity, cooperation and teamwork visible in art educational discourse now, and a greater emphasis is being placed on difference: on issues of race, culture and gender. In this chapter I want to pursue the notion that while the 'content' of art education has become more feminine, the larger systems and structures within which art pedagogy exists continue, in metaphorical terms, to operate as hidden patriarchal power. These structures are becoming increasingly authoritarian, unified, and bureaucratic and are invisible, non-conscious and are not easily available to criticism and reform.

Shifting modes of discourse and power

Art education, unlike the old established university disciplines of English, History or Philosophy, is not a unified academic discipline; it has been an interdisciplinary project that has always drawn its authority from other well-established fields. Historians have emphasized that, as well as being shaped by Romanticism and Classicism, art education's growth in the modern world has also been moulded by the influences of industry, manufacturing and increasing bureaucratization. As it emerged in the late nineteenth century, art education borrowed its rhetoric and style from the contingent, traditionally stable, economically successful and more powerful social discourses that surrounded it to legitimize itself as a new practice.

Patricia Hills has demonstrated how, by the same processes, modernist art criticism borrowed its images from international finance, technology, scientific management and business to add legitimacy to its project. She identified the same languages of individualism, exploration, enterprise, freedom, evolutionary development and self-expression adopted by art criticism that had been prevalent in capitalist business corporations. Hills has stressed that it was not the actual practices of capitalism that were necessarily borrowed, but the aesthetic: the look, the languages and the style.[1]

Art education, attempting to establish itself at the end of the nineteenth century, borrowed its rhetorics from systems organization in business: it took on the techno-ideological coding of mass production processes in its notions of creativity. It adopted the look and the 'feel' of technology and science in its discursive practices in which schemes for art education were represented in analytic diagrams and through scientific-like methodologies of aims, objectives and outcomes. It was not in itself scientific, but scientistic.

Children may have learned some specific manual skills in art education to fit them for 'the needs of industry', but on the whole, as Robert Moore has argued, it was not so much skills as ideological attitudes that were passed on to children. School values were couched within the same systems of value and meanings as the world of work. Manufacture, business and industry offered to education what he has called 'occupationalist educationalist ideologies'.[2] The economically successful organization of modern work and productive employment, of technology and scientific achievement lent their rhetorics to the less secure discourses of education. And in the negotiation of these ideological structures and systems, identities and predispositions were formed so that by the time they left school, children's identities would be broadly formed within the values and structural modern attitudes to work.

With the gradual decline in Britain's industrial base after the second half of the twentieth century, and as masculinized manufacture and industry have lost their economic and ideological power, industrial occupationalist ideologies are losing their rhetorical authority in education. In spite of the fact that manufacture and production are still crucial economic activities, their productive languages, their paternal styles of authority and their skills seem 'old fashioned'. Traditional men's jobs – in shipbuilding, engineering, and mining – are in decline. The ideologies of 'a man's wage', 'a job for life', 'pride in a job well done', and the associations of the constructive skills of 'forging', 'constructing' and 'building' in heavy industry no longer have ideological force. The successful postmodern male identity promoted in advertising and men's magazines is that of the entrepreneur, the jet-setting business man having the skills of 'communication', 'responsiveness', 'flexibility' and 'creativity', a cleaner, better dressed, younger image based in new economic realities.

Education is increasingly drawing its occupationalist educationalist ideologies from new relations and work practices found in the powerful image of global corporate culture and consumption to replace the 'old fashioned' masculine legitimizing discourses of science, industry and productivity.

Business discourses and art education

Business and arts education are finding reciprocal power and legitimizing authority in each other's practices. The Getty Education Institute for the Arts, which supports American Discipline Based Art Education, vigorously promotes this relationship:

> At a national level, the business community has joined with teachers, school administrators, artists and arts and cultural organizations, parents and students in a focused effort to make sure the arts are included in state-level plans to implement America's education goals. The business community has been deeply invested in this effort, called the 'Goals 2000 Arts Education Partnership' . . . So business is a key player – and a key partner – in our efforts to find a solid education in the arts to every child in America.[3]

Some art courses in higher education in Britain are shifting their educational priorities in line with new business imperatives: the aims of the five key skills at Camberwell College of Art, for instance, and those of Birmingham Institute of Art and Design are the same as those promoted by the Confederation of British Industry (CBI): 'initiative, self-motivation, creativity, communication and teamwork'. These are now considered the necessary skills for arts graduates 'in a flexible labour market'.[4] As Turkle and Papert have observed, the paradigm of economic man in the modern era was the rigorous, analytical scientist. The paradigm of postmodern economic man is the playful, creative, risk-taking, entrepreneurial artist.[5]

There is hardly a contemporary text on school art education in Britain and the United States today that does not have some reference to new business values and skills: flexibility, holism, teamwork, cooperation, empathy, communication, creativity empowerment, responsiveness, listening skills and so on.[6] In Art, Design and Technology education, the rhetoric has shifted from the teaching of masculine, individualist manual skills towards the valuing of interactive team skills, groupwork and cooperation.[7] The teacher's role has been shifting from authoritarian models to 'flatter' management styles of 'enabling', 'empowering' and 'negotiating' with the student in an 'interactive' and 'holistic' way.[8]

In an economic context, where art education in particular is finding it hard to survive, what better can it do than hitch its ideological wagon to successful images and patronage of business management and global corporate culture?

What follows in this chapter is a brief survey of the gendered social discourses within which contemporary art education is sited and from which it is taking its values and meanings. I make no attempt to survey the whole field of influence that is being brought to bear on art education, but I focus on the particular effects that occupational educationalist ideologies based on consumer capitalism and global corporate power are having on the feminization of working class identities, and the feminization of art education and the feminization of the profession of teaching art.

The feminization of work

There has been a widespread and well-documented change in postmodern work and labour relations and culture in the West towards feminized work.[9] Richard Gordon has identified feminized work as those tasks and restructured jobs that have traditionally been carried out by mothers in the patriarchal household: cleaning, catering, nursing, entertainment, textile work and so on. Not only are more women going out to work, but also eight out of ten jobs created now are 'women's jobs'. More work is available, and more working class children are entering feminized work in services, light industry, leisure and consumption.[10]

'Feminization' has meant increased employment in jobs that are described in management theory as 'contingent': casual, part-time, temporary, seasonal or involving practices such as flexi-time, piece-working, job-sharing and homeworking.[11] During the period between 1982 and 1996, 90 per cent of new jobs available were feminized contingent work, and this appears to be the future of all new work.[12] Feminized skills are usually undervalued, underpaid, low status and often menial with unsocial hours.[13] Donna Haraway has described feminized work as

> both literally female and feminized, whether performed by men or women. To be feminized means to be made extremely vulnerable; able to be disassembled, reassembled, exploited as a reserve labor force; seen less as workers than as servers; subjected to time arrangements on and off the paid job that make a mockery of a limited work day; living an existence that always borders on being obscene, out of place, and reducible to sex.[14]

Feminized work can be seen today in globally organized craft, textile and electronics industries – making trainers, domestic products, fashion goods, personal computers, television sets, mobile phones and so on – based on the old 'slopwork' employment practices. Immigrant women, feminized men and their children are working in nineteenth century patriarchal traditions, concentrated in new sweatshop conditions in Britain and the United States as well as in China and South East Asia.[15] Feminized work has moved to global areas of the urban West, with high immigrant populations where patriarchal family values are still strong, where Enlightened modernity's discourses of emancipation and rights, labour laws and education are not so well established and where women and children's structural position in the family can be easily exploited.[16] Evan Watkins has argued that the nineteenth century garment industry has served as a model to which these global corporations now aspire:

the organisation of management, the increasingly complex chain of subcontracting work, the development and use of new technologies, and the hiring patterns of the garment industry resemble nothing so much as . . . a negative afterimage of the worst sweatshops of the industrial 'past'.[17]

Patriarchal power continues to operate in feminized work: men continue to dominate in the ownership and control of business, high finance and law, and their organizational principles, their financial dealings, and their lines of authority, management and communication are becoming increasingly inaccessible and invisible to the ordinary worker.

The feminization of identity

Feminized work requires different attitudes and expectations from those required by older masculine forms of employment. People with fewer options – working class, older, immigrant and non-white men as well as women – are having to learn different behaviours, personal identifications and work conditions in hierarchical relations that have historically and traditionally been associated with women's work. Feminized work relies on less powerful individual men and women, particularly men, letting go of masculine behaviours – such as criticism, control, aggression, manual skill, productivity – and adopting complex clusters of feminine attributes: flexibility, cooperation, the ability to work in teams, good social skills. Those who refuse feminine identifications, who continue to deploy and enact assertive, individualistic and confrontational behaviours, who seek 'a job for life', 'a man's wage' and who question and criticize their roles, are less likely to find employment. According to surveys, British young men are showing themselves reluctant to abandon 'machismo' behaviours, compared with their continental counterparts, and are consequently finding themselves excluded from new forms of feminized work.[18]

The values that are increasingly being seen in art education, and which are being promoted in some feminist methodologies, such as flexibility, cooperation, creativity and a notion of art as leisure and self-fulfilment, it can be argued, continue to produce socially convenient identities that correspond to those required in a feminized, contingent labour force.[19]

Consumption and art education

Art education is increasingly engaging with the discourses of consumption. In the late nineteenth century, as Romans has shown, the teaching of taste was central to art education, in elevating and informing the buying potential of future consumers.[20] During the twentieth century and particularly in the period between 1940s and early 1970s, consumer education was specifically targeted to girls. Today, consumer rhetorics are spreading right across Art and Design discourses. The languages of consumption, appreciation, discrimination, discussion, responsiveness and altruism, once common in girls' textile crafts, are appearing more often in art educational texts and are being taught to both boys and girls.

The fragmentation of the curriculum

The delivery of art has become fragmented and packaged. A pluralist, diverse and consumerist 'freedom of choice' is evident in British national curricula as well as in North American Discipline Based Art Education (DBAE) and it is becoming more difficult to teach in-depth skills or sustained ideas.

As an example, I quote at length from a small section of the English version of the 1992 National Curriculum. Here the authors suggest models of practice for teachers of 12-year-old children:

– discuss and compare the various ways in which artists have represented journeys; e.g. Chinese scroll paintings, Aboriginal dream maps, Turner's note books and Richard Long's walks.
– recognise and value representations of similar forms in different cultures; e.g. the kite in Chinese, Japanese, Indian and European traditions.
– compare the wall paintings of muralists working in different cultures; e.g. Giotto, Diego Rivera.
– compare the way that letters and symbols have been used to convey information and ideas in graphic form in different cultures; e.g. Egyptian hieroglyphics, Islamic calligraphy, Chinese characters, Bauhaus designs.
– write a review of a local exhibition using words in their specialist sense; e.g. asymmetry, opaque, gradation, rhythm, harmony.
– consider how artists contributed to the decoration of public buildings; e.g. Greek and Roman wall panels, Byzantine mosaic, Gothic stained glass and stone carving.
– study how artists exploited the use of oil paint to create texture and surface effects.
– consider the work of artists such as Simone Martini, Donatello, Dürer, Rembrandt, Poussin, Gainsborough, Turner, Cézanne, Picasso and Dali and analyse the distinctive contribution of several of them.
– design and make a wall hanging in mixed media exploiting colour and surface, referring to the work of Jackson Pollock, Alan Davie and Patrick Heron.

– translate a seventeenth century interior by Vermeer or de Hooch into a collage combining source material from magazines and newspapers with photograms and drawings.[21]

This list represents one part of one stage of study towards required attainment targets in 'Knowledge and Understanding' for children at Key Stage 3. Another different range of practices for other stages as well as another set of practices given as examples for the subject of Design and Technology are also available in the document. Not all subjects are of course expected to be taught to all children, but together, national curricula discourse – the textbooks, teaching packages and the classroom practices it has spawned – cover a vast terrain of historical, cultural and geographically disparate art and craft practice. The fragmentation of the school timetable, the division of art into behavioural objectives and attainment targets, the limited amount of time and resources in state education suggest that no one subject can be understood in any depth, nor can the different subjects be situated contextually and related to each other as historical, social and symbolic practices. Visiting museums and galleries where advice is given on 'how to look at art' also encourages a consumer approach. Children acquire the accomplishments of knowing many different skills and genres superficially.

Art education is offering more choice and diversity and apparent freedom for the teacher and the pupil, but access to critical skills, to historical and contextual knowledges and information which would empower the teacher or the child to critique or suggest alternatives to the system as a whole are not supplied or even indicated.

'Critical Studies'

A critical approach to studying art has for some time in Britain been promoted in through the agenda of a field of art pedagogic practice known as *Critical Studies in Art Education*. Critical Studies, as it is called, explicitly asserts the value of critical thinking, research and contextual study for children, and would appear to be the place where some understanding of art educational rationales could be found. But Critical Studies takes criticism only so far.

Critical Studies' concerns and limitations can be identified in a collection of its key themes in the publication *Critical Studies and Modern Art*.[22] This collection of articles, many from prominent art educators, includes contributions from political, postcolonial and psychoanalytic theory, from philosophical aesthetics and contemporary art practice. (There are significantly no articles directly concerned with gender or class relations in school art education.) There are critiques of notions such as the unity of identity,[23] the perceptualist tradition,[24] teleological narratives of history and the subjectivist position inherent in art education.[25] Together the articles represent cogent concerns of art education, and it would seem to be the place from which a fundamental critique and examination of the theoretical concepts that underpin national curricula could be mounted. But the way the book – and the discourse of critical studies – has been structured makes it difficult for the reader to understand how the different views relate to each other. There is no explicit stated project; in the book there is no editorial map of the different intellectual genealogies and ideological perspectives from which each position has been formed. There is a reluctance on the part of the editors to assume an authorial voice or to contextualize Critical Studies itself within a wider historical and economic context. The introduction stresses the 'opportunity to change the socio-political agenda'. It invites the reader to challenge 'the discourses of modern art' and 'the nature of patriarchal culture' and to acknowledge modern art's challenge to 'normal perception'. But there is little guidance or further reading recommended on contemporary analyses of socio-political or patriarchal culture on which to make informed choices. Readers are encouraged to take their pick, 'to reflect on the multiplicity of differing theories, approaches and practices'. But without an engagement in critical ideas, it has no position from which to produce arguments for privileging any point of view or evaluate critically the educational value of different artistic practices. It falls back into the modernist consumerist concept of 'freedom of choice', bricolage, and the liberal acceptance of all perspectives as 'equal but different'. Critical Studies in practice in schools, it is often observed, has become absorbed back into modernist paradigms and has been largely ineffective as criticism.

The art curriculum allows for choice and diversity but its knowledges and practices have become fragmented and disassociated from one another, the reasons why they were introduced in the curriculum in the first place have been hidden.

The cumulative curriculum

Over the years the curriculum has become overloaded with a variety of competing and contradictory practices with earlier modern systems and ideologies of art education continuing unproblematically alongside the postmodern. Sonia Landy-Sheridan has described the contemporary art curriculum as an accretion of unrelated practices:

> For the most part, art-educational changes are occurring in layered increments. Although new areas of interface between art, science and technology are sprouting up all over the world, the vast majority of institutions are only adding new media to old structures – in the 1950's printmaking was added to painting and sculpture, in the 1960's photography

was added to printmaking, painting and sculpture. In the 1970's video was added to photography, printmaking, painting and sculpture. In the 1980's computers were added to make a neat technological stack.[26]

There is a multiplicity of piecemeal and unrelated practices available on the curriculum and a corresponding lack of a culture of criticism and research.[27] Leslie Perry has suggested that curricular change in art has been 'an amateur enterprise', a gross mixture of politics, administration, economics, fashion and contingency, rather than being based on recent developments in educational and psychological ideas. In a similar vein John Swift has identified the absence from government discussions or interventions, any reference to educational research. Indeed, he argued, 'any attempts to employ such arguments have been met with the response that "experts" were biased because they were too intellectually and emotionally involved'.[28] Howard Hollands has suggested that part of the failure of art education to take a critical stance is due to the lack of interest in educational issues by contemporary cultural theorists.[29] This suggests that school art education has been shaped in a cultural context where mainstream art educators have little contact with contemporary debates in aesthetics, art criticism or cultural theory, and where contemporary intellectuals and artists have little interest in art education. The values and interests of business and consumer culture find little resistance.

Consumption in schools

Unlike productive work, which usually separates the workplace from leisure in the home, consumption breaks down the barriers between work and home; through television and magazines it enters people's personal lives, their intimate desires, hopes and fantasies; as Mica Nava argued, identities and imaginations are knotted inextricably to consumption.[30]

The culture industries reach the child through provision of school teaching aids, through art and design 'projects' which engage with popular branded institutions and products that familiarize children with the pleasures and habits of consumption as current and potential customers.[31] Art and Design education cannot compete with the mass resources, seductive imagery and sensuous pleasures offered by expensively produced images in popular music, culture and entertainment, and to a certain extent borrows from popular culture to make its practices seem more 'relevant'. Sheila Harty has described the processes by which businesses attempt to influence school curricula through the free distribution and use of materials in line with their own corporate profit motives, and how schools, starved of funding, have been willing to collude in this process.[32] In the Design curriculum, for instance, the drawing of corporate logos, designing packaging, advertising and promotions and working in cooperation with existing institutions are all common practice.[33]

In Britain, the main art teachers' professional body is sponsored by a traditional art materials company. Their products and practices using their materials are uncritically accepted in teaching packs and conferences.

Museum study, if uncritically taught, as Watkins has argued at length, provides students with sufficient superficial 'packaged' and conventional knowledges about art which allows them to do no more than be discerning consumers in new leisure activities of gallery going, visiting heritage centres, tourist shops, and stately homes and shopping.[34]

Children can form identities only through 'available symbolic materials', by consuming knowledges and making choices with what is available.

The feminization of boys

Advertising that was once directed mainly to women as the main consumer spenders is now targeted at children, particularly boys, who are seen as an important and growing sector to be drawn into consumer activity. In the 1970s, the textile and clothing industry, for instance, was aware that women's consumption of fashion had been 'saturated': there were relatively fewer new market options available, so the industry explicitly began to view young boys as an untapped resource for opening markets.[35] Men and boys were regarded as 'naive' targets for advertisers of consumer products. Unused to shopping, unsure and unstable in their modern masculine roles and cultural identities, boys have been ripe for exploitation. The force of advertising's fast changing fashion markets, combined with boys' learned competitive behaviours, sense of loyalty and peer solidarity ensured that its niche cultures – for brand-label clothes, trainers, sports goods, music, computer games, mobile phones and fast foodstuffs – were targeted at their vulnerabilities and their lack of any other real options. The glossy, superficial, fragmented and trivialized styles of journalism and art education that once characterized women's magazines and girls' crafts are now spreading to boys' activities. Male identities are in certain aspects becoming feminized as advertising draws them into its 'personal' regimes of style, make-up, body-image, shopping, fashion, dance, cooking and interior design.

Paul Willis has provided a case study of creative identity forming enactments of consumption by British black working class boys. He has shown how they relate reflexively to knowledges acquired from different sources; how they subvert and manipulate, misuse and redeploy what he calls 'available symbolic materials'. Representations from popular culture – sports and music heroes – are combined with 'school meanings', which then are made sense of in relation to traditional values of family life. Through a bricolaging process of bringing together into an imaginary whole, disparate and contradictory aspects of everyday life, in line with fantasies and aspirations, boys' new identities are constructed.[36]

Evan Watkins has suggested that consumption is assuming a primary pedagogic role. At one time, education was believed to give access to power, agency and choice, access to what Bourdieu called 'cultural capital', and was assumed to be a passport to a job.[37] But acquiring a better life is no longer imagined to be obtained through qualifications, or by laboriously acquiring specialist knowledges and skills. 'Performance' is sufficient. By engaging in creative consumption in activities such as joining the right gang, 'being in fashion', having the knowledges, knowing 'who's who' and acquiring the jargons of style, of sports, of popular music, shared experiences establish and communicate social position.[38] Changing one's appearance, accent and attitude and acquiring performative skills – ways of walking, talking, dressing and acquiring personal possessions to surround oneself – make it appear *as if* we possess relevant knowledges and skills. Performance, through the choice and deployment of objects and knowledges, rather than carefully researched understanding, becomes the means by which social positions and relationships are constructed.[39] 'Lifestyles', David Chaney has argued, 'are best understood as characteristic modes of social engagement, or narratives of identity, in which the actors concerned can embed the metaphors at hand'.[40]

Boys are appearing with all the signs of the 'fashion victim' identity, the silliness – 'laddism' – that has been typical of the image of the modernist, working class girl. To be serious, intellectual or studious is to be 'boring', an 'anorak' or a 'nerd'. Willis has argued that working class masculinity has been constructed in opposition to a culture of learning and school authority, and Jeff Hearn deduced from his research that 'there is for some boys and young men an antagonism between educational attainment, even attentiveness, and the performance and achievement of particular and valued masculinities'.[41]

Although arguments such as Willis' in creative lifestyle performance suggest that children are not merely passive victims of advertising and consumer culture, the 'available symbolic materials' that children have to work with are limited. The modernist discourses of art education that encouraged in-depth criticism, excellence, autonomy, disinterestedness, accuracy, rigour, sustained research, 'planning' modes of creativity and effort and hard work are considered in liberatory and postmodern terms to be old fashioned, 'modernist' and repressive.

Modern values have given way to the privileging in art education and in postmodern art of the values of the feminine: intuition, emotion, pluralism, relativism, eclecticism and 'bricolage' modes of creativity. Art education's critics have begun to dismantle modernist narratives of reason, science and progress. In the subsequent loss of faith in overarching modernist theories – as Karen Hamblen has concluded in her review of art education's histories – educationalists have not believed it possible or desirable to put any new postmodern theories in their place.[42]

Creative work as contingent labour

Many of the jobs that children will be doing in the future will be in 'creative and knowledge' industries. The number of people engaged in the creative industries is set to rise by 5 per cent a year. As one newspaper summary of the government report *Different Jobs, Different Lives* put it:

> Well meaning parents should advise their children to head for the stage – or the screen, the music business, design, journalism or professional sport. The creative professions will be the fastest growing source of new jobs between now and 2006 . . . the increase in the demand for people with literary, artistic and sporting skills will even outpace the need for more computer programmers and lawyers . . . by the year 2006, there are as likely to be as many luvvies as construction workers in Britain and they will also outnumber engineers or security guards. . . . traditional craft and manual jobs will shrink in numbers.[43]

This rise in creative employment is significant in that it is being called on to legitimize growth and investment in the arts and in art education. But what kind of work will children be educated for? And what meanings about art and artists are being produced in art education?

Creative work itself continues to be gendered as feminine. And the feminized individuals who do creative work are economically subordinated.

On the plus side, creative industries, like other feminized industries, break down the barriers between home and work; the work is pleasant, requires self-motivation and entrepreneurial skill, is glamorous and always has the lure of fantasies of fame, status and big prizes. But feminized creative work relies on commitment, highly developed skills and intensive self-training of creative individuals. Original research, as Anne Oakley has argued, is feminized work: 'the housework and also the motherhood' of the academic world, 'the undervalued bread and butter of knowledge development'. She demonstrates that researchers are contingent workers; they

> suffer from job insecurity, inequality of opportunity, low status and low pay, exclusion from many aspects of university life, isolation and lack of access to training. The trend is towards shorter and shorter contracts . . . Like housework, contract research is severely undervalued and under-supported in relation to its actual importance.[44]

Most painters, sculptors, craftworkers, actors, writers, musicians, computer software designers, television programme producers, performers and fashion designers and those who work in 'knowledge development' work as 'freelance' or 'self-employed' often working and training in their own home, and in their own time. Artists' lives are often insecure, non-unionized, without career structures, health benefits or pensions. 'Much art activity is run on a voluntary basis with little consideration for contracts, rates of pay or conditions of service.' Strictly speaking most artists' attitudes are on a par with nineteenth century bourgeois feminine leisure craft ideologies. Their jobs are seen as superficial to 'real' life, as inessential decoration and leisure. The creative employee, as the economist Hillman-Chartrand has argued, 'provides research and development for the commercial arts': they produce innovative and new ideas and products for the media, advertising, journalism and fashion industries to dip into, and bricolage into more popular and profitable forms for mass consumption.[45] This kind of work is what businesses aspire to achieve: low paid workers who are creative, skilled, self-motivated as well as cheap and easily disposable. The artist provides the paradigm of the postmodern worker.

The artist as contingent worker

Individuals who have been educated in the bourgeois child-centred belief that 'art' is for self-development, rather than being an essential social and economic activity, and who are kept ignorant of 'boring' or masculine concerns of criticism, finance, business, law, politics and power, are easily exploited.

The popular image of the artist is one who is not intellectual, socially committed or analytical, but is represented as feminine and dependent: irresponsible, spontaneous, wayward and unpredictable, 'naughty' and troublesome. The art critics Simon Ford and Andrew Davies, in criticizing the lack of political awareness of the Young British Artists phenomenon, illustrated in their choice of language how 'hungry artists and cash-strapped institutions are in weakened positions', unable to refuse the patronage of business: 'Soon they were begging for it . . . Poorly prepared in matters of business, the artists' desperation for any type of exposure is often exploited'.[46] The art critic Cindy Nemser described in the 1970s the lack of power of the artist in the same gendered and familial terms:

> Artists, both male and female, are equated with the women of our culture and therefore their contributions receive little serious attention or remuneration in proportion to other members of our society. Artists adorn our existence, but like women, they have no voice in constructing or controlling it. For the most part, they do not even have individual economic autonomy, but remain ever at the beck and call of rich patrons, striving to please them with fetching new creations as women strive to please their husbands and lovers with fetching new clothes.[47]

Postmodern art's aim has been described by some critics as 'pure pleasure: it has no moral ambition and no educational or creative purpose'.[48] There are many artists who are happy to collude with business and to take on the aesthetic values of consumerism and the marketplace. There are aspects of postmodern art that have been characterized by 'sensationalism, titillation, frilliness, pastiche, dumbness and narcissism': as postmodern art becomes bound up with business, popular culture, fashion and consumption, art criticism follows its lead:

> The scholarly monograph, the temporary exhibition, the discipline of art history, galleries and museums have become in consumer culture essentially celebratory entities, and that these institutions and discourses which collectively function to construct the object called 'art' have become themselves allied to the material determinations of the market place. They only serve to establish and confirm the commodity status of the work of art. There is no place from which relatively disinterested criticisms can be made.[49]

Postmodern artistic practice, however, is anything but monolithic, and it would be a mistake to assume that all postmodern art is uncritical, but the more critical forms of postmodern practice are less well known. Critical art practice is often pejoratively associated with earlier, 'old fashioned' modernist ideals, with a passé feminism, or with 'worthy', joyless or otherwise 'politically correct' art and therefore no fun at all.[50]

Critical postmodern art can be found in the work of artists like Martha Rosler, Andrea Fraser, Anne Tallentire and Mona Hatoum. It is not necessarily art that is explicitly 'political' or 'issue based'. Critical work can be described as art practice that challenges existing oppressive norms and holds out imaginative possibilities for something different. It can be found in the work of Mary Kelly, who traced the reciprocal construction of the identities of mother and child and in doing so challenged the norms of the 'maternal instinct'. Ingrid Pollard, as a black woman photographer, challenged the image of rural pastoralism within which so many English fantasies have been based. Sheila Clayton's tea parties and the boiling of her husband's suits in wax made problematic the assumptions of the traditional family. The discourse of textiles has been asserted and reactivated as a postcolonial, critical practice. Cindy Sherman's photographic work, which questions the notion of fixed identity, is an example of an artist whose work has been identified as critical, yet who herself did not have a particularly critical intention. She shows how gender identity is constructed through practices such as makeup and photographic technique. Other work such as that of Cathy de Monchaux's hybrid sculptures, Pauline Cummins' and Louise Walsh's video installations on the body, Della Grace's lesbian photographs, the dance performances of Delta Streete – all suggest alternatives to dominant modernist concepts of binary difference, oppressive distinctions of gender and generation that could help children to construct their own identities differently.

School art education's mainstream texts seem unaware of the differences between stylistic and critical postmodern art, and there is little information available for art teachers or time given to them for research that would help in making evaluative judgements, or gain access to ethical and critical art agencies and the currents of contemporary fine art practice which question the Cartesian viewing subject, the primacy of reason, capitalist art markets, consumer and fashion values.[51]

Art teachers as feminized

The role of the art teacher is that of a feminized service worker. They have the executive role of carrying out and 'managing' the delivery of curricula that have been written and structured centrally, by unknown others, 'elsewhere'.

Service work is recognized in business theory in areas such as retail and shop work, in delivering goods, repairing equipment, answering phones, communicating with the public as waiting staff or office cleaners, cooking fast food. Teaching, nursing, therapy, entertaining and sex-work are all kinds of services, based on the work traditionally carried out by women in the family.[52]

Service work requires different skills and different relationships from those of productive work. It is more concerned with mental performance and 'process'; there is no final product to be considered. Service usually involves 'the whole self': a bodily involvement and often close bodily proximity with the customer or client. Service workers often enter the homes or private emotions and personal spaces of the client. It requires a 'good presentation', cleanliness, good manners and willingness. The intimate style, the speech, demeanour and behaviour of the worker are embodied in the service performed. Service workers are expected to suppress or conceal their own opinions and feelings, and align their opinions with the company who employs them. They are often required in their jobs to smile, to flatter, to be friendly and to care.[53] The paradigm of the service worker is found in the image of the nineteenth century domestic servant.

Amanda Hochschild, in her influential case study of airline staff, demonstrated that it is not enough for the worker to do a job in service, but they must also bring their personalities, their 'niceness', charm, humour, attractiveness and benevolence to bear on interactions with the public.[54] This bringing of personal and feminine caring behaviours into work practices is referred to as 'emotional labour';[55] it is now accepted as part of labour strategy and is typically seen in teaching. The 'good teacher' displays all the behaviours of service workers in that they are always aware of the importance of their behaviour and appearance and may modify their language in school. They learn to control and repress their own feelings, spontaneous criticisms and angers, and suppress their own attitudes in dealing with children. They learn to bring care and even love to the teaching relationship. Good humour, listening skills, smiling and affection are part of the progressive teacher's practice as a service worker.

Maternal authority

The leading management theorist, Geerte Hofstede, has analysed in detail the way that the relationships of the family have provided a model for establishing relationships of emotionally suffused power in service and management work practices.[56] In the image of the traditional patriarchal family, the mother is executive manager. She is subject to and dependent on the economic and social authority of the father. It is her responsibility to control and socialize children into the norms of culture. The image of the ideal mother is one who puts the interests of the children before her own. Instead of using overt authority, punishment, anger and violence, the mother controls the child through her personal skill of kindness, love, care, flattery, humour, 'wheedling' and affection. She may also control children by negatively manipulating emotions: by the withdrawal of love, by silence and tacit disapproval.

The performance of maternal behaviours is explicitly recognized in new management strategies where it is no longer acceptable to display naked power as punitive, combative, confrontational or aggressive. The authoritarian figure of the boss-as-father is seen as both old fashioned and oppressive, but more importantly it is recognized as less effective in managing and controlling employees.

There has been an explicit shift in the organization of large corporations away from masculine and authoritarian 'command and control', hierarchical modes, towards feminine 'flatter', 'transformational' modes. Good management is now valuing maternal and feminine values of collaboration and consultation, power sharing, teambuilding, prioritizing and praising staff, caring for the physical environment, a holistic approach, flexibility and good listening skills.[57]

Many women are finding new and satisfying roles in middle management; they see themselves as already possessing the more caring, sharing skills and can encourage cooperation and non-confrontational techniques of managing disputes and promoting teamwork. Women's management styles, it is being argued, are empowering and enabling, energizing and participating.[58]

Feminine methodologies in art education provide support for this shift to the feminine and argue for the introduction of a similar system of maternal values in education.[59] Renée Sandell for instance has asserted the value of empowerment and student–teacher cooperation.[60] Val Walsh has expressed it:

> Feminist pedagogy develops collaboratively and creatively. It highlights the sharing of experience, information, ideas, feelings and skills; a sense of mutuality and reciprocity; an equalising of power relations between student and tutor.[61]

Maternal pedagogy has always been part of the discourse of child-centred art education. Valerie Walkerdine analysed at length the history of the introduction of women teachers at the beginning of the twentieth century, who were specifically recruited for their maternal and nurturing capacities in pro-gressive education.[62] These pedagogies drew their authority and theoretical basis from theories of child development, and creativity from object-relations theories from Melanie Klein and D. W. Winnicott, and from psychotherapeutic models from psychologists such as Carl Rogers and E. L. Kelly.[63] Diana Dosser has taken these ideas into new feminist art pedagogy which, she asserts, values listening skills, collective endeavour, interaction between teacher and student, and empowerment of students, stressing that 'The abilities to play, to be flexible, to take risks and to judge their own work are widely recommended as routes to creative visual thinking, . . . the art student needs above all to feel safe to work to full potential'.[64]

Critiques of maternal pedagogy

There are more recent feminist educators who are beginning to question the value of maternal pedagogies.[65] Jean Elshtain suggests that the authority of the maternal teacher is hidden and therefore not open to question which can give rise to what she terms 'psycho-pedagogy': 'within a manipulative environment, where a teacher has a hidden agenda, students are treated with less dignity and respect, for all the pedagogical cards are not out on the table'.[66]

Feminist notions of empowerment can be positive, they can make for a more satisfying and personally involving job, and give the art teacher scope to feel creative and an active agent. On the other hand, when the wider picture of the institution is considered, empowerment does not appear so beneficial to the individual: John Kaler, writing from a perspective in Business Ethics, concluded in his analysis:

> All in all empowerment would seem to be a one sided deal . . . if empowerment works, then management gains by an enhancement of the productive capacities of staff . . . Thus employees do more without getting anything from empowerment except the rather dubious privi-lege of having more to do.[67]

But whether they are called 'feminine' or 'feminist', teachers appear to be losing much of their autonomy and authority to centralized paternal powers who delegate responsibility for teaching national curricula. Like mothers in the maternal family, they are being allotted a merely executive role, often reduced to the bureaucratic managerial position of delivering curriculum decisions made by higher authorities and experts to whom they are ultimately responsible, but who are invisible and to whom they have no access.[68] The art teacher, who in secondary school has often had a professional training as an artist or designer in their own right, is subordinated, not expected to be highly creative or skilled themselves, but to have the capacity for creating 'family' and domestic home-like conditions where the child can grow and learn. The teacher is being reduced to a feminized maternal service worker.

Business art and education

Art education has borrowed from the powerful contemporary discourses of business and management, but as the art world becomes more financially successful itself, and as cheap and contingent labour of artists becomes a model for the entrepreneur and creative worker, the images and employment practices of art lend themselves to the creative and entrepreneurial image of business. The feminized maternal pedagogic skills and practices and the psychological models of progressive art pedagogy, which were once considered appropriate only for the caring control of the very young child, are now being recognized as effective in the control and organization and the infantalizing and disempowering of personnel in business and management. Hugh Willmott in a seminal article in business studies has critiqued the process of feminine management styles in deliberate practices of manipulative control at work where employees are infantilized: encouraged, praised, rewarded by managers but at other times kept in the dark, uninformed, excluded and made to experience stress, anxiety, self-doubt, guilt and helplessness.[69]

Business and the arts

Businesses are learning from the arts, and harnessing the power of the imagination, bodily pleasures and private emotions into the interests of business and management practices through psychology, the arts and aesthetics.[70] In 1972 the feminist art critic Cindy Nemser wrote:

> American society; with its traditional emphasis on the logical, the practical, the ordered, all supposedly 'masculine' virtues, has awarded all its big prizes to business, science and technology which supposedly embody all these traits. It has turned its back on the arts which it has stigmatised as 'female' or intuitive, subjective, capricious, emotional etc.[71]

Today business does not 'turn its back' but totally embraces the arts, appreciating how they serve as a model of cheap and creative labour as well as improving corporate performance and image and ultimately, increasing profits for shareholders.[72]

Modernist art was marginalized, but its position on the margins meant that the arts could represent a relatively autonomous alternative to corporate consumer values and the aesthetic desires of consumer capitalism. Postmodern art and postmodern education now often collude with big business as the work of artists, researchers and academics is now actively drawn into their discourses.[73]

The educational psychologist, Edward de Bono, for instance, whose work influenced the teaching of creativity in art education in the 1970s, now teaches the same ideas in high level creativity courses to managers and bureaucrats.[74] Business studies in universities throughout the Western world are now running courses in poetry, theatre and painting, and corporations now employ arts managers to liaise with individual artists and artists' groups.[75] Artists, poets and performers are being employed in business organizations to teach body language, role-playing and creating art works as a team project. 'The work environments are transformed as installations: offices are wrapped in bubble wrap; windows are covered in; the theory was that by changing the environment people's creativity would be stimulated'. Art in business has the same function as in progressive pedagogies: it can 'unlock creativity' and encourage innovatory thought. It is thought to turn 'boring' office workers from conformist, security-seeking, linear-thinking individualists into people who will take chances, work in teams, accept ambiguity and change and initiate new ideas.[76]

As the discourses of progressive art pedagogy are shaping business and management, business and management theory are shaping art education.[77] Art education is losing its relative autonomy as an educational force and is becoming part of the economic and bureaucratic system of global corporate culture. It becomes more difficult for the individual teacher to provide alternatives or other knowledges which would make any critical difference or any alternatives imagined.

There is no essential reason why art education should not be related to external and economically powerful organizations. Artists Richard Layzell, the ethical arts organization 'Platform' and Edwina Fitzpatrick, for instance, all work within multinational corporations, but are informed about the full implications of their work. They act strategically, on their own well-informed terms and with a critical agenda.[78]

There are many kinds of 'business' as there are many kinds of art and art criticism. There are cooperatively run businesses, charitable businesses and businesses that try to be ethical and genuinely socially concerned. Perhaps art education could be more informed in selecting which businesses and which models of personnel management as well as which models of art would most appropriately promote its own educational aims.[79]

Global corporations

Global corporations are by definition international and cross traditional boundaries of time, geography and cultural difference; their organization and lines and networks of communications are instant and invisible. Their structures no longer have a physical 'centre' and it is not easy to understand how the people who head corporations do their work. Corporations reach around the world as monolithic entities, yet they are also fragmented and enter, through consumer activities, our most private and intimate concerns. Educational research in Australia has shown how the success of corporate culture's organization has been influencing educational structure and management. It has been argued that corporate management is essentially a framework which has as its major concern greater discipline and control: 'through limiting goals, focusing on what are perceived as key programmes, and reducing waste through tying work to the achievement of narrowly prescribed outputs', to achieve 'increased central control and greater homogeneity'. The essential strategy in the public domain is to obtain more from public sector workers at less cost.[80] Decentralizing and fragmentation are achieved within a framework of control.

Corporate culture has a stronger hold in business institutions in the United States than it has in Britain, but nonetheless it is having a particularly powerful impact on secondary school art education in Britain and Australia as well as North America. Its influence as a new systems approach and as management strategy for dealing with the teaching of centralized national curricula to large numbers of children is creeping into all levels of art educational discourse. Its influence and rhetorics, its values and meanings of logical operation, of measurement, surveillance and evaluation, can be seen in the very heart of art education from the early years to further and higher levels in universities.

Corporate culturism

The abiding concern of large multinational corporations is to win over the 'hearts and minds' of employees and consumers into the values and meanings of the corporation. The aim of corporate culture in work is to make working life appear enjoyable and emotionally satisfying; to bring the desires, aspirations and identities of individuals in line with those of the aims of the institution.[81] In this way, the employee benefits from better and more meaningful working conditions and the corporation has more efficient workers. Corporate culture is recognized in a complex of managerial practices that identify, recognise and exploit employees feelings, fantasies, aspirations and emotions, and harness them to its profit-making ends. Corporate culture maintains that

> the ability to grasp and use people's aspirations, irrationality and self-motivation is the secret of management success. Flexibility, adaptability, experimentation and informality are the buzzwords, backed up by a pop-psychological imagery of people as self-realising and self-fulfilling. New techniques of capital accumulation are thus accompanied by new techniques for inculcating self-monitoring and self-managing capacities.[82]

Employees are selected carefully and their motivations and personal aspirations, their irrational desires, their drives, motivations and needs discovered. Psychological profiles are produced through interview aptitude tests, through questionnaires, corporate retreats, individual performance reviews, informal managerial monitoring and surveillance.

Employee loyalty, group identification and solidarity are formed through techniques of informal pleasure and relaxation, enabling employees to enjoy their work. One established method that has been adopted in educational management strategy is to remove selected managers from the workplace to a luxurious environment for an exclusive seminar, workshop or conference, where corporate norms can be passed on and loyalties formed, reciprocal bonds established and affectionate ties stimulated. Managers then go back to their place of employment, recharged and re-enthused to spread the corporate word, and inspire their subordinates. Corporate culturism has a missionary-like zeal. As its critics have argued, it relies on belief rather than on any real knowledge or understanding about how the corporation works. The financial dealings or decision-making procedures are usually invisible to the employee.

Corporate culturism and the arts

In the 1960s and 1970s corporate culture promoted its aims by training for leadership, aggression, competition, toughness and individualism through the encouragement of manly sports, rugged adventure trials and oppositional team games. Leaders in management were expected to be tough, hard, competitive and authoritative. Employers today are increasingly aware that coercive, bullying and intimidating styles of management do not achieve overall cooperation and willingness to work. New transformative business styles of feminine management, adopted from therapeutic psychologies and small group interactions, have been more successful in fostering cooperation, teamwork, flexibility and creativity in the workplace. Instead of competitive games, arts activities are now deployed in corporate retreats: dance, theatre, music and crafts encourage innovatory thinking, collaboration, teamwork, emotional bonding and a fusion of individual creative energy with the aims aspirations of the corporation. Art is now being drawn into the institutional practices of corporate culture.

Corporate culturism in North American art education

Discipline Based Art Education has been structured within a corporate culture model. The management strategy of corporate culture is to appear to give more autonomy, diversity and freedom but hiding strong central control.[83] The actual structures are not visible or made explicit. There is in

DBAE and in British national curricula no possibility for teachers to question, criticize or challenge the larger system within which they are expected to work. Like corporate culture, procedures are structured in art education within a monolithic systems model of behavioural objectives and no reference or theoretical argument is supplied to give access to any founding theoretical or aesthetic rationales. Like corporate culture, DBAE works through the promotion of a powerful corporate identity, a strong image, a simple message and a messianic zeal promoted in a well-funded public relations organization.[84] Its teachers are invited to summer institute programmes, seminars and conferences where they are motivated, led and inspired with appropriate instructional methods of approaching DBAE, which they then take away to diffuse among their colleagues in schools throughout North America. Individual mentors and 'evaluators' are established ensuring continuity and reliable transmission of values. Exemplars and models of best practice are listed and illustrated in textbooks which are distributed with glossy advertising literature to ensure correct orthodoxies. The teacher is reduced to a technician, a service worker who 'delivers' the curriculum, and manages choice and diversity within its established parameters, of behavioural objectives and examinations.

DBAE in the United States appoints district coordinators and evaluators with authority to initiate, facilitate and monitor the pedagogic process. 'The higher up the coordinator is in the district hierarchy, the more assurance that the rest of the factors will be put in place.' In Britain, the Office for Standards in Education (Ofsted) and the establishing of national curricula both play a similar part in normalizing monolithic standards and transmission of shared values through peer pressure, and regulating practices of assessment, so complicated that they inhibit change and deflect criticism.

DBAE's activity, on the other hand, is not visibly aggressive and authoritarian. It is represented as gentle and natural, an evolutionary process, democratically involving women and minority groups. Its internal structures are loose and allow for choice, flexibility and diversity. Its image is 'quiet', yet all embracing:

> A quiet evolution is taking place in thousands of elementary and secondary classrooms throughout the nation . . . The overarching outcome of the Getty Education Institute's ambitious regional consortium . . . principals are using the DBAE initiative to re-organise entire elementary school curricula.[85]

The global corporate values of diversity-in-unity of corporations like Coca-Cola and Benetton, as Giroux has described, are entering into education.[86] Their rhetoric is of diversity and cultural difference, but ultimately they seek to unify, to bring all differences happily into a larger, paternal, authoritarian corporate fold, 'empowered' as 'shareholders and partners' with a common mission.[87]

There is no absolute reason why art education should not borrow from other successful practices such as business management and successful organizations in order to structure its own systems. The problems of teaching a shared and assessable art education to large numbers of children, however, has to be planned and organized but it does not necessarily have to be based on large corporations.

The problem of the 'too creative' individual

Creative and innovatory thinking, combined with research and informed analysis and criticism, are the most important tools in education for understanding and challenging existing systems and providing a basis for putting into place an art education that has educational rather than economic aims.

Creativity is the new buzzword in business and management, but what is meant by 'creative' in business is not necessarily the same as for art; however, many of the assumptions about creativity in business are finding their way into school management.

In corporate business, employees are encouraged to be creative, flexible, and innovatory, but it is recognized that creativity, criticism, free thinking and knowledge must have limits. People who think too much, are too creative and who question and disagree, or have different ideas from the institution they serve, become a personnel and management problem. In business, creativity has to be 'fostered and harnessed'. As one management consultant expressed it: 'the question is, with tight budgets and lithe competition, how do we balance creative exploration with the constant need to deliver bottom line results?'[88]

Creative people, management theory suggests, are essential to any business, but 'they are not like the rest of us', they have to be treated with 'fingertip sensitivity' and a 'sure instinct'. The question for employers is how to produce managers and employees who are creative, responsive and flexible and who have good ideas, but are not so creative that they undermine, criticize or destabilize the company they work for.

DBAE and centralized national curricula management follow this business model of 'limited creativity' for art education's management. In DBAE 'the lone ranger', the person who disagrees or questions, has become an explicit object of concern. Management training and intensive group activities for art teachers function to keep awkward and critical attitudes and 'other' inconvenient knowledges at bay, as Swift found in his training course in a similar process in English art education:

I experienced two days of management training . . . which offered means of manipulation to prevent personal conflict arising. It offered techniques in receiving or giving criticism by deflecting, diverting or otherwise refocusing the situation to avoid conflict.

Swift cites too the example of debates on a national curriculum agenda where objections were disallowed as 'negative': 'In fact anyone suspected of holding such views were screened out of any Working Group member-ship'.[89]

Those managers or teachers who do not fit in to DBAE's overriding aims are counselled as having a 'personality' problem. Those – and this includes critical feminists and critical pedagogues – who question the creed of DBAE or national curricula do not need to be punished or argued with, but can effectively be silenced by remaining unrepresented, not mentioned, their knowledges 'disallowed' or overlooked. Silent disapproval, exclusion and peer ostracism operate more effectively than threats and punishment in management techniques. In effect, as Willmott has argued, corporate culture programmes are designed to deny or frustrate the development of conditions in which critical reflection and knowledges can be fostered. 'They commend the homogenisation of norms and values within organisations'.[90] Group work encourages peer group pressure, lowering of standards and conformity as well as cooperation.

The same problem of the 'too creative' art teacher is evident in art edu-cation. Art teachers are required to be creative people and teach creativity, but they must also deliver national curricula and DBAE directives. Like managers:

> The overriding goal is to select those who are prepared to undertake their tasks in a compliant, dutiful, and reliable manner. The required behaviour of middle managers is to perform 'satisfactorily' rather than 'outstanding' . . . Staff recruitment therefore focuses upon those who can demonstrate an ability to learn the rules, who are prepared to be compliant within roles of superordination and subordination, and who are able to work with others within a functionally independent division of labour. They are not expected to be 'creative' or 'entrepreneurial' . . . since those qualities can lead to an undermining of the bureaucratic culture upon which modern administrative techniques are established . . . Hence they are inclined to select middle-class white males (and increasingly females) who are perceived to be capable of ultimately fill-ing 'middle' management positions.[91]

Teacher training often produces art teachers with

> specific cognitive management styles; with certain personalities and characters which enabled them to act as managers and as human beings without contradiction. The cognitive style required emphasises depen-dency, conformity, co-operation, and 'satisfactory' job performance.[92]

Built into the British national curricula and Discipline Based Art Education are structural safeguards against 'too much creativity', too much initiative and too much critical thinking, which are typical of corporate management.

First, effective creativity can be limited by devaluing and demoting the morale, self-image and social status of the art teacher. By changing them from a potentially critical, autonomous, creative, meaning-making and intellectual force, which their higher education as art students putatively encouraged, into conforming 'managers' through an intensive period of teacher training where they undergo an ideological initiation. They learn to shift their identity from self-centred, entrepreneurial artists to become maternal teachers, who give all their emotional energies to 'the job' and who put the immediate interests of the children first.

Teacher creativity is further hampered by the rigid structures and frameworks within which they are forced to operate. They have to learn a whole new language of behavioural objectives of 'tangible projects', 'definable goals', 'careful planning' and 'early prototyping and testing'. Structures of staff monitoring, moderation and the careful assessment of attainment targets are explicitly set in place in business practice, 'to keep the fun and freedom from degenerating into non-productive anarchy'.[93] They are the same processes by which the creativity of the art teacher can be 'harnessed' and controlled. The constant stopping to evaluate, to monitor and defer to a system of values established outside the classroom, on theoretical models that are not open to investigation, inevitably limit creative alternatives. Furthermore, the limiting of in-service training and the reducing art teacher education to studies of curriculum implementation, classroom practice and the control of children's behaviour means that the teacher has little time to keep in touch with their own art practice or contemporary ideas. Demoted to a manager:

> The teacher determines neither the ends nor the means ... from the behavioural point of view it is not necessary for teachers to know anything about the theoretical traditions from which their prescribed practices are derived.[94]

Creativity can also be limited by shifting the definitions of good artistic practice away from rigorous 'planning' modes, and colluding in ideologies that represent critical and radical art practices as 'boring' and old fashioned. Ideologies that relegate critical feminist art and radical modernist practices to a past era that is now 'over', and which promote a notion of creativity within discourses of fun, play, and as a 'personal' attribute, inevitably disallow investigation into any critical and challenging knowledges.

I suggest too, although only from anecdotal evidence, that the 'artists in schools' programme could be unwittingly demoting the status of the teacher. Bringing in 'real' artists and 'real' historians and critics to work alongside the teacher produces in the child's mind, and perhaps the teacher's too, the comparison that the teacher is not herself a 'real' artist, critic or contributor to knowledges about art but is merely a manager *of* artists and art knowledges.

Corporate culture as patriarchal power

Corporate culture operates as a hidden and masculine force. Its structures transmit meanings about order, sequence, logical and rationalized, systemizing procedures. Its inherent values are concerned with maximization of profits, social control and the naturalizing of the powers of invisible authority.

School 'subjects' of art may be inclusive of difference but antiracist and feminist initiatives are subsumed under the larger systems of corporate structures. Initiatives from antiracism and feminism can be drawn into the corporate fold. Capitalist consumer culture, service work and the creative industries need a diverse workforce; they require the 'blurring of gender boundaries' and more feminine styles of identification.

> A diverse workforce has clear competitive advantages . . . since women and people of color can offer insights and ideas that would not be tapped in the 'old boy' network . . . a culturally diverse workforce can help to secure an increasingly diverse market for corporate products and services. Not only do women know better than men what women 'need', for example, but they know best how to play on their insecurities to sell it to them.[95]

There is no conflict between multiculturalism, gender de-differentiation and corporate culture; on the contrary, postmodern art education helps to promote diversity, pluralism and difference. Capitalism does not care who does the work, and corporate culture is dedicated to making work pleasant and seemingly the only and natural way that work can be organized. What corporate culture and a consumer economy do *not* need and what they effectively suppress are people who are critically aware, and who can creatively imagine and construct alternatives. To put it in patriarchal metaphorical terms, it does not matter if the children squabble among themselves about introducing this or that new subject into the art curriculum, or how they teach, providing the overall and hidden structures of paternal power remain untouched and their aims and targets maintained.

Signs of resistance

There have, of course, always been those who creatively and critically resist dominant versions of art education that have been offered by centralized programmes of instruction. Practically every teacher I have encountered in the course of writing this book has some private strategy for 'negotiating' or subverting national curricula, and bringing to bear their own expert and experienced knowledges and their own assessment of the needs of the children they teach and meanings about art. Attempts to manipulate and reduce teacher autonomy, power and creativity of teachers and educators have not been complete. Behavioural and therapeutic models of psychology, liberal and progressive educational ideals of freedom and even the values of corporate culture are double edged, and can be deployed to serve other interests including those of marginalized and silenced groups.

Centralized efforts to control, and the often ineffective application of corporate culture into the older collegiate systems of education produces contrary and unwanted effects. They produce in certain individuals ridicule, disbelief, mockery, cynicism and scepticism. Business research has uncovered the existence of creative and subversive strategies by employees who appear to conform, but who go their own way. They operate on the basis of what has been called 'calculative compliance',[96] or 'creative refusal', or what Berger and Luckmann have called 'cool alienation'.[97] They resist manipulation and incorporation by adopting different strategies: 'dropping out' (taking early retirement, creating an 'alternative' lifestyle, 'downsizing'), 'refusing to play the game'. Child-like strategies include sulking and avoiding power and responsibility, indulging in mischievous behaviour. They engage in sabotage. Juliet Mitchell observed such guerrilla tactics in the behaviour of girls and women through feminine passive/aggressive behaviours of giggling and gossiping.[98] By 'sitting at the back', being quiet, acting dumb and silly, employees avoid the responsibility and complete identification with oppressive forces over which they have no control. Instead of always producing committed, enthusiastic and cooperative subjects who go along with nationally organized curricula, there is the production of some identities of teachers (and children and parents) who comply with the explicit demands of the institution and curriculum, without internalizing their values. Through the discourses of nationally organized curricula, subjects are constructed who are divided between outward performance and internal belief, who have an ironic and detached, yet also a committed and creative identity of a modern teacher. The notion of 'masquerade' and performance comes in here, as well as the feminine concept of 'faking it'.

But these strategies are often individual and idiosyncratic, and often go unsupported and unrecognized. The difficulty of reconciling inward belief with outward performance has been recognized by business psychologists as a site of employee stress and inefficiency. It may destabilize the necessary unitary narratives of the self that are important for personal well-being.

6 Beyond gendering: tactics and strategies

In this book, with the help of empirical evidences, insights and interpretations, I have created a narrative of art education which pictures it as developing towards increased feminized identification. Women's art, pluralism and diversity of subject matter, 'other' perspectives and multicultural initiatives are now part of a postmodern curriculum. Feminist methodologies and a cultural re-evaluation of 'the feminine' have meant that rhetorics of cooperation and care rather than individualism and competition, fluidity and flexibility rather than rigid subject boundaries, and bricolage or gathering and eclectic modes of creativity are appearing more often instead of linear, scientific, 'planning' modes. The methods of the delivery of art education have changed: power relations between the teacher and the taught have become 'flatter'. Children are empowered and they 'work together' with teachers to achieve common aims. Children are putatively becoming 'active agents' in their own education.

At the same time in this picture, there lurks in the shadows an invisible and inaccessible power of patriarchal authority to which this happy relationship of maternal art teachers and their creative children are subject. This power is exerted in the workings of the state and the continuing influences of industry, and corporate power and their twin interests in consumption. It is active in the organization of the curricula, in the way that art is packaged and delivered. It is enacted in the everyday processes of regulating children, organizing materials and plans for the lesson, in systems of evaluation and assessment, the meeting of attainment targets, and the marking of examinations.

Teachers and children are both subject to the invisible Laws of the Father. They carry out and their identities are constructed within larger systems over which they themselves have no authority or knowledge. These systems are based in psychological concepts that have been buried over time and are virtually inaccessible. The uncritical, romantic modernist 'artist' (who believes that research and criticism are not their affair) and the disempowered maternal teacher are cut off from critical inquiry and useful knowledges and from the dominant meaning-making structures of power.

Oedipal narratives in the art world

The institutions within which art education is shaped are steeped through with patriarchal metaphors of power and natural-seeming authority. Oedipal male inheritance provides a 'logical' process for the reproduction and transmission of knowledge and culture and a way of explaining gradual change. Historicist accounts of art, for instance, suggest that change is brought about by struggles for power between the established Old Masters – the Fathers – who are threatened by the radical arts of the 'young Turks', their 'murdering sons'. The history of the establishment of modernist art and avant gardism has been told in this way: as a series of temporary established orders, punctuated by challenges to the status quo by new, young, male upstarts who in turn become the established order, in part of what Mulvey has called 'the short term radicalism of youth'.[1]

The naughty antics of a Damien Hirst – who, as a typical Oedipal son, cut in half a cow, the universal symbol of the mother – will soon become the new orthodoxy, displacing in turn the struggles to establish modernist abstraction, with which its revolutionary fathers usurped *their* artistic fathers. Looking at the discourses of art education, at the individuals who head its institutions, who edit and control the knowledges about art education, it can be seen that most are men who have inherited their positions and their ideas from other men. They have tended to look inwards and build on ideas that have gone before, rather than looking outwards at what is going on in the contemporary aesthetic and cultural field. There are many women in art education, but few reach the highest positions of authority.[2] Women are admitted on special 'women's issues' of journals and in specific women's conferences, but by and large the concerns of their maternal antecedents in feminist critical theory have not been integrated into the mainstream concerns of art education.

What has to be remembered in such family narratives is that the sons inherit to become conservative and conforming fathers – repudiating their mothers and their maternal inheritance – in their turn. Artists who are implicated in Oedipal avant gardism are not known for questioning the power and social relations of art itself: they may work outside the gallery system, but they keep one eye always on it and their place in history. They do not fundamentally challenge the gallery system, the modes of viewing, production and consumption of art or the way that art and audiences relate. They have a very material stake in inheriting the authority of the dominant culture and cannot be expected to challenge the systems of art so thoroughly that they undermine the inheritance they hope one day to gain. The Oedipal artist, as Kuspit says, may be boyish, 'naughty' or rebellious, but he is less likely to put himself beyond the reach of the prizes and rewards that the legitimate art world bestows.[3]

Women's inheritance

The effect of the ideology of constant newness, male inheritance and omission from the main plot has been to cut women off from earlier knowledges and experiences gained by their 'maternal' antecedents in feminism. The patriarchal cultural rejection of the values of old people, and in particular the older woman, has meant that communication between present day girls and older feminist knowledges has been constantly undermined. In modernist education, girls had never been taught that early twentieth century women had had their own newspapers, clubs and restaurants and had been active in political, artistic and knowledge-making activity throughout the modern era. The discourse of feminism and the achievements of women were hidden, and only the knowledges that had no power to disturb the status quo were reproduced. The same process of omission, silence and repression continues today.

The modernist discourse of newness and ever changing fashion, and the belief in the notion of a 'generation gap', cut girls off from building on their inheritance. Feminism and its work is considered old fashioned in a version of 'newness' that is essentially modernist, which 'demands experiment but nevertheless compels repetition'.[4] Present day students are repeating the same work and the same mistakes, unaware of historical precedent. The terms 'old fashioned', 'out of date' and 'passé' are used ideologically in that they prevent examination of the experiences and knowledges of the recent past. To have one's art work designated 'old fashioned' has a particular resonance for girls, and is a devastating critique for young female students. Recent history – last year's or the last decade's ideas in particular – have to be left behind. In the postmodern critical frame it is not the new that is truly disturbing, unattractive and bad taste – we are accustomed now to newness. What really disturbs is the Shock of the Old-fashioned.

Feminist art strategies

Women artists and academics have positioned themselves as the non-inheriting daughters, having nothing to gain from an establishment that passes the torch of Great Art and Big Ideas on from father to son. Kristeva has suggested that some women have succeeded in exploiting their unsymbolized, non-inheriting position, cast as 'outside' culture and paternal logic: 'isn't a woman also the most radical atheist, the most committed anarchist, when she is carried away by what the symbolic order rejects?'[5] From a position of having nothing to inherit, nothing therefore to lose, feminists have seen themselves in a symbolic position to disrupt, disturb, subvert and sabotage, needle and embarrass established fine art categories and hierarchies of value and meaning. The environmental and strategic art practices of women at Greenham Common, for instance, were ignored by mainstream art, but represented new modes of artistic intervention. In the 1970s and 1980s, many women ignored the 'gallery scene'; they made work for each other and for female audiences.[6] They turned their backs on the paternal 'master narratives' of art and theory. They had been left out of the discourses of the brotherhood of left wing political activity and developed a concept of 'sisterhood' to validate their practice and from which to subvert the dominant aesthetic and visual regime. The illegitimate, as Donna Haraway said, are 'often exceedingly unfaithful to their origins. Their fathers are, after all inessential'.[7]

Yet this 'girl power' has its limitations. Women can gain access to existing power structures this way, but not alter the terms on which they have been constructed, nor can they alter the critical conventions and financial value transactions within which their art and themselves as artists are given value and meaning. The power of artists such as Tracey Emin, who shocked the art world with her explicitly personal and sexual work, was constrained in its potential meanings by the surrounding discursive field criticism, media interests and consumer values. Her work has been recognized as equivocal in its power to disrupt existing consumer values and gender relations.[8] To be always on the outside, fighting to get in to a hierarchy that men have designed for themselves and accepting of a position as 'naughty girl' is to accept a proper place in the patriarchal plot. Rebellious daughters have the chance to disrupt and subvert, to needle and annoy, to amuse and provoke, but not to actively construct dominant meanings about art and education, and assume authority and a central place in history as of right.

The limitations of performances

Feminist activists and artists have often had little choice but to act tactically and strategically. In the modernist scheme of things and in patriarchy, they have the options of being 'an embarrassing nuisance', trying to become 'one of the (inheriting) boys' or remaining in a sulk and going mad.[9] In the Oedipal story, it is only when a woman is very old – like the radical modernist artist Louise Bourgeois – that she is given a voice, as 'crone' or 'wise woman' to be interpreted by men.

In this book I have reproduced the image of modernity that has shown it as consisting of a dominant discourse of paternal power and masculine reason as constantly being undermined by a feminine, subversive underside.

A picture of life after modernization and modernity could be constructed that could make patriarchal metaphors of masculine and feminine binary differences and generational power redundant.

Alternatives to nature

The biological family and the Oedipal metaphor have provided a natural and powerful structuring pattern for modernity's social organization within which we are psychically formed. Patriarchal language may (or may not) be our inheritance, but that does not mean that all our everyday interactions and social institutions have to be imagined as structured in the same way. As Fredric Jameson has suggested, people need metaphors and stories to explain things, to cognitively organize information by which to live. We need metaphors and narratives. But metaphors have a limited life and the Oedipal narrative has been around in one form or another for a long time.[10] Other images and experiences could provide the metaphors for structuring thought and identity. Haraway has rejected the natural family as metaphor and suggests that human beings are essentially technological. She ironically proposes that we could adopt the metaphor of the cyborg: half machine, half human organism for postmodern imaginary structures and relationships. There is no space to discuss these radical alternatives here, but what it implies is that evolutionary, biological narratives and other natural phenomena, whilst they have a place in nature, are not always appropriate for imagining human social relationships, cognitive change or art-making which are social symbolic, rather than natural activities.[11] Other metaphors can take their place.

Instead of modelling social and work relationships on the relations between fathers, mothers and sons, we could instead, at a pragmatic level, drop familial, gendered and generational references altogether. In art education we could instead begin by making critical evaluations of the human, ethical rights and responsibilities of people with different jobs, at different ages, and with needs and possibilities. In education it is necessary to seek to determine and define the nature of the professional relationship between teachers and the taught in relation to wider social power and economic concerns. (A revisiting of the radical education's discourses of children's rights could be a starting point here.) The workplace is different from a home and its relationships and power structures may be similar but are specific to education. The differences need to be understood and made explicit. Teachers, managers, curators and bosses are not parents. Clients, customers, workers, schoolchildren and artists are not sons and daughters. Although many of the aspects of care, responsibility, authority and status are the same for teachers as they are for parents, their roles are specific and in other respects they are different. We do not, for instance, love our students as we love our children; we should not be expected to tolerate behaviour in school that we would tolerate in the home. We do not expect to involve ourselves as teachers in children's private and intimate lives.

As postmodern psychology suggests, we do need metaphors, narratives, images and identifications on which to build imaginary social structures and behaviours, but we need to question whether modelling social life, institutional practices and work relationships on nature and the patriarchal family is the best we can do.

We need, too, a different metaphor for thinking about the relationship of art to human life. I suggest that the concerns and interests of the feminine, of art and those of real women and girls could be better served by a return to the discourses of philosophic aesthetics for art education.

A return to aesthetics

One of the ways that Enlightened thinking achieved to 'resolve' the binary paradox of the fear of subversive feminine breaking through the rational authority of masculine civilization, was through the concept of 'the aesthetic'. Aesthetics emerged as an Enlightenment discourse not in opposition to science's inquiring and critical spirit, but as an attempt to make rational sense of all those human areas of existence that are beyond the realm of the empirical gaze, measurement and categorization:

> It is as though philosophy suddenly wakes up to the fact that there is a dense, swarming territory beyond its own mental enclave which threatens to fall utterly outside its sway. That territory is nothing less than the whole of our sensate life together – the business of affections and aversions, of how the world strikes the body on its sensory surfaces, of that which takes root in the gaze or the guts and all that arises from our most banal, biological insertion into the world. The aesthetic concerns this most gross and palpable dimension of the human, which post-Cartesian philosophy, in some curious lapse of attention, has somehow managed to overlook.[12]

It is the 'underside' of modernity, the countermodern discourses, the private and the bodily realm, that exist in the realm of the aesthetic. Notions of the aesthetic-as-feminine find their echo in contemporary French feminist psychoanalytic theories and in Kristeva's idea of the feminine 'abject', where the unimaginable, timeless, realm of the unconscious rules and where the rules of language and logic remain unsymbolized.[13]

Used in this broader and original sense, aesthetics is not just concerned with conventions of art and art history, connoisseurship and acquiring knowledges about art – which is the way that DBAE and critical studies have employed it. Aesthetics represents an approach to knowledge and a way of organizing ideas that must always be unfinished, always on the move in that it attempts to account for the private, invisible, unconscious and 'messy' areas of human life.

The German feminist philosopher, Hilde Hein, suggested aesthetics as a possible model for feminist practice, 'Because it embraces a domain that is invincibly pluralistic and dynamic', and because it has to cope with those private, hidden illogical, irrational areas of life that have been assigned to the feminine.[14] Aesthetics, Hein argues, is the one philosophic discourse which, although it is bound by an ideal of rational theorizing, has to be always open ended, responsive and has to preserve and even privilege as essentially human, the diverse, the non-rational and the disorderly. It has to explain somehow logically the importance of contradiction, accept paradox, diversity and plurality. Aesthetics represents 'the first stirrings in post Cartesian philosophy of lived experience; primitive materialism . . . of the body's long inarticulate rebellion against the tyranny of the theoretical'.[15]

Aesthetic discourse and art education

It is this notion of 'the aesthetic' that could serve as a model paradigm for thinking of art education. At present, art education is built on scientific and systems models drawn from economic concerns and management systems of corporate culture.

It is not possible to describe here what an art educational system based on aesthetics would look like. Perhaps the imaginative model of philosophical aesthetics, a masculine discourse of reason and science that always has to listen, be receptive and privilege the always elusive feminine 'aesthetic' realm, would be more appropriate to arts educational aims and more inclusive of the creative and interventionist values which represent the interests of real women. This would mean listening to and privileging and giving a central place to feminist discourse. It is feminist discourse that has had at the centre of its theorizing and interested concerns the feminine aesthetic and it has constructed different methodologies and models for investigating and traversing the difficulties, paradoxes and contradictions of the aesthetic realm.

Tactics and strategies

One of the strengths of feminism has been the diversity of its approaches. Like art education, it contains contradictions and constantly changing positions, many different influences and discursive modes, yet all committed to a progressive emancipatory aim. In feminism there have been no leaders, no corporate bodies, no 'system' or structure, no 'rules' dominating centralized power structures, no single overarching theories. Yet there is a recognition that there is a powerful movement, a complex discourse called 'feminism' that works for women and which has made fundamental changes to women's lives.

Critical feminism as a strategy for education is appropriate and does not imply a unified force based on a biological notion of a unified notion of 'woman' as a distinct category. Instead it bases its action in common ideals and aims – however imaginary – with people working together, as Haraway suggests, 'not on the basis of natural identification, but only on the basis of conscious coalition, of affinity, of political kinship'.[16]

Feminism – and art education – need not aim to unify all experience into 'fundamental' accounts which apply at all times, nor need it be held together by fantasies of a lineage of great male or female geniuses. It can reappropriate, rework and repair older ideas in relation to the new. It can continue to work in the modernist tradition of masculine research and criticism, in being responsive to what already exists, recognizing and reorganizing existing material, subverting the original meanings of things to our own ends but doing criticism and research within an agreed value system of ethics and responsibility.

Criticism and research

One of the things that feminist historical scholarship has made clear is that women's rights for education, the vote and equal pay did not come about as a result of natural evolutionary change or the goodwill of men. The achievements that have promoted the interests of women, such as education, the vote, equal rights in law, medical and welfare improvements, may have been the unlooked-for results of Enlightenment thinking by men, but they have been redeployed by women in strategies of planned effort, struggle, through difficulty and suffering, and those efforts are by no means over. Feminist art education needs to continue this difficult and unglamorous work and take a wider perspective to address itself continually to deconstructing power relations between real people in art institutions, even in the 'old-fashioned', empirical traditions of quantifiable research. In order to plan change there needs to be information about the work that women and men do in the art world. More information is needed in making explicit such things as male female ratios of staffing, about which sex edits journals and heads art education institutions. Information about relative pay and conditions of men and women in the art world, and the career structures and range of authority of male and female lecturers and teachers. Not only at an art professional level, but also the invisible work of working class women needs to be taken into account in structuring the art world. As Cynthia Cockburn has put it:

> the agenda for change needs to be broadened from its current focus on removing barriers . . . to an admittedly more diffuse project of identifying the means whereby men's power is reproduced. This would include

among other things, understanding how gender may be implicated in changes in status between discipline areas, the split between private domestic and public career responsibilities and the role of secretaries, cleaners and cooks, librarians in the maintenance of education.[17]

It is easy to get the impression that because the female body is more visible, that real women are doing well, but we need to have more statistical information about the relative responsibilities of teachers and art educationalists and about who gets to make the important decisions. We need to make the workings of the gendered practices of curating, criticism, connoisseurship and the art market clear so that female students have a realistic picture of the difficulties they are likely to come across and who themselves need information as to how to proceed tactically and strategically.

Research means finding out things, seeking out knowledges that have been hidden, are difficult to find or inaccessible, and then dismantling the rationales that have been erected to hide them. Critical feminist knowledges are less likely to be found in popular magazines on the racks of supermarkets, yet it appears that these are where most people obtain their ideas about feminism. It is harder work looking for suppressed knowledges, but after all, it is the things that are suppressed that in psychoanalytic terms are the most disturbing, yet necessary to reveal for psychic health. Why do I find, for instance, that so many critical feminist art books are out of print? Why can I find so few slides of women's art in slide collections? Why don't the auction houses produce glossy monographs on critical modernist or feminist work? Why is the work of the same male art educators – Herbert Read, Rudolph Arnheim, Eliot Eisner – cited in journals over and over again? Why are the same books and photographs and postcards of French Impressionist art reprinted and circulated? The reasons are not part of a conspiracy to subordinate women, and marginal and inaccessible material is not necessarily better than mainstream art, but the question has to be asked how and why is it that some ideas, images and practices become marginalized? Whose interests are served? Who do they threaten? Each omission on its own means little and can be pragmatically explained, but taken together, the invisibility of women's history begins to appear to operate as apart of a system of gendering, of a continuation of a modernist practice of suppression that benefits a certain minority of powerful older male interests.

Tactics

A tactic is a calculated action determined by the absence of a proper locus . . . it does not have the options of planning general strategy and viewing the adversary as a whole within distinct, visible and objectifiable space. It operates in isolated actions blow by blow. It takes advantage of 'opportunities' and depends on them . . . it must vigilantly make use of the cracks that particular conjunctions open in the surveillance of the proprietary powers. It poaches on them. It creates surprises in them. It can be where it is least expected. It is a guileful ruse.[18]

A tactical approach is a 'grassroots' approach, one that puts 'theory' into a supportive place. This description of tactics envisages a sort of oppositional guerrilla activity against ruling ideas, but it is an approach that can be employed by anyone at any level of power and authority. It does not have to be overt, violent or visibly disruptive, but it can often be a slight shift, an altering of conventional meanings. There are many ways of acting tactically that keep within the regulations yet disturb expected conventions. Operating tactically is sometimes the only option available to those who are oppressed or whose lives are limited and constrained by forces over which they have no control. The art work of the *Guerrilla Girls* who use existing systems and visual conventions of advertising is tactical. Artists who exhibit their work in supermarkets, in leisure centres, fitness centres and crèches are tactically using existing spaces to reach different audiences. In a recent exhibition in Birmingham, an installation showed how some South African mothers and elderly women bared their breasts and flaunted their old, fat and naked bodies, successfully embarrassing and dis-arming English white colonial male authorities.[19] And Chilean women made small domestic patchworks, telling their stories through the sale of their craftwork to Europe. Women dying of AIDS in Uganda are writing the story books of their lives to pass on to their children so they do not disappear from history. The tactics of many Third World feminists

> depend upon an ability to read the current situation of power and of self-consciously choosing and adopting the ideological form best suited to push against its configurations, a survival skill well-known to oppressed peoples.[20]

Tactics can be employed by the busy classroom teacher on a day-to-day basis, indeed tactics are already widely used by the consumers of national curricula and behavioural objectives of DBAE, who are obliged to follow the letter of curriculum policy, but who freely resist, alter or subvert their implicit aims. Tactics have been used and are used by schoolchildren to gain some control over their own lives, from dumb insolence, to refusal, to simple non-attendance and non-participation, or they can be used by single parents acting in groups or by just being visible and asserting their rights, being 'a problem'. There are few points of powerlessness where some tactical advantage cannot be imagined and practised. The feminist movement offers precedents and it has been tactical in that it has 'poached on' and subverted, played with existing meanings and worked from the 'cracks', the margins and the spaces that the dominant male culture has made available for women.

Acting tactically means deploying what is already available and changing its meanings for other ends. Any discourse can be utilized tactically: feminist theory, academic research, romantic fiction, left wing texts, children's art, astrology, new technologies, modernism, postmodernism, 'the Design system', drawing, DIY, and so on. Every discourse is a consumer resource, which can deployed either critically or conservatively.

This tactical use of existing resources is not new and postmodern. It is an established practice theorized in the early twentieth century in left political thought:

> One of the tasks of radical critique, as Marx, Brecht and Walter Benjamin understood, is to salvage and redeem for left political use whatever is still viable and valuable in the class legacies to which we are the heirs. 'Use what you can' is a sound enough Brechtian slogan – with of course, the implicit corollary that what turns out to be unusable in such traditions should be jettisoned without nostalgia.[21]

Working tactically also means using what we have available personally. Identities have all been constructed within different social constraints and contexts in terms of skills, money, gender power, energy, education, class and race. There are some situations where being working class, black or a woman can be used to advantage. The 'ideal' school, curriculum package or lesson never exists, we always have to manage and make do, but we can begin to use our personal and social resources and as Dick Hebdige says, we can 'draw on small lessons from unsuspected sources'.[22]

Strategies

A strategy is an exercise of formal and accepted power by an institution, or an individual over other people who are separate and distinct from itself. Adopting and performing political, economic and scientific and educational performances and behaviours of rationality have been strategies for some feminists: sometimes, acting masculine can get results. A strategy often implies working to get power within 'the system'. In feminism it is represented by establishing struggles, arguments, organizing coalitions of interest to bring about equal pay, access to equal opportunities, to representation in galleries and museums, to publishing, criticism, attaining careers which lead to wider economic control and political power within established political parties and business institutions. Strategies require research, planning, shared aims and actions, knowledges about how power, money, the law and authority work.

Change in art education can come about either by tactical moves, by children, parents and teachers or by the subversive actions of art educators, theorists and critics; or it can come about by individuals gaining 'legitimate' access to power, by working towards a responsible and accountable position and to have an active say in the shaping and designing of national curricula, of writing educational policy, or by having power in legislation and economic activity. Using strategies and tactics implies that change is not evolutionary or natural, but neither does it have to be destabilizing. It does not involve the sweeping away of old ideas and replace them with the new, but a careful consideration of the full implications of all strategic acts, particularly within an ethics of care and responsibility for children and their education.

Formalist modernisms

Modernism abstraction and formalism have often been seen as the epitome of all that was rejected by feminist art of the 1970s. But revisiting formalist modernist critical themes of the past can provide starting points for transformative models of practice in postmodern art education. There are, even within Greenbergian formalism, some elements that are useful. The modernist values of encouraging students to be objective, although it has tended to be in favour of a masculine fixed identity, can be strategically important in that it enables children, however temporarily, to imagine themselves through art-making outside of culture, outside of race and gender relations and conventional morality, to 'forget themselves' for a while and visualize how things could be better and different. One of the things about modernist art education was that its masculine objective discourses meant that there were moments when girls could forget they were girls and could imagine themselves as boys – as human beings with full potentials. There is no gender in the imaginary: being forced to watch boys' films, play boys' games, and being identified in masculine terms, girls are already familiar with practices of distanciation, alienation, irony and masquerade. In the family, as mothers, they are always being asked to put their own interests on hold, to see things from a male perspective and imagine other points of view and feelings of their children. Women have been subtly trained in 'empathy' and so-called 'intuition' in anticipating other people's wants. Part of art and art education's purpose is to develop the capacity to negotiate cognitively other ways of being, of imagining different and better ways of living and relating to the world than those offered by the present regimes of power and consumption, and bring them into some kind of creative production. This sometimes means a suspension or interruption of the existing practices and dominant identifications with fixed gender (or racial or class) roles and a 'modernist', objective, autonomous and even elitist position where a relative disassociation of knowledges from power can be attempted.

'Ostranenie'

Russian formalist theories could be revisited here. Russian formalist art included 'the social' into its formal concerns; it was not a purely visual theorizing of formalism as was the Greenbergian version that has been the dominant form of modernist art inherited in art education. Maybe a re-theorizing of a different kind of formalism may yield some insights advantageous to a socially contextualized art education.[23]

The Russian Formalists developed in 1917 the notion of *Ostranenie* (making strange),[24] the idea of deliberately interrupting visual expectations, looking behind appearances, in order to stimulate creative activity in abstract devices such as 'laying bare' and 'defamiliarization': art used in this sense 'is a way of restoring conscious experience, of breaking through deadening and mechanical habits of conduct and allowing us to be reborn to the world in all its freshness and horror'.[25]

These are not necessarily radical devices in themselves: they are often used by advertisers and mainstream film-makers these days, to shock and disrupt habits of consumption. But used critically and within an ethical framework of researched understanding, and a thinking through of their political and gendered implications, the habits of interrupting conventional lines of thought, of questioning and uncovering hidden meanings could be fostered in children by the use of some of these early modern critical formal devices. Grizelda Pollock showed how such strategies influenced feminist art of the 1970s. 'Dis-identificatory practices', she argued,

> displaced the spectator from identifying with the illusory fictional worlds offered in art, literature and film which engages us on behalf of oppressive regimes of class, sexist, heterosexist and racist classifications and placements.[26]

Brecht's plays do not carry the audience through in a seamless continuous narrative, with which they emotionally identify, but constantly interrupt, are uneven, the actors speak to the audience, the audience can see the construction of the stage set and the scene movers.[27] Different media, film, back projections are employed which refuse to blend smoothly and often contradict the spoken text. As soon as the audience settles into following a recognizable narrative of familiar gender or class relationships – 'the king and his subjects', romance and 'happily-ever-after' themes – identification is disrupted, by techniques such as collage, juxtaposition, or by revealing to the audience the way the story and the play has been put materially together. Interruption is introduced as an aid to creative thinking.

Rethinking the pleasurable

Brechtian ideas and devices of *Ostranenie* could also have some value for disturbing the illusory narrative and structures of art education. Strategies of 'alienation effect' could jolt the school children from an unquestioning habitual response and easy pleasurable identification with gendered plots.

In my experience as a teacher of art, the interruption of visual pleasure in this way with students often elicits groans as their absorption in the plot is interrupted. Analysing art, they complain, 'spoils it' and they do not want the 'obvious' questioned. But they quickly see the point of what is going on and they achieve a new kind of pleasure in 'seeing the joins': in mastering the material workings and apparatus of film, in understanding how things like films, paintings and advertising are constructed and how they work on emotions, fears and desires. As Mulvey said in the 1970s, we need to destroy existing pleasures and identifications in order to create new and non-oppressive forms.

Pleasure has political and economic implications, our pleasures are not necessarily natural or harmless but are, as Harvey argues, 'produced through codes of desire in consumption', through 'the production of needs and wants, the mobilization of desire and fantasy, of the politics of distraction'.[28] To find pleasure in something is not alone a necessary justification for doing it (child abuse, smoking and violence are pleasurable for some). This does not mean a rejection of the pleasurable in art itself, or a rejection of humour, sex, play and fun (as postfeminist critics seem determined to maintain) but a constructing of different kinds of pleasures.[29] Women whose wants and needs have been constructed by a masculine male desiring gaze and a modernist scopic regime, have been sceptical of the pleasures on offer and feminist artists are learning to construct and imagine new and totally different kinds of pleasure not bound up in masculine circles of power.

Jacqueline Rose has argued in a similar vein, that it is adults who have decided what children like, what their art consists of and what they ought to find pleasure in.[30] Children's desires and fantasies have been constructed out of the fantasies and economic needs of adults. Children need to be made sceptical of the pleasures and easy identifications with 'childhood' that are on offer. Art education, which deals with images and artefacts, could be one of the ways by which children learn to use alternative and different symbolic materials to imagine alternative ways of being young, to learn to negotiate and resist easy identifications with dominant structures of power, to invent and construct ethical and emancipatory alternative identities.

Repair

Evan Watkins uses the technological metaphor of repair – of making use of the socially designated obsolete, both technologically and ideologically.[31] 'Repair' carries with it ethical concerns about waste, the environment and overproductivity and so on. The concept of 'natural wastage' was coded into the design process. Waste and the continual consumption of materials are some of the consequences and by-products of productive modernist art education; through modernist art education we have familiarized children with waste, continuous consumption and inbuilt obsolescence. Watkins proposes 'repair' as a strategy:

> Oppositional consciousness must instead learn the skills of repair, and where these skills can be most usefully deployed. The repair of the obsolete can be strategically inventive, even if the invention will never count as 'innovative' in the dominant coding of obsolescence/innovation.[32]

Instead of a creative process that aims to make new products, bricolage forms of creativity could be thought of in the context of an ethical practice of repairing or reworking the old, the rejected, the overlooked, the unlovely and the discarded. Critical postmodern artists have been engaging in such ethical forms of non-wasteful practice, like the performances of Dominique Mazeaud in *The Cleansing of the Rio Grande River* project.[33]

This too means re-using ideas: even 'working on the discarded ideologies and conceptual relics of modernity'.[34] This does not mean making things out of garbage just to shock – yet again – but changing the meanings of things: using the familiar, the overlooked, or the common, the readily available in new and different contexts. This is the 'make do and mend' ideology of wartime consumption.

It can also mean rethinking the feminine aesthetic, re-evaluating and giving new meanings to past old-fashioned and traditional practices, or to use Norman Bryson's words 'Looking at the Overlooked', the title he gave to his essays on still life painting.[35] This suggests a very different notion of creativity and creative process.

Refusal

A refusal to take part or to play the games that we have had no hand in constructing has always been an option. Consumer culture has to constantly change its tactics to deal with those consumers who 'switch off', who refuse 'loyalty' incentives, who throw away junk mail, who do not answer questionnaires or provide information about themselves in psychological profiles. 'From the standpoint of the individual, the distancing of self from corporate values may be the preferred means of preserving and asserting self-identity'.[36] A significant number of women are already refusing dominant modes of consumption and are taking to Green, vegetarian or ethical shopping, resisting easy and obvious consumer identifications often going out of their way to make ethical and aesthetic choices. In market terms their individual acts of refusal (interestingly referred to by marketers as 'promiscuous' and 'disloyal', like unfaithful wives) are collectively changing the priorities of supermarkets and politics.[37]

Even knowledge is not necessarily progressive. Knowledge is power, but some knowledges have more power than others. There are certain knowledges that work to uphold oppressive gender, race and class relations. We can avoid these knowledges. Whose interests are served by knowing for instance how to address a bishop, the correct way to lay a table or the exact significance of brand labels on T-shirts or the latest knowledges about cars? Reproducing redundant and exclusive knowledges reproduces the gender relations and class hierarchies which presuppose them.

Finding spaces

It is partly from positions of structural weakness that feminists have found ways to be effective.[38] Teaching, with its emphasis on feminine qualities of care and its socially unglamorous image, has traditionally been one of the areas where women have been allowed to carve out a space for themselves, and the teaching of art has always had its significant female and feminist art educators. The history of modernist practices has many of these spaces in the gaps left by more fashionable men, in the margins, in the unpopular and unfashionable areas of welfare, social work and nursing. But it is from these margins and spaces between the disciplines that fertile ideas come.

The notion that it is only 'big ideas' and rational progression that shape history has been challenged and feminists have brought to the fore at a theoretical level, the hidden aspects of power:

> the small scale actions and receptions taking place at the margins: the pleasures of conversations, the conflicts of domesticity, the agony of rejection and failed love, the spreading of rumours, the support systems that promote ideas and make activity in the public sphere feasible. All the low moments which invariably precede and follow the high moments. All of the moments and all of the emotions which make up the fabric of Modernism just as surely as the great drama of 'the birth of Cubism' ever did. So conditioned are we by the hierarchical values of what constitutes serious cultural endeavour, that we either co-opt these small-scale narratives into the great schemes of cultural activity or we allow them to slip into a kind of domesticated netherworld, to undo the lofty categories in which we have all been working.[39]

New art and new radical theoretical concerns emerged in the 1970s from a place least expected – from working mothers. The exhibitions *Feministo* in the 1970s, and *Mother's Pride, Mother's Ruin,* the film *Nightcleaners* and Mary Kelly's *Post Partum Document,* were concerned with the art of the 'trivial' and took the concerns of the private and personal and service work into the dominant arena of art amidst popular and critical protest. What is commonplace in art practice now, and practices that students take for granted, were then seen as embarrassing and ridiculous and just 'bad art'.[40] The new politics and art practices for the postmodern era did not come from the theories of the 'hard left' nor from the established lineage of gallery art and mainstream criticism but were initiated most coherently and consistently from the feminist politics and critiques of domesticity, work and consumption. Today, it is in the marginal and vulnerable areas in the academy – in literary studies, women's studies, media and film studies and in art history – once the most conservative 'feminine' areas, which now seem to embrace and revisit the most radical and threatening social ideas.

New art forms did not naturally emerge as linear development from abstraction, but emerged in opposition to formalism from feminism, mainly from the kitchens and domestic spaces of mothers. Perhaps now it is among the places and the people least likely, least imagined that signs of change and new artistic and educational practices are emerging. Not necessarily from Gallery Artists of London, or the salerooms of New York, from educationalists writing national curricula, but, as Haraway suggests, 'Ironically, it might be the unnatural cyborg women making chips in Asia and spiral dancing in Santa Rita after an anti-nuclear reaction whose constructed unities will guide effective oppositional strategies'.[41]

New ideas and meanings about art and art education may be found in the midst of electronics piece-workers of South East Asia, from the social contexts where old women dance in the townships of South Africa or even from feminized teachers and working class girls in schools.

What to do?

It is not always possible to know how to act on an everyday basis. We do not always have access to information nor can we always know what the full implications of our acts are. But there are certain approaches which could be adopted. There is nothing intrinsically better about 'marginal' practices and knowledges (fascism is after all marginal) but a seeking out of hidden discourses of art and art education, of the 'feminine' within an ethical frame of educational aims could be a place to begin to act.

Julia Kristeva's words offer a guide:

act first with all those who 'swim against the tide', all those who refuse – all the rebels against the existing relations of production and reproduction. But neither take the role of revolutionary (male or female); to refuse all roles, in order on the contrary, to summon this timeless; 'truth' – formless, neither true or false, echo of our jouissance, of our madness, of our pregnancies – into the order of speech and social symbolism. But how? By listening: by recognizing the unspoken in speech, even revolutionary speech; by calling attention at all times to whatever remains unsatisfied, repressed, new, eccentric, incomprehensible, disturbing to the status quo.[42]

Kristeva's psychoanalytic approach suggests that, in order to have an active and meaning-making role in the world, working class girls will need to have access to and understanding of dominant law-making and symbolic cultural forms which are at present in the hands of men, and which circumscribe everyday lives and everyday actions. Working class girls need to be taught in art how to understand, use and manipulate symbolic material effectively in order to gain access to the hitherto middle class and male dominated control of areas such as media, art history, art education and criticism as well as to assert rights of inheritance to the dominant, feminine forms of contemporary artistic practice.

Notes and references

Introduction

1 I have drawn in this text from established histories of art education: S. Mac-Donald (1970) *The History and Philosophy of Art Education*. London: University of London Press; R. Carline (1968) *Draw They Must*. London: Edward Arnold Publishers; A. D. Efland (1989) *A History of Art Education*. New York: Teacher's College Press.

2 I am using the model offered by D. K. Kondo (1990) *Crafting Selves: Power, Gender and Discourses of Identity in a Japanese Workplace*. Chicago: University of Chicago Press.

3 See for instance G. Chalmers (1990) South Kensington in the farthest colony, in D. Soucy and M. A. Stankiewiez (1990) *Framing the Past: Essays in Art Education*. Reston, VA: National Association of Education in Art.

4 The term 'subject' is a problem here. In education the term 'subject' usually refers to a specific area of study in school. In post-Lacanian psychoanalytic discourse the term 'subject' is used to replace the terms 'individual' or 'the person' of humanist psychology. I intend that the meaning should be clear in the context in which it is being used.

5 The school subject 'Art' and other disciplines in the school curriculum will be designated by use of an initial capital.

6 For statistics on gender difference in art education see G. Collins and R. Sandell (1992) *Women and Art Education*. Reston, VA: National Association of Education in Art; J. Hatton, Art, in J. Whyld (ed.) *Sexism in the Secondary Curriculum*. London: Harper & Row.

7 See for example the omission of any critique of Art in the curriculum from D. Spender (1987) *The Education Papers*. London: Routledge & Kegan Paul; S. Riddell (1990) Gender and the politics of the curriculum, in K. Thomas (ed.) *Gender and Subject in Higher Education*. Buckingham: Open University Press; K. Archer (1984) *Women and Education*. London: Routledge & Kegan Paul.

8 See P. Dalton (1978) The reproduction of patriarchal structures in art education. Unpublished Masters paper. University of Sussex.

9 N. Claude-Mathieu (1977) Notes towards a sociological definition of sex

categories, in *Ignored by Some Denied By Others*, trans. A. M. Sheridan-Smith. London: Women's Research and Resource Centre Publications. p. 22.

10 Ministry of Education (1959) *15–18: A Report of the Central Advisory Council for Education* (Newsom report). London: HMSO p. 392.

11 Collins and Sandell, op. cit.

Chapter 1   Theoretical perspectives

1 See P. Kirkham (ed.) (1996) *The Gendered Object*. Manchester: Manchester University Press.

2 A. Chave (1990) Minimalism and the rhetoric of power, *Arts Magazine*, 64(5): 44–63, p.53.

3 V. Walkerdine (1988) *The Mastery of Reason*. London: Routledge.

4 B. Marshall (1994) *Engendering Modernity: Feminism, Social Theory and Social Change*. Cambridge: Polity. I have deployed Marshall's analysis of the gendered structures of modernity throughout this section.

5 D. Gittins (1985) *The Family in Question*. London: Macmillan.

6 J. Mitchell (1974) *Psychoanalysis and Feminism*. Harmondsworth: Penguin, p. 409. See also B. Eherenreich (1992) Life without father, in L. McDowell and R. Pringle (eds) *Defining Women*. London: Polity/Open University.

7 M. Arnot (1993) The emergence of a new orthodoxy, *Gender and Education*, 4(1–2): 7–24.

8 See for instance, J. Rose (1986) *Sexuality in the Field of Vision*. London: Verso; J. Lacan (1949) The mirror stage as formative of the function of the I as revealed in psychoanalytic experience, in Lacan (1977) *Ecrits: A Selection*, trans. A. Sheridan. London: Tavistock.

9 H. Foster (1985) Introduction, in Foster, *Recordings: Art, Spectacle, Culture Politics*. Port Townsend, WA: Bay Press, p. 9.

10 L. Kipnis (1986) 'Refunctioning' reconsidered: towards a left popular culture, in C. McCabe (ed.) *High Theory/Low Culture*. Manchester: Manchester University Press.

11 Mitchell, cited in Gittins, op. cit., p. 36.

12 Gittins, op cit., pp. 92–111.

13 L. Althusser (1969) Ideology and ideological state, in J. Evans and S. Hall (1999) *Visual Culture: The Reader*. London: Sage/Open University Press.

14 G. Debord, cited in L. Kipnis op. cit., p. 19.

15 R. Coward (1976) Psychoanalysis and patriarchal structures, *Papers on Patriarchy Conference: London 76*. Lewes: Women's Publishing Collective.

16 J. Mitchell (1974) *Psychoanalysis and Feminism*. Harmondsworth: Penguin, p. 390.

17 L. Mulvey (1989) The Oedipus myth: beyond the riddles of the sphinx, in Mulvey, *Visual and Other Pleasures*. London: Macmillan. p. 199; R. Braidotti (1991) *Patterns of Dissonance*. London: Polity. p. 170.

18 L. Irigaray (1985) *The Speculum of the Other Woman*. Ithaca, Cornell University Press. pp. 90–123.

19 A. Jardine (1991) cited in Braidotti, op. cit., p. 167.

20 S. Alexander (1976) Capitalist modes of production and the sexual division of

Labour, in J. Mitchell and A. Oakley (eds) *The Rights and Wrongs of Women*. London: Pelican.

21 M. Roper (1989) *Masculinity and British Organizational Man*. Oxford: Oxford University Press.

22 G. Hofstede (1994) *Cultures and Organizations*. London: Harper Collins.

23 M. Tierney (1995) Negotiating a software career: informal work practices and 'the lads' in a software installation, in K. Grint and R. Gill (eds) *The Gender Technology Relation*. London: Taylor & Francis.

24 J. Wajcman (1993) *Feminism Confronts Technology*. Oxford: Polity. See also essays in G. Kirkup and L. Smith-Keller (eds) (1992) *Inventing Women: Science Technology and Gender*. Cambridge: Polity/Open University Press.

25 C. Cockburn (1993) *Brothers: Male Dominance and Technological Change*. London: Pluto.

26 For debates in critical feminism in relation to pedagogy, see C. Luke and J. Gore (eds) (1992) *Feminisms and Critical Pedagogy*. New York: Routledge.

27 In this section I am drawing on the writings of A. Assiter (1996) *Enlightened Women*. London: Routledge; L. Kauffman (ed.) (1989) *Gender and Theory*. London: Blackwell; S. Benhabib and D. Cornell (eds) (1987) *Feminism as Critique*. Cambridge: Polity.

28 bell hooks (1984) cited in G. Weiner (1994) *Feminisms and Education*. Buckingham: Open University Press. Weiner gives an account of the different feminisms that have shaped education.

29 Liberal feminism is discussed in P. Rothfield, 'Feminism, subjectivity and sexual difference'; radical feminism in R. Rowland and R. D. Klein, 'Radical feminism: critique and construct'; socialist feminism in L. C. Johnson 'Socialist feminisms'; all in S. Gunew (ed.) (1990) *Feminist Knowledge: Critique and Construct*. London: Routledge.

30 See review of debates in feminist education M. Arnot and K. Weiler (1993) (eds) *Feminism and Social Justice in Education*. London: Falmer.

31 C. Luke and J. Gore. Women in the academy: strategy, struggle and survival, in Luke and Gore, *Feminisms and Critical Pedagogy*, op. cit.

32 See debates on feminism's relation to theory in S. Harding (1992) The instability of the analytical categories of feminist theory, in H. Crowley and S. Himmelweit (eds) *Knowing Women: Feminism and Knowledge*. Cambridge: Polity/Open University Press; J. Wolff (1994) The artist, the critic and the academic: feminism's problematic relation with 'theory', in K. Deepwell (ed.) (1995) *New Feminist Art Criticism*. Manchester: Manchester University Press.

33 V. Walsh (1995) Eyewitnesses, not spectators/activists, not academics: feminist pedagogy and women's creativity, in Deepwell, op. cit.

34 W. Januszczak, cited in Wolff, The artist, the critic and the academic, op cit., p. 92.

35 G. C. Spivak (1987) Feminism and critical theory, in Spivak (ed.) *In Other Worlds: Essays in Cultural Politics*. New York: Methuen, p. 77.

36 Ibid.

37 G. Pollock (1988) Feminist interventions in the histories of art: an introduction, in Pollock, *Vision and Difference*. London: Routledge.

38 S. Hall (1992) Cultural Studies and its theoretical legacies, in L. Grossberg, C. Nelson and P. A. Treichler (eds) *Cultural Studies*. London: Routledge. p. 282.

39 This next section draws on M. Jay (1973) *The Dialectic Imagination*. Boston, MA: Heinemann; P. Slater (1974) The aesthetic theory of the Frankfurt School,

in Birmingham Centre for Contempory Cultural Studies (eds) *Cultural Studies 6*. Nottingham: Russell Press; A. Arato and E. Gebhardte (eds) (1977) *The Essential Frankfurt School Reader*. New York: Urizen; R. Wiggershaus (1994) *The Frankfurt School*. Cambridge: Polity.

40 See modernist debates on art in C. Harrison and P. Wood (eds) (1992) *Art in Theory, 1900–1990*. Blackwell. Oxford.

41 E. Fromm (1932), cited in Marshall, op. cit., p. 98.

42 K. Soper (1989) Feminism as critique, *New Left Review*. July/August. (176): 91–112.

43 See A. Huyssens (1986) Mass culture as woman, in Huyssens, *After the Great Divide*. London: Macmillan.

44 Ibid., p. 47.

45 A. Rühle-Gerstel (1933) Back to the good old days?; H. Støcker (1930) Marriage as a psychological problem; V. Baum (1927) People of today; L. Landau (1929) The companionate marriage; L. Reissner (1923) Schiffbek: all reprinted in A. Kaes, M. Jay and E. Dimendberg (eds) (1994) *The Weimar Republic Sourcebook*. Berkeley, CA: University of California Press.

46 J. Benjamin (1977) The end of internalisation: Adorno's social psychology, *Telos*, 32: 42–64; J. Benjamin (1978) Authority and the family revisited: or, a world without fathers?, *New German Critique*, 13: 35–58.

47 S. Benhabib (1987) The generalised and the concrete other, in Benhabib and Cornell, op. cit.

48 E. Grosz. Theories of subjectivity, in S. Gunew (ed.) (1990) *Feminist Knowledge: Critique and Construct*. London: Routledge.

49 For introductions to Lacan and feminism, see C. Clément (1983) *The Lives and Legends of Jaques Lacan*. New York: Columbia University Press; E. Grosz (1990) *Jacques Lacan: A Feminist Introduction*. New York: Routledge; R. Minsky (1996) *Psychoanalysis and Gender*. New York: Routledge.

50 M. Foucault (1970) *The Order of Things*. New York: Random House.

51 M. Foucault (1975) *Discipline and Punish: the Birth of the Prison*. New York: Pantheon; M. Foucault (1978) *History of Sexuality*. New York: Pantheon.

52 Cited in Grosz, *Jacques Lacan*, op. cit.

53 M. Foucault (1978) Politics and the study of discourse, *Ideology and Consciousness*, 1(3): 7–26.

54 K. Freedman (1992) Structure and transformation in art education: the Enlightenment project and the institutionalization of nature, in D. Thistlewood (ed.) *Histories of Art and Design Education*. London: Longman.

55 See Foucault, cited in Grosz, *Jacques Lacan*, op. cit., p. 91.

56 D. Sharpe (1978) *The Bauhaus*. London: Visual Publications.

57 G. Orenstein (1973) Women of surrealism, *Feminist Art Journal*, 2(2): 1, 16–21. See also Women's History Research Center (1974) *Female Artists Past and Present*. Berkeley, CA: Women's History Research Center; *Heresies: A Feminist Publication on Art and Politics* (biannual journal), New York.

58 For a review of modernist feminist art and its descendants, see M. C. De Zegher (ed.) (1996) *Inside the Visible: An Elliptical Traverse of 20th Century Art*. Boston, MA: Institute of Contemporary Art; R. Parker and G. Pollock (eds) (1987) *Framing Feminism: Art and the Women's Movement 1970–1985*. London: Pandora; N. Broude and M. Garrard (1994) *The Power of Feminist Art*. New York: Harry. N. Abrams.

59 See R. Krauss (1987) Introduction, in Krauss, *October: The First Decade*. Cambridge, MA: MIT Press. See T. Atkinson (1969) Editorial, art and language, reprinted in Harrison and Wood, op. cit.

60 S. Hall (1992) Cultural studies and its theoretical legacies, in L. Grossberg, C. Nelson and P. A. Treichler (eds) *Cutural Studies*. London: Routledge, p. 276.

61 See in this context J. Wolff (1995) Memoirs and micrologies: Walter Benjamin, feminism and cultural analysis, in Wolff, *Resident Alien: Feminist Cultural Criticism*. Cambridge: Polity.

62 P. Dunn and L. Leeson (1979) The fire and the fireplace, *Block*. 1: 15–33.

63 C. Tisdall and S. Nairne (1981) *Conrad Atkinson: Picturing the System*. London: Pluto.

64 Artists referred to and other artists can be found in Parker and Pollock. op. cit., pp. 201, 206–14; G. Elinor, S. Richardson, S. Scott, A. Thomas and K. Walker (eds) (1987) *Women and Craft*. London: Virago; Broude and Garrard. op. cit.

65 These artists are documented in S. Gablik (1991) *The Re-enchantment of Art*. New York: Thames & Hudson.

66 Hall, op. cit.; J. Wolff (1995) The female stranger, in Wolff, Resident Alien, op. cit.

67 A. Gramsi (1971) *Selections from the Prison Notebooks of Antonio Gramsci*, ed. and trans. Q. Hoare and G. Nowell-Smith. London: Lawrence & Wishart; I. Illich (1971) *Deschooling Society*. London: Calder and Boyars; P. Freire (1972) *Pedagogy of the Oppressed*, trans. M. B. Ramos. Harmondsworth: Penguin.

68 P. Bordieu and J-C. Passeron (1970) *Reproduction in Education, Society and Culture*, trans. R. Nice. London: Sage.

69 P. Bordieu (1966) Educational knowledge and creative project, in M. F. D. Young (ed.) (1971) *Knowledge and Control*. London: Collier-Macmillan; I. Illich (1981) Opening speech of the World Congress. New York: INSEA report.

70 See for example *Radical Education* (1974–5) 2; Walkerdine, op. cit.

71 Young, op. cit.; S. Bowles and H. Gintis (1976) *Schooling in Capitalist America*. New York: Basic Books.

72 For example see T. Harcup (1974–5) The frozen Arabs sock story, *Radical Education*, 2; P. Willis (1977) *Learning to Labour: How Working Class Children Get Working Class Jobs*. London: Saxon.

73 P. Willis (1979) An extract from symbolism and practice (A theory for the social meaning of pop music), in *Schooling and Culture*, 6. London: Cockpit Theatre Arts Workshop, p. 39.

74 See for example the teaching pack *Photography, Painting and Realism* produced by the Educational Advisory Service of the British Film Institute (1978–9) and debates in the journal *Screen Education*.

75 B. Kanpol (1994) *Critical Pedagogy: An Introduction*. London: Bergin and Garvey, p. 74.

76 J. Gore (1993) *The Struggle for Pedagogies*. New York: Routledge, p. 37; H. Bromley (1989) Identity politics and critical pedagogy, in *Educational Theory*, 39(3); H. Giroux (1994) *Disturbing Pleasures: Learning Popular Culture*. New York: Routledge.

77 D. Trend (1992) *Cultural Pedagogy: Art Education/Politics*. New York: Bergin & Garvey; E. Watkins (1993) *Throwaways: Work, Culture and Consumer Education*. Stanford, CA: Stanford University Press.

78 For an introduction to deconstruction and feminism, see Grosz, *Jacques Lacan*,

op. cit., See also P. Lather (1992) Post-critical pedagogies, in Luke and Gore, *Feminisms and Critical Pedagogy*, op. cit.

79 C. Norris (1987), cited in S. Kvale (ed.) (1992) *Psychology and Postmodernism.* London: Sage, p. 122.

80 L. Nochlin (1973) Why have there been no great women artists?, in T. Hess and E. Baker (eds) *Art and Sexual Politics.* New York: Collier; G. Greer (1979) *The Obstacle Race.* London: Secker & Warburg.

81 J. Derrida (1976) *Of Grammatology*, trans. G. C. Spivak. Baltimore, MD: Johns Hopkins University Press, p. 24.

82 For debates on modernity, modernization and modernism, see P. Berger (1977) Towards a critique of modernity, in Berger, *Understanding Modernity.* Harmondsworth: Penguin, pp. 101–12; J. Habermas (1981) Modernity: an incomplete project, in T. Docherty (ed.) (1993) *Postmodernism: A Reader.* Hemel Hempstead: Harvester; P. Anderson (1984) Modernity and revolution, *New Left Review*, 144: 96–128; R. Williams (1989) When was modernism?, in Harrison and Wood, op. cit.; J. Wolff (1990) Feminism and modernism, in Wolff, *Feminine Sentences: Essays on Women and Culture.* London: Polity; A. Giddens (1991) *Modernity and Self Identity.* Stanford, CA: Stanford University Press.

83 P. Madsen (1992) 'Postmodernism' and 'Late Capitalism': on terms and realities, in Kvale, op. cit., p. 209.

84 See T. Docherty (1993) Postmodernism: an introduction, in Docherty, op. cit.

85 Z. Bauman (1989) *Modernity and the Holocaust.* Cambridge: Polity.

86 Berger, op. cit., p. 101.

87 Huyssens, op. cit.

88 J. Kristeva, cited in J. Donald (1992) *Sentimental Education: Schooling, Popular Culture and the Regulation of Liberty.* London: Verso, p. 60.

89 Williams, op. cit.

90 Anderson, op. cit., p. 103.

91 Pollock, *Vision and Difference*, op. cit.

92 For an introduction to these practices, see B. Taylor (1995) *The Art of Today.* London: Weidenfeld & Nicholson.

93 Kipnis, cited in Donald, *Sentimental Education*, op. cit., p. 562.

94 T. Eagleton (1996) *The Illusions of Postmodernism.* Oxford: Blackwell, p. vii.

95 R. Usher and R. Edwards (1994) *Postmodernism and Education.* London: Routledge, p.2.

96 For further reading on this position, see Habermas, op. cit. See also N. Fraser and L. Nicholson (1988) Social criticism without philosophy: an encounter between feminism and postmodernism, *Theory, Culture and Society*, 5(2–3) 380–9; A. Solomon-Godeau (1990) Living with contradiction: critical practice in the age of supply side aesthetics, in C. Squiers (ed.) *The Critical Image.* London: Lawrence & Wishart.

97 For discussions of this position see T. Eagleton (1996) *The Illusions of Postmodernism.* Oxford: Blackwell.

98 A. Wellmar (ed.) (1991) *The Persistence of Modernity.* Oxford: Polity/Blackwell.

99 See arguments in T. Modelski (1986) Femininity as mas[s]querade: a feminist approach to mass culture, in McCabe, op. cit.

100 A. Jardine (1985) *Gynesis: Configurations of Woman and Modernity.* Ithaca, NY: Cornell University Press, p. 207.

101 L. Irigaray (1993) *An Ethics of Sexual Difference.* London: Athlone.

102 J. Flax (1990) *Thinking Fragments*. Oxford: University of California Press, cited in Usher and Edwards, op. cit.

103 Giroux, op. cit.

Chapter 2 Nineteenth century contexts

1 R. Usher and R. Edwards (1994) *Postmodernism and Education*. London: Routledge, p. 2.

 2 B. Marshall (1994) *Engendering Modernity: Feminism, Social Theory and Social Change*. Cambridge: Polity; A. Assiter (1996) *Enlightened Women*. London: Routledge.

 3 Marshall, op. cit., pp. 10–11.

 4 J. B. Landes (1974) Women and the public sphere: a modern perspective, *Social Analysis*, 15 August 1984: 20–31.

 5 See P. Dalton (1978) The reproduction of patriarchal structures in art education. Unpublished Masters paper, University of Sussex.

 6 C. Heward (1988) *Making a Man of Him*. London: Routledge, p. 30.

 7 Ibid., p. 31.

 8 J. Kristeva (1989) *Black Sun: Depression and Melancholia*, trans. L. S. Roudiez. New York: Columbia University Press, p. 45.

 9 L. Mulvey (1989) The Oedipus myth: beyond the riddles of the sphinx, in Mulvey, *Visual and Other Pleasures*. London: Macmillan; N. Bryson (1992) Géricault and masculinity, in N. Bryson, M. A. Holly and K. Moxey (eds) *Visual Culture*. Hanover, NH: University Press of New England.

10 P. Bordieu and J-C. Passeron (1970) *Reproduction in Education, Society and Culture*, trans. R. Nice. London: Sage, p. 19.

11 Heward, op. cit.

12 For examples see V. Walkerdine (1990) *Schoolgirl Fictions*. London: Verso.

13 Bordieu and Passeron, op. cit.

14 See arguments in M. Weiner (1985) *English Culture and the Decline of the Industrial Spirit 1850–1980*. Cambridge: Cambridge University Press.

15 Cited in R. Carline (1968) *Draw They Must*. London: Edward Arnold, p. 158.

16 M. Romans (1998) Political, economic, social and cultural determinants in the history of early to mid-nineteenth century art and design education in Britain. PhD thesis, University of Central England. Romans gives an account of the discourses of the Classical in shaping the education of taste.

17 Carline, op. cit.

18 V. Burgin (1991) Geometry and abjection, in J. Donald (ed.) *Psychoanalysis and Cultural Theory*. London: Macmillan.

19 See essays in D. Petherbridge and L. Jordanova (1997) *The Quick and the Dead* (exhibition catalogue). London: National Touring Exhibitions; L. Jordanova (1985) Gender, generation and science: William Hunter's obstetrical atlas, in W. F. Bynum and R. Porter. (eds) *William Hunter and the 18th Century Medical World*. Cambridge: Cambridge University Press.

20 S. Harding (1992) The instability of the analytical categories of feminist theory, in H. Crowley and S. Himmelweit (eds) *Knowing Women: Feminism and Knowledge*. Cambridge: Polity/Open University Press; Marshall, op. cit.; Jordanova, op. cit.

21 Carline, op. cit.

22 In this section I have used the work of M. Foucault (1977) *Discipline and Punish*. London: Tavistock; K. Jones and K. Williamson (1979) The birth of the school-room, *Ideology and Consciousness*, 6: (autumn): 59–111; J. Tagg (1980) Power and photography – a means of surveillance: the photograph as evidence in law, *Screen Education*, 36 (autumn): 17–55; N. Rose (1990) *Governing the Soul: The Shaping of the Private Self*, London: Routledge.

23 See A. Huyssens (1986) Mass culture as women, in Huyssens, *After the Great Divide*. London: Macmillan.

24 J. Swift (1995) Controlling the masses: the reinvention of a 'national' curriculum, *Journal of Art and Design Education* (JADE), 14(2): 115–27.

25 Ibid., p. 120.

26 A. D. Efland (1989) *A History of Art Education*. New York: Teacher's College Press; P. Smith (1996) *The History of American Art Education*. Westport. CT: Greenwood.

27 P. Willis, S. Jones, J. Canaan and G. Hurd (1990) *Common Culture: Symbolic Work at Play in the Everyday Cultures of the Young*. Buckingham: Open University Press.

28 L. Beyer (1996) The arts as personal and social communication: popular/ethical culture in schools, *Discourse: Studies in the Cultural Politics Of Education*, 17(2): 257–69.

29 S. Brown (1978) *Romanticism*. Key Concepts: An Arts Foundation Course Unit 21. Milton Keynes: Open University.

30 D. Thompson, cited in Brown, ibid., p. 20.

31 P. Wollen (1987) Fashion/orientalism/the body, *New Formations*, spring: 1.

32 See A. Bonshek (1987) Feminist romantic painting: a re-constellation, in H. Robinson (ed.) *Visibly Female*. London: Camden Press.

33 See arguments in R. Parker and G. Pollock (1981) *Old Mistresses*. London: Routledge.

34 See C. C. Orr (1995) Vistas of pleasure; women, art and the public sphere, in Orr (ed.) *Women in The Victorian Art World*. Manchester: Manchester University Press.

35 J. Ruskin (1868) *Sesame and Lilies*. London: Oxford University Press.

36 These descriptions are taken from P. Marks (1976) Femininity in the classroom, in J. Mitchell and A. Oakley (eds) *The Rights and Wrongs of Women*. Harmondsworth: Penguin.

37 See B. Turner (1974) *Equality for Some*. London: Ward Lock, p. 59.

38 R. Walkham (1865), cited in Turner. op. cit., p. 43.

39 J-J. Rousseau (1762/1974) *Emile*, trans. B. Foxley. London: Dent, p. 332.

40 Ibid., p. 331.

41 L. Davidoff, H. L'Esperance and H. Newby (1976) Landscape with figures: home and community in English society, in Mitchell and Oakley, op. cit.

42 J. Collier (1753), cited in Mitchell and Oakley, op. cit., p. 157.

43 Mrs Merrifield (1855) On design as applied to ladies' work, *The Art Journal*, February: 37.

44 L. Davidoff and C. Hall (1983) The architecture of public and private life: English middle-class society in a provincial town 1780–1850, in D. Fraser and A. Sutcliffe (eds) *The Pursuit of Urban History*. London: Edward Arnold; J. Wolff (1990) The culture of separate spheres, in J. Wolff, *Feminine Sentences: Essays on Women and Culture*. London: Polity; Orr, op. cit.

45 J. Attfield and P. Kirkham (eds) (1995) *A View From the Interior: Feminism Women and Design*. London: Woman's Press, p. 180.
46 A. Callen (1979) *Angel in the Studio: Women in the Arts and Crafts Movement*. London: Astragal, p. 26.
47 L. Tickner (1991) Men's work: masculinity and modernism, in N. Bryson, M. A. Holly, K. Moxey (eds) *Visual Theory*. Cambridge: Polity.
48 In 1998 in a petition from some MA Fine Art students asking for an amateur art exhibition to be removed from their college walls.
49 S. Alexander (1976) Capitalist modes of production and the sexual division of Labour, in Mitchell and Oakley, op. cit., pp. 81–2.
50 T. Modelski (1986) Femininity as mas[s]querade: a feminist approach to mass culture, in C. McCabe (ed.) *High Theory/Low Culture*. Manchester: Manchester University Press, p. 54.
51 Callen, op. cit.
52 M. Garrard (1976) Of men, women and art: some historical reflections, in N. Broude and M. Garrard (1994) *The Power of Feminist Art*. New York: Harry N. Abrams, p. 327.
53 E. McGregor (1995) The situation of women curators, in K. Deepwell (ed.) *New Feminist Art Criticism*. Manchester: Manchester University Press.
54 These examples are cited in S. Macdonald (1970) *The History and Philosophy of Art Education*. London: University of London Press, p. 146; A. Yoxall (1914) *A History of the Teaching of Domestic Subjects*. London: Methuen, p. 13.
55 Cited in S. King (1990) Technical and vocational education for girls, in P. Summerfield and E. J. Evans (eds) *Technical Education and the State since 1850*. Manchester: Manchester University Press.
56 A. Davin (1978) Imperialism and motherhood, *History Workshop*, 5 (spring): 9–67; D. Attar (1990) *Wasting Girls' Time*. London: Virago; A. Yoxall (1914) cited in P. Dalton (1979) Issues in the role and status of needlecrafts. MEd thesis, University of Sussex.
57 H. Sillitoe (1933) *A History of the Teaching of Domestic Subjects*, London: Chivers, p. 8.
58 See arguments developed in P. Dalton (1979) Issues in the role and status of needlecrafts. MEd thesis, University of Sussex.
59 Romans, op. cit.
60 P. Berger (1977) Towards a critique of modernity, in Berger, *Understanding Modernity*. Harmondsworth: Penguin; A. Giddens (1991) *Modernity and Self Identity*. Stanford, CA: Stanford University Press.
61 A. Tolson (1977) *The Limits of Masculinity*. London: Tavistock Publications.
62 M. Arnold (1879), cited in Carline, op. cit.
63 D. Chaney (1996) *Lifestyles*. London: Routledge, p. 126.
64 See J. Wolff (1990) The invisible flâneuse, in Wolff, *Feminine Sentences*, op. cit.
65 See arguments about the male gaze in J. Berger, S. Blomberg, C. Fox, M. Dibb and R. Hollis (1972) *Ways of Seeing*. London: BBC/Penguin; G. Pollock (1988) Feminist interventions in the history of art: an introduction, in Pollock, *Vision and Difference*. London: Routledge.
66 R. Taylor (1992) *Visual Arts in Education*. London: Falmer, p. 17.
67 Davidoff *et al.*, op. cit.
68 P. Sparke (1995) *As Long as its Pink: The Sexual politics of Taste*. London: Pandora, p. 163.

69 J. Baudrillard (1970) Consumption, in M. Poster (ed.) (1988) *Jean Baudrillard: Selected Writings*. Cambridge: Polity, p. 46.

70 Sparke, op. cit.

71 Callen, op. cit.

72 For a construction of the concept of the 'artisan', see Romans, op. cit.

73 MacDonald, op. cit., p.147.

74 Ibid., p. 148.

75 Attfield and Kirkham, op. cit.

76 S. Dodd (1995) Art education for women in the 1860s: a decade of debate, in Orr, op. cit.; Callen, op. cit.

77 The arguments in this section are drawn from V. Walkerdine (1986) Progressive pedagogy and political struggle, in C. Luke and J. Gore (eds) (1992) *Feminisms and Critical Pedagogy*. New York: Routledge; V. Walkerdine (1990) *Schoolgirl Fictions*. London: Verso.

78 Walkerdine, Progressive pedagogy, op. cit., p. 16.

79 Walkerdine, *Schoolgirl Fictions*, op. cit., p. 20.

80 N. Rose (1990) *Governing the Soul*. London: Routledge. See also J. Henriques, W. Holloway, C. Urwin, C. Venn, V. Walkedine (1984) *Changing the Subject*. London: Methuen.

81 See Callen, op. cit.

82 Board of Education (1926) *Report of the Consultative Committee on Education of the Adolescent* (The Hadow report). London: HMSO, p. 229.

83 Attfield and Kirkham, op. cit.

84 Ibid.

85 D. Thistlewood (1993) Herbert Read: a critical appreciation at the centenary of his birth, *Journal of Art and Design Education*, 12(2): 143–59.

86 Summerfield and Evans, op. cit.

87 Hadow Report, op. cit., p.113.

88 See Callen, op. cit.

89 See Dalton, op. cit.

Chapter 3 Psychology in art education

1 V. Walkerdine (1985) Psychological knowledge and educational practice: producing the truth about schools, in G. Claxton (ed.) *Psychology and Schooling: What's the Matter?* Bedford Way Papers, London: Institute of Education, University of London.

2 See P. Light and P. Barnes (1995) Development in Drawing, in V. Lee and P. Das Gupta (eds) *Children's Cognitive and Language Development*. Buckingham: Open University Press.

3 F. Goodenough (1926) *Measurement of Intelligence by Drawings*. New York: World Book.

4 K. Machover (1949) *Personality Projection in the Drawing of the Human Figure*. Springfield, IL: C. C. Thomas.

5 D. Harris (1963) *Children's Drawings as Measures of Intellectual Maturity*. New York: Harcourt Brace.

6 S. G. Feinberg (1976) Conceptual content and spatial characteristics in boys and girls' drawings of fighting and helping, *Studies in Art Education*, (18)2: 63–72.

7 M. Ostle (1924) Educational methods, in P. Rea (ed.) *Woman's Year Book*. London: Woman's Publishers.

8 For a desription of the shortcomings of behavioural psychology in human sciences, see S. Frosh (1989) *Psychoanalysis and Psychology*. London: Edward Arnold.

9 R. MacMillan, Preface, in J. Swanson (1913) *Educational Needlecraft*. London: Arnold.

10 M. Klein (1930) The importance of symbol formation in the development of the ego, in J. Mitchell (ed.) (1986) *The Selected Melanie Klein*. Harmondsworth: Penguin; D. W. Winnicott (1957) *The Child, the Family and the Outside World*. London: Tavistock.

11 M. Milner (1971) *On Not Being Able to Paint*. London: Heinemann; C. Rogers (1971) *Encounter Groups*. London: Allen Lane.

12 C. Rogers, cited in D. Dosser (1990) Gender issues in tertiary art education, *Journal of Art and Design Education*, 9(2): 63–71.

13 M. Ross (ed.) (1978) *The Creative Arts*. London: Heinemann.

14 V. Walkerdine (1986) Progressive pedagogy and political struggle, in C. Luke and J. Gore (eds) (1992) *Feminisms and Critical Pedagogy*. New York: Routledge, pp. 15–24.

15 Ibid., p. 50.

16 Ibid.; see also Walkerdine, Psychological knowledge and educational practice, op. cit.

17 R. Harré and G. Gillett (1994) *The Discursive Mind*. London: Sage, p.4.

18 E. W. Eisner (1988) The biological basis of learning, *The Role of Discipline-Based Art Education in America's Schools*. Los Angeles: Getty Center for Education in the Arts.

19 See C. Merchant (1980) *The Death of Nature*. New York: Harper & Row; E. Fee (1981) Women's nature and scientific objectivity, in M. Lowe and R. Hubbard (eds) *Woman's Nature: Rationalizations of Inequality*. New York: Pergamon; E. F. Keller (1985) *Reflections on Gender and Science*. New Haven, CT: Yale University Press. J. Wajcman (1991) *Feminism Confronts Technology*. Cambridge: Polity.

20 For an account of the implications of the separation of mind and body see J. M. Stoppard (1998) Dis-ordering depression in women, *Theory and Psychology*. 8(1): 79–99.

21 J. R. Morss (1990) *The Biologising of Childhood*. Hove: Erlbaum.

22 As recounted by E. Gombrich (1950) *The Story of Art*. London: Phaidon.

23 See F. Frascina and C. Harrison (1982) Editorial text to K. Popper (1957) Historical interpretation, in Frascina and Harrison (eds) *Modern Art and Modernism*. London: Chapman/Open University Press.

24 H. Spencer, cited in A. D. Efland (1989) *A History of Art Education*. New York: Teacher's College Press, p. 158.

25 R. Witkin (1978) Expressivist theories of art and ideologies of arts education, in M. Ross (ed.) *The Creative Arts*. London: Heinemann.

26 See S. Malvern (1994) Recapping on recapitulation, *Third Text*, 27: 21–31.

27 V. Walkedine (1988) *The Mastery of Reason*. London: Routledge.

28 V. Lowenfeld and L. Brittain (1947/1970) *Creative and Mental Growth*. New York: Macmillan.

29 P. Smith (1996) *The History of American Art Education*. Westport, CT: Greenwood.

30 H. Gardner (1973) *The Arts and Human Development*. New York: Wiley. See

debates and critiques in M. Bornstein (1984) Developmental psychology and the problem of artistic change, *Journal of Aesthetics and Art Criticism*. XLIII (2): 131–45; Morss, op. cit.; E. Burman (1994) *Deconstructing Developmental Psychology*. New York: Routledge.

31 Gardner, op. cit., pp. 233 and 293.
32 R. Clement (1993) *The Art Teacher's Handbook*. Cheltenham: Stanley Thornes, p.32.
33 See debates in Light and Barnes, op. cit., p.7.
34 C. Gilligan (1982) *In a Different Voice*. Cambridge, MA: Harvard University Press. See also N. Noddings (1984) *Caring: A Feminist Approach to Ethics and Moral Education*. Berkeley, CA: University of California Press.
35 F. Newman and L. Holzman (1993) *Lev Vygotsky: Revolutionary Scientist*. London: Routledge.
36 Walkerdine, *The Mastery of Reason*, op. cit.
37 R. Williams (1976) *Keywords*. Glasgow: Fontana; A. Weate (1993) The economics of creativity, in E. Errington and P. Edward (eds) *Arts Education*. Geelong, Vic.: Deakin University Press.
38 See S. Turkle and S. Papert (1990) Epistemological pluralism: styles and voices within the computer culture, *Signs*, autumn: 128–57; E. Fox Keller (1985) *A feeling for the Organism: Reflections on Gender and Science*. New Haven, CT: Yale University Press.
39 L. Hudson (1967) *Contrary Imaginations; A Psychological Study of the English Schoolboy*. Harmondsworth: Penguin.
40 N. Bryson (1983) *Vision and Painting*. London: Macmillan, p. 21.
41 D. Haraway (1985) A manifesto for cyborgs: science, technology and socialist feminism in the 1980s, in L. Nicholson (ed.) (1990) *Feminism/Postmodernism*. New York: Routledge.
42 E. Watkins (1993) *Throwaways: Work, Culture and Consumer Education*. Stanford, CA: Stanford University Press; Haraway, op. cit.
43 M. Landau (1984) Human evolution as narrative, *American Scientist*, 72: 262–8, p. 262.
44 J. S. Eggleston (1973) An international perspective of design education, in J. S. Eggleston (ed.) *International Perspectives of Design Education*. Keele: Keele University Press, p. 6.
45 Weate, op. cit.; see also D. Rushton and P. Wood (1979) *The Politics of Art Education*. London: Studio Trust.
46 See M. Boden (1990) *The Creative Mind*. London: Abacus.
47 J. P. Guilford (1968) The structure of intelligence, in D. K. Whitlea (ed.) *Handbook of Measurement and Assessment in the Behavioral Sciences*. Reading, MA: Addison-Wesley; L. Hudson (1967) *Contrary Imaginations: A Psychological Study of the English Schoolboy*. Harmondsworth: Penguin.
48 D. Child (1973/1997) *Psychology and the Teacher*, 6th edn. London: Cassell, pp. 276–97.
49 J-F. Lyotard (1992) Answering the question: what is postmodernism?, in T. Docherty (ed.) (1993) *Postmodernism: A Reader*. Hemel Hempstead: Harvester.
50 Turkle and Papert, op. cit., p. 136.
51 E. Eisner (1972) *Educating Artistic Vision*. New York: Macmillan.
52 See R. Gregory (1966/1998) *Eye and Brain*, 5th edn. Oxford. Oxford University Press.

53 R. Fry (1920/1961) An essay in aesthetics, in Fry, *Vision and Design*. Harmondsworth: Penguin, p. 37 and p. 36.

54 One of the often used texts, which has recently been reprinted, is M. De Saumarez (1964) *Basic Design: The Dynamics of Visual Form*. London: Studio Vista.

55 Fry, op. cit., p. 28, p. 25.

56 C. Greenberg (1967) cited in M. Ginsborg (1998) Coming to terms with values, in P. Hetherington (ed.) *Artists in the 1990s: Their Education and Values*. London: Wimbledon School of Art/Tate Gallery, p. 78.

57 Bryson, *Vision and Painting*, op. cit., p. xiii.

58 V. Burgin (1976) Modernism in the work of art, in Burgin (1986) *The End of Art Theory: Criticism and Postmodernity*. London: Macmillan.

59 See the evolutionary model of teaching drawing, from mark-making to realism, in D. Atkinson (1993) Representation and experience in children's drawing, *Journal of Art and Design Education*, 12(1): 41–51.

60 N. Macadoo (1993) The ATs for Art: a philosophical perspective, *Journal of Art and Design Education*, 12(1): 41–51.

61 N. Stanley (1993) Objects of criticism: a contribution from the new museology, *Journal of Art and Design Education*, 12(3) 317–34.

62 Documented in A. Fraser (1991) Museum highlights; a gallery talk, *October*, summer (57). See also website www.mishmash.co.uk

63 L. Mulvey (1975) Visual pleasure and the narrative cinema, in Mulvey, *Visual and Other Pleasures*. London: Macmillan

64 M. Jay (1973) *The Dialectic Imagination*. Boston, MA: Heinemann.

65 C. Metz (1982) *The Imaginary Signifier*, trans. C. Britton *et al.* Bloomington, IN: Indiana University Press.

66 G. Pollock (1988) Feminist interventions in the histories of art: an introduction, in Pollock, *Vision and Difference*. London: Routledge.

67 Mulvey, Visual pleasure and the narrative cinema, op. cit.

68 C. Pajaczkowska (1983) Structure and pleasure, *Block*, 9: 13; J. Rose (1986) *Sexuality in the Field of Vision*. London: Verso.

69 See M. Jay (1988) Scopic regimes of modernity, in H. Foster (ed.) *Vision and Visuality*. Seattle, WA: Bay Press. See also V. Burgin (1982) The absence of presence: conceptualism and postmodernisms, in Burgin (1986) *The End of Art Theory*, op. cit.

70 J. Tagg (1980) Power and photography – a means of surveillance: the photograph as evidence in law, *Screen Education*, 36 (autumn): 17–55.

71 Haraway, op. cit.

72 L. Mulvey (1989) The Oedipus myth: beyond the riddles of the Sphinx, in Mulvey, *Visual and Other Pleasures*. London: Macmillan.

73 Jay, op. cit., p. 8.

74 L. Irigaray (1978) cited in Pollock, Feminist interventions in the histories of art, op. cit., p. 50.

75 For a view of twentieth century critical women's art practices, see M.C. De Zegher (1994) *Inside the Visible*. Boston, MA: MIT Press.

76 R. Taylor (1992) *The Visual Arts in Education*. London: Falmer.

77 For more detailed critique of implementation of critical studies, see A. Hughes (1993) Don't judge pianists by their hair, *Journal of Art and Design Education*, 12(3): 279–89.

78 Pollock, Feminist interventions in the histories of art, op. cit., p. xii.
79 For an accessible introduction to social constructionist and other new currents in psychology, see R. Stevens (ed.) (1996) *Understanding the Self*. Buckingham: Open University Press.
80 J. Shotter (1993) *The Cultural Politics of Everyday Life*. Buckingham: Open University Press.
81 Bakhtin, cited in Shotter, ibid., p. 109.
82 Ibid.
83 See for example as theorised by W. Holloway (1984) Gender difference and the production of subjectivity, in J. Henriques, W. Holloway, C. Unwin, C. Venn and V. Walkerdine, *Changing the Subject*. London: Methuen.
84 J. Butler (1990) *Gender Trouble: Feminism and the Subversion of Identity*. New York: Routledge, p. 142.
85 D. Chaney (1996) *Lifestyles*. London: Routledge.
86 Watkins, op. cit.
87 C. West and D. Zimmerman (1987) Doing gender, *Gender and Society*, vol. 1(2): 125–51, p. 126.
88 See reciprocal construction of identies in everyday practices in M. Kelly (1983) *Post Partum Document*. London: Routledge.
89 Butler, op. cit.

Chapter 4 Modernist art and design education

1 See H. Read (1943) *Education Through Art*. London: Faber & Faber; M. Richardson (1948) *Art and the Child*. London: London University Press; D. Thistlewood (1993) Herbert Read: a critical appreciation at the centenary of his birth, *Journal of Art and Design Education*, 12(2) 143–59.
2 F. E. Kast and J. E. Rosenzweig (1972) The modern view: a systems approach, in J. Beishon and G. Peters (eds) *Systems Behaviour*. Milton Keynes: Open University Press.
3 M. J. Rouse (1970) Art: meaning, method, and media: a six year elementary art curriculum based on behavioural objectives, in D. J. Davies (ed.) *Behavioural Emphasis in Art Education*. Reston, VA: National Association of Education in Art.
4 E. Broughton (1971) Home Economics, in B. Aylward (ed.) *Design Education in Schools*. London: B. Evans, p. 98.
5 P. Dalton (1979) Issues in the role and status of needlecrafts. MEd thesis, University of Sussex; see also D. Attar (1990) *Wasting Girls' Time*. London: Verso.
6 Attar, op. cit.
7 C. Tipping (1972) *The Design Education Myth*. London: Middlesex Polytechnic.
8 See Department of Education and Science (1971) *Education Survey 11: Art in Schools*. London: HMSO.
9 J. Pratt, J. Bloomfield and C. Seale (1984) *Option Choice: A Question of Equal Opportunity*. London: Nelson.
10 Tipping, op. cit., p. 119.
11 P. Willis (1977) *Learning to Labour: How Working Class Children Get Working Class Jobs*. London: Saxon
12 Ministry of Education (1959) *15–18: A Report of the Central Advisory Council for Education* (Newsom Report). London: HMSO, p. 34.

13 Schools Council (1971) *Home Economics Teaching*. Curriculum Bulletin 4. London: Evans/Methuen.
14 Attar, op. cit., p. 21.
15 Cited in M. Adams and M. Arnot (1986) *Investigating Gender in Secondary Schools*. London: Inner London Education Authority.
16 See Pratt *et al.*, op. cit.
17 Willis, op. cit., p. 159.
18 Dalton, op. cit., p. 60.
19 Ibid.
20 G. Collins and R. Sandell (1992) *Women and Art Education*. Reston, VA: National Association of Education in Art.
21 Attar, op. cit.
22 Dalton, op. cit.
23 B. Aylward (ed.) (1973) *Design Education in Schools*. London: B. Evans, p. 109.
24 Careers information leaflet, cited in Dalton, op. cit., pp. 62 and 67.
25 Ibid.
26 N. Rose (1979) President sees education cuts as a threat to healthy survival of home economics, *Housecraft*, November: 265.
27 G. Wills and D. Midgeley (1973) *Fashion Marketing*. London: Allen & Unwin.
28 D. K. Kondo (1990) *Crafting Selves: Power, Gender and Discourses of Identity in a Japanese Workplace*. Chicago: University of Chicago Press.
29 M. Romans (1998) Political, economic, social and cultural determinants in the history of early to mid-nineteenth century art and design education in Britain. PhD thesis, University of Central England.
30 B. Friedan (1963) *The Feminine Mystique*. Harmondsworth: Penguin.
31 R. S. Cowan (1976) The industrial revolution in the home: household technology and social change in the twentieth century, *Technology and Culture*, 17(1): 1–23.
32 T. Veblen (1971) cited in K. Galbraith (1974) *Economics and the Public Purpose*. Harmondsworth: Penguin, p. 48.
33 R. Thompson (1968) *The Pelican History of Psychology*. Harmondsworth: Penguin.
34 National Economic Development Office (1970) *Your Future in Clothing*. London: HMSO, p. 70.
35 Newsom Report, op. cit., p. 135.
36 Ibid., p. 187.
37 Galbraith, op. cit., p. 49.
38 Ibid., p. 30.
39 W. Bull (1954) *Basic Needlework*. London: Longman, p. 174.
40 Ibid., p. 180.
41 C. Greenberg (1965/1982) Modernist Painting, in F. Frascina and C. Harrison (eds) *Modern Art and Modernism*. London: Chapman/Open University Press.
42 V. Walkerdine (1988) *The Mastery of Reason*. London: Routledge
43 K. Freedman (1992) Structure and transformation in art education: the Enlightenment project and the institutionalization of nature, in D. Thistlewood (ed.) *Histories of Art and Design Education*. London: Longman.
44 P. Fuller (1998) The art of England, in Fuller (ed.) *Theoria: Art and the Absence of Grace*. London: Chatto & Windus.
45 S. Hall (1988) *The Hard Road to Renewal*. London: Verso, p. 164.
46 See R. Wiggershaus (1994) *The Frankfurt School*. Cambridge: Polity; A. Arato

and E. Gebhardte (eds) (1977) *The Essential Frankfurt School Reader*. New York: Urizen.

47 D. Fielding (1970) *The Black Mountain Book*. New York: Croton.

48 V. Burgin (1976) Modernism and the work of art, in V. Burgin (ed.) (1986) *The End of Art Theory*. London: Macmillan.

49 P. Anderson (1969) Components of the national culture, in A. Cockburn and R. Blackburn (eds) *Student Power*. Harmondsworth: Penguin.

50 M. Weiner (1985) *English Culture and the Decline of the Industrial Spirit 1850–1980*. Cambridge: Cambridge University Press.

51 H. Read (1951) *The Meaning of Art*. Harmondsworth: Penguin; H. Read (1975) The limits of permissiveness, in P. Abbs (ed.) *The Black Rainbow*. London: Heinemann.

52 Rea, *The Meaning of Art*, op. cit., p. 59.

53 See P. Sparke (1995) *As Long as It's Pink: The Sexual Politics of Taste*. London: Pandora.

54 Ibid., p. 74.

55 Ibid., p. 534.

56 P. Dalton (1980) Housewives, leisure crafts and ideology, in G. Elinor, S. Richardson, S. Scott, A. Thomas and K. Walker (eds) (1987) *Women and Craft*. London: Virago.

57 A. Huyssens (1986) Mass culture as woman, in Huyssens, *After the Great Divide*. London: Macmillan.

58 L. Tickner (1991) Men's work: masculinity and modernism, in N. Bryson, M. A. Holly, K. Moxey (eds) *Visual Theory*. Camridge: Polity.

59 C. Greenberg (1939) Avant garde and kitsch, in C. Harrison and P. Wood (eds) (1992) *Art in Theory, 1900–1990*. Blackwell: Oxford.

60 Greenberg, cited in Burgin, op. cit., p. 2.

61 A. Partington (1989) The designer housewife in the 1950s, in J. Attfield and P. Kirkham (eds) (1995) *A View from the Interior: Feminism, Women and Design*. London: Women's Press, p. 212.

62 C. Steedman (1977) Writing the self: the end of the scholarship girl, in J. McGuigan (ed.) *Cultural Methodologies*. London: Sage.

Chapter 5 The feminization of art education

1 P. Hills (1993) The modern corporate state, the rhetoric of freedom, and the emergence of modernism in the United States: the mediation of language in critical practice, in M. Gee (ed.) *Art Criticism Since 1900*. Manchester: Manchester University Press.

2 R. Moore (1987) Education and the ideology of production, *British Journal of Sociology of Education*, 8(2): 227–42.

3 ArtsEdNet (2000) *Educating for the Workplace through the Arts*. Getty Education Institute for the Arts: www.artsednet.getty.edu/ArtsEdNet/Advocacy/Workplace/three.html

4 M. O'Connor (1998) Colleges are keeping Britannia cool, *National Association for Teachers in Further and Higher Education Journal*, May: 12–13.

5 S. Turkle and S. Papert (1990) Epistemological pluralism: styles and voices within computer culture, *Signs: Journal of Women in Culture and Society*, 16(1): 212–18.

6 G. Hofstede (1994) *Cultures and Organizations: Software of the Mind*. London: Harper Collins.

7 G. Roberts and R. Ritchie (1990), cited in H. G. Denton (1990) Managing rapid change: the role of staff teamwork in technology delivery, *Design and Technology Teaching*, 23: 25–34. A. Skelton (1990), cited in Denton, ibid.

8 M. Buchanan (1990) Issues for implementation and the role of art and design, *Design and Technology Teaching*, 23: 5–12.

9 B. Harrison (1994) *Lean and Mean: The Changing Landscape of Corporate Power in the Age of Flexibility*. New York: HarperCollins.

10 R. Gordon (1983) The computerization of daily life, the sexual division of labour, and the homework economy. Paper delivered at the Silicon Valley Workshop Group Conference, cited in Haraway (1985) A manifesto for cyborgs: science, technology and socialist feminism in the 1980s, in L. Micholson (ed.) (1990) *Feminism/Postmodernism*. New York: Routledge.

11 Harrison, *Lean and Mean*, op. cit.

12 Editorial (1996) Working Men, *Achilles Heel*, 20(4).

13 See M. Noon and P. Blyton (1997) The social construction of skill, in their *The Realities of Work*. London: Macmillan

14 Haraway, op. cit., p. 108.

15 See contributions in P. D'Onofrio-Flores and S. M. Pfafflin (1982) *Scientific-Technological Change and the Role of Women in Development*. Boulder, CO: Westview; M. P. Fernandez-Kelly (1983) *For We Are Sold, I and my People*. New York: State University of New York Press; A. Fuentes and B. Ehrenreich (1983) *Woman in the Global Factory*. Boston, MA: South End Press.

16 Haraway, op. cit; Harrison, *Lean and Mean*, op. cit., ch. 9.

17 E. Watkins (1993) *Throwaways: Work, Culture and Consumer Education*. Stanford, CA: Stanford University Press, p. 30.

18 G. Hofstede (1984) *Culture's Consequences*. London: Sage, p. 201.

19 For feminist methodologies in art education, see G. C. Collins (1981) Feminist approaches to art education, *Studies in Art Education*, 15(2): 83–94; E. Garber (1990) Implications of feminist art criticism for art education, *Studies in Art Education*, 32(1): 17–26; R. Sandell (1991) The liberating relevance of feminist pedagogy, *Studies in Art Education*, 32(3): 44–57.

20 M. Romans (1998) Political, economic, social and cultural determinants in the history of early to mid-nineteenth century art and design education in Britain. PhD thesis, University of Central England.

21 Department of Education and Science (1992) *Art in the National Curriculum (England)*. London: HMSO, pp. 8–9.

22 L. Dawtry, T. Jackson, M. Masterson and P. Meecham (eds) (1996) *Critical Studies and Modern Art*. New Haven, CT: Yale University Press with the Open University.

23 G. Bennett (1996) The non-sovereign self (diaspora identities), in Dawtry *et al.*, ibid.

24 S. Clive (1996) Thoughts on visual literacy, in Dawtry *et al.*, op. cit.

25 D. Best (1996) The rationality of artistic feeling, in Dawtry *et al.*, op. cit.

26 S. Landy-Sheridan (1990) Editorial: Why new foundations?, *Leonardo*, 23(2–3): 165–7.

27 L. Perry (1993) Theoretical comments, *Journal of Art and Design Education*, 12(3): 343–55.

28 J. Swift (1996) Editorial, *Journal of Art and Design Education*, 15(2): 119–24.
29 H. Hollands (1995) Art: chance, opportunity and entitlement in R. Andrews. (ed.) (1996) *Interpreting the National Curriculum*. London: Middlesex University Press, pp. 158–70.
30 See E. Carter (1984) Alice in consumer wonderland, in A. McRobbie and M. Nava (eds) *Gender and Generation*. London: Macmillan; C. Steedman (1986) *Landscape for a Good Woman*. London: Virago; K. Mercer (1987) Black hair/style politics, *New Formations*, 3.
31 H. Giroux (1994) *Disturbing Pleasures: Learning Popular Culture*. New York: Routledge.
32 S. Harty, cited in Giroux, ibid., p. 51.
33 See for typical example B. Treadwell (1994) Flamin' team Slug: drawing into design at Key Stage 2, in Caloustie Gulbenkian Foundation (eds) *Young at Art*. Birmingham: National Primary Centre.
34 Watkins, op. cit.
35 J. Farns (1979) Intertex report, *International Textile Management Newsletter*, 20(18): vi–viii.
36 P. Willis, S. Jones, J. Canaan and G. Hurd (1990) *Common Culture: Symbolic Work at Play in the Everyday Cultures of the Young*. Buckingham: Open University Press, p. 52.
37 Watkins, op. cit.; P. Bourdieu (1966) Educational knowledge and creative project, in M. F. D. Young (ed.) (1971) *Knowledge and Control*. London: Collier-Macmillan.
38 D. Chaney (1996) *Lifestyles*. London: Routledge.
39 Ibid., p. 50.
40 Ibid., p. 94.
41 Willis *et al.*, op. cit.; J. Hearn (1998) Troubled masculinities, in J. Popjay and J. Hearn (eds) (1998) *Men, Gender Divisions and Welfare*. London: Routledge, p. 42.
42 K. Hamblen (1989) Research in art education as a form of educational consumer protection, *Studies in Art Education*, 31(1): 37–45.
43 D. Coyle (1999) *Independent*, 16 April: 1.
44 A. Oakley (1995) *Public Visions, Private Matters*. London: The Institute of Education, University of London.
45 J. Hillman-Chartrand (1987) The arts: consumption skills in the postmodern economy, *Journal of Art and Design Education*, 6(1): 35–50.
46 S. Ford and A. Davies (1998) Art capital, *Art Monthly*, February: 213.
47 C. Nemser (1972) Art criticism and gender prejudice, *Arts Magazine*, March: 43–6.
48 W. Januszczak, cited in J. Wolff (1994) The artist, the critic and the academic: feminism's problematic relation with 'theory', in K. Deepwell (ed.) (1995) *New Feminist Art Criticism*. Manchester: Manchester University Press, p. 92.
49 A. Solomon-Godeau (1990) Living with contradiction: critical practice in the age of supply side aesthetics, in C. Squiers (ed.) *The Critical Image*. London: Lawrence & Wishart.
50 For a fuller debate on critical or oppositional postmodernism art, see Mary Kelly and Griselda Pollock in conversation, in K. Campbell (ed.) (1992) *Critical Feminism: Argument in the Disciplines*. Buckingham: Open University Press; see also Solomon–Godeau, op. cit.

51 For a review of different contempory art practice, see B. Riemschneider and U. Grosenick (1999) *Art at the Turn of the Millenium*. Cologne: Taschen.

52 S. Fournier, cited in V. Griffith (1998) Knowing when to be of service, *Financial Times*, 12 February.

53 R. Pringle (1992) Women and consumer capitalism, in L. McDowell and R. Pringle (eds) *Defining Women*. Cambridge: Open University/Polity.

54 A. R. Hochschild (1983) *The Managed Heart*. Berkeley, CA: University of California Press.

55 See M. Noon and P. Blyton (1997) Emotion work, in their *The Realities of Work*, op. cit.

56 Hofstede, *Culture's Consequences*, op. cit., p. 201; Hofstede, *Cultures and Organizations*, op. cit.

57 J. McGregor (1978) *Leadership*. New York: Harper & Row; B. Bass (1985) *Leadership and Peformance*. New York: Free Press; J. B. Rosner (1990) Ways women lead, *Harvard Business Review*, November–December: 119–125.

58 Rosner, op. cit.

59 See debates in J. Jipson (1995) Teacher-mother: an imposition of identity, in Jipson, *Repositioning Feminism and Education*. Westport, CT: Bergin & Garvey.

60 R. Sandell (1991) The liberating relevance of feminist pedagogy, *Studies in Art Education*, 32(3): 44–57.

61 V. Walsh (1995) Eyewitnesses, not spectators/activists, not academics: feminist pedagogy and women's creativity, in Deepwell, op. cit., p. 55.

62 V. Walkerdine (1998) *The Mastery of Reason*. London: Routledge. See also J. Miller (1992) More has meant women: the feminization of schooling, in *Papers from the Institute of Education*. London: University of London.

63 C. Rogers (1971) *Encounter Groups*. London: Allen Lane; E. L. Kelly (1967) *Assessment of Human Characteristics*. Belmont, CA: Brooks Cole.

64 D. Dosser (1990) Gender issues in tertiary art education, *Journal of Art and Design Education*, 9(2): 63–71.

65 Jipson, op. cit., P. Dalton (1999) Oedipal dramas in art education, *Journal of Art and Design Education*, 18(3): 301–6; L. Moreley (1997) All you need is love: feminist pedagogy for empowerment and emotional labour in the academy, *Inclusive Education*, 2(1): 15–27.

66 J. Elshtain (1991) The therapeutic classroom: a critique and an alternative, in B. Scott (ed.) *The Liberal Arts in a Time of Crisis*. New York: Praeger, p. 71.

67 J. Kaler (1999) Does empowerment empower?, in J. Quinn and P. Davies (eds) *The Ethics of Empowerment*. London: Macmillan, p. 110.

68 P. Brown and R. Scase (1994) *Higher Education and Corporate Realities: Class, Culture and the Decline of Graduate Careers*. London: UCL Press.

69 H. Willmott (1993) Strength is ignorance; slavery is freedom: managing culture in modern organizations, *Journal of Management Studies*. 30(4): 515–51.

70 See A. Strati (1999) *Organization and Aesthetics*. London: Sage.

71 C. Nemser (1972) Art criticism and gender prejudice, *Arts Magazine*, March: 43–6.

72 A. Thorncroft (1998) New tunes and more harmony, *Financial Times*, 30 June. T. Brown [European Director of Ideo, a product development company] (1997) Nurturing a culture of innovation, *Financial Times*, 17 November; A. Rawsthorn (1984) Art, but not just for Art's sake, *Financial Times*, 17 March.

73 A. Thorncroft (2000) Commerce and the arts swap skills for their mutual benefit, *Financial Times*, 17 February.
74 E. De Bono (1994) *Parallel Thinking*. Harmondsworth: Penguin; A. Ahuja (2000) Are you an innovative thinker?, *The Times*, March 14.
75 B. Warnolf (1996) Business needs artists, *Artists Newsletter*, March.
76 A. Garrett (1997) Show business means business, *Observer* Business Section, 30 March.
77 R. K. Lester, M. J. Piore, and K. M. Malek (1998) Interpretive management: what general managers can learn from design, *Harvard Business Review*, March–April: 86–96.
78 See *Contextual Arts Network*: for information, email contextual-practice-network@mailbase.ac.uk
79 For introduction to different kinds of businesses see G. Chryssides and J. Kaler (1993) *Introduction to Business Ethics*. London: Chapman & Hall; *Business Ethics Quarterly*, the journal of the society for business ethics, for issues on consumption, the environment, employment rights, gender and so on.
80 Paraphrased from P. Watkins. (1996) Decentralising Education to the point of production: Sloanism, the market and the schools of the future, in *Discourse: Studies in the Cultural Politics of Education*, 17(1): 85–95.
81 Willmott, op. cit., T. J. Peters and R. H. Waterman (1982) *In Search of Excellence*. New York: Harper & Row.
82 J. Donald (1992) *Sentimental Education: Schooling, Popular Culture and the Regulation of Liberty*. London: Verso, p. 164.
83 Watkins, op. cit., p. 86.
84 The management structures of the Getty Education Institute for the Arts is based on a corporate model. See B. Wilson (1997) *The Quiet Evolution: Changing the Face of Arts Education*. Los Angeles: Getty Education Institute for the Arts.
85 B. Wilson, ibid., p. 1.
86 H. Giroux (1994) *Disturbing Pleasures: Learning Popular Culture*. New York: Routledge.
87 Wilson, op. cit.
88 P. Horn (1997) Creativity and the bottom line, *Financial Times*, 7 November, p. 12.
89 J. Swift (1996) Editorial, *Journal of Art and Design Education*, 15(2): 119–24.
90 Willmott, op. cit., p. 534.
91 Brown and Scase, op. cit., p. 4.
92 Ibid.
93 T. Brown (1997) Nurturing a culture of innovation, *Financial Times*, 17 November.
94 Moore, op. cit., p. 236.
95 S. Thiederman (1991), Profiting in America's multicultural marketplace, cited in E. Watkins and L. Schubert (1991) The entrepreneurship of the new: corporate direction and educational issues in the 1990s, in C. Newman and R. Strickland (eds) (1995) *After Political Correctness*. Boulder, CO: Westview, p. 94.
96 Willmott, op. cit., p. 537.
97 P. Berger and T. Luckmann (1966) *The Social Construction of Reality*. Harmondsworth: Penguin.

98 J. Mitchell (1972) Women's liberation and the new politics, in Mitchell, *The Body Politic*. London: Stage 1 Press.

Chapter 6 Beyond gendering: tactics and strategies

1 L. Mulvey (1989) The Oedipus myth: beyond the riddles of the Sphinx, in Mulvey, *Visual and Other Pleasures*. London: Macmillaan, p. 181. See also S. Noyes-Platt (1985) *Modernism in the 1920's: Interpretations of Modern Art in New York from Expressionism to Constructivism*. Ann Arbour, MI: University Michigan Research Press.

2 E. Dickinson (1998) *Gender Discrimination in the Art World*. Published privately, San Francisco, CA: E. Dickinson.

3 D. Kuspit (ed.) (1994) *Ideosyncratic Identities*. New York: Cambridge University Press.

4 M. Kelly (1981) Re-viewing modernist criticism, *Screen*, 22(3): pp. 41–61.

5 J. Kristeva (1974) *About Chinese Women*, trans. A. Barrows. London: Marion Boyars/Open Forum, p. 41.

6 L. Lippard (1980) Sweeping exchanges: the contribution of feminism to the art of the seventies, *Art Journal*, 41(1–2): 362.

7 D. Haraway (1985) A manifesto for cyborgs: science, technology and socialist feminism in the 1980s, in L. Nicholson (ed.) (1990) *Feminism/Postmodernism*. New York: Routledge.

8 S. Drury (1999) A review of the critical response to the world of Tracey Emin. Unpublished paper submitted for MA. University of Central England, Birmingham.

9 Kristeva, *About Chinese Women*, op. cit.

10 F. Jameson (1972) *The Prison House of Language*. Princeton, NJ: Princeton University Press.

11 Haraway, op. cit.

12 T. Eagleton (1990) *The Ideology of the Aesthetic*. Oxford: Blackwell, p. 13.

13 Cited in J. Donald. *Sentimental Education: Schooling, Popular Culture and the Regulation of Liberty*. London: Verso, p. 92; D. Cornell (1991) *Beyond Accommodation: Ethical Feminism, Deconstruction and the Law*, New York: Routledge.

14 H. Hein (1993) Refining feminist theory: lessons from aesthetics, in H. Hein and C. Korsmeyer (eds) *Aesthetics in Feminist Perspective*. New York: Hypatia.

15 Eagleton, op. cit., p.13.

16 Haraway, op. cit.

17 C. Cockburn (1989) Technology, production and power, in G. Kirkup and L. Smith-Keller (eds) (1992) *Inventing Women*. Buckingham: Open University Press/Polity.

18 M. de Certeau (1984) *The Practice of Everyday Life*. London: University of California Press.

19 Exhibition of South African art held at the Birmingham Central Museum, England in 1998.

20 Haraway, op. cit.

21 Eagleton, op. cit., p. 8.

22 D. Hebdige (1988) *Hiding in the Light*. London: Comedia/Routledge.
23 See V. Burgin (1976) Modernism in the work of art, in Burgin (1986) *The End of Art Theory: Criticism and Postmodernity*. London: Macmillan.
24 V. Shklovsky (1917) Art as technique, cited in P. Rice and P. Waugh (eds) (1989) *Modern Literary Theory*. London: Edward Arnold; V. Shklovsky (1970) *Sentimental Journey*. New York: Cornell University Press.
25 Jameson, op. cit., p.51
26 G. Pollock (1998) Feminist interventions in the histories of art: an introduction, in Pollock, *Vision and Difference*. London: Routledge, p. 158.
27 See R. Taylor (trans. & ed.) (1977) *Aesthetics and Politics: Debates Between Ernst Bloch, George Lukacs, Bertold Brecht, Walter Benjamin, Theodor Adorno*. London: New Left Books; S. Heath (1974) Lessons from from Brecht, *Screen*, 15(2): 108–9.
28 L. Mulvey (1973) Visual pleasure and the narrative cinema, in L. Mulvey (ed.) (1989) *Visual and Other Pleasures*. London: Macmillan, p. 16; D. Harvey (1989) The condition of postmodernity, p. 61, cited in T. Docherty (1993) Postmodernism: an introduction, in Docherty (ed.) *Postmodernism: A Reader*. Hemel Hempstead: Harvester, p. 94.
29 See M. Kelly (1982) Sense and sensibility in feminist art practice (exhibition catalogue essay). Nottingham: Midland Group.
30 J. Rose (1994) *The Case of Peter Pan: or the Impossibility of Childen's Fiction*. London: Macmillan.
31 E. Watkins (1993) *Throwaways: Work, Culture and Consumer Education*. Stanford, CA: Stanford University Press, p. 11.
32 Ibid., p. 11.
33 S. Gablik (1991) *The Re-enchantment of Art*. New York: Thames & Hudson.
34 Watkins, *Throwaways*, op. cit., p. 214
35 N. Bryson (1994) *Looking at the Overlooked: Four Essays on Still Life Painting*. Cambridge, MA: Harvard University Press.
36 H. Willmott (1993) Strength is ignorance; slavery is freedom: managing culture in modern organizations, *Journal of Management Studies*, 30(4) 515–51.
37 V. Griffith (1998) Knowing when to be of service, *Financial Times*, 12 February; M. Nava (1991) Consumerism reconsidered: buying and power, *Cultural Studies*, 5(2): 157–73.
38 Pollock, Feminist interventions in the histories of art, op. cit.
39 I. Rogoff (1996) Gossip as testimony: a postmodern signature, in G. Pollock (ed.) *Generations, Geographies and the Visual Arts*. London: Routledge, pp. 59–60.
40 See P. Dalton (1984) Housewives, leisure crafts and ideology, in G. Elinor, S. Richardson, S. Scott, A. Thomas and K. Walker (eds) (1987) *Women and Craft*. London: Virago.
41 Haraway, op. cit., p. 195.
42 Kristeva, *About Chinese Women*, op. cit., p. 38.

Index